THE EIGHTEENTH CENTURY

[CROWNED BY THE ACADÉMIE DES
SCIENCES MORALES ET POLITIQUES]

BY

CASIMIR STRYIENSKI

TRANSLATED FROM THE FRENCH BY

H. N. DICKINSON

LONDON
WILLIAM HEINEMANN

London : *William Heinemann*, 1916

CONTENTS

FIRST PART—REGENCY OF THE DUC D'ORLEANS

SECOND PART—THE DUC DE BOURBON AND CARDINAL FLEURY

THIRD PART—LOUIS XV

CONTENTS

FOURTH PART—LOUIS XVI

FIFTH PART—THE ARTISTIC AND LITERARY MOVEMENT

FIRST PART
THE REGENCY OF THE DUC D'ORLEANS

CHAPTER I

THE COMMENCEMENT OF THE REGENCY
1715

The death of Louis XIV. The Royal family. The Duc du
Maine. The Duc d'Orléans : his character. The late King's
will disregarded. The new King's *Lit de Justice* on September 12 ;
his portrait ; the popularity of Louis XV.

LOUIS XIV is dead and his courtiers breathe again.
The last years of the King had been mournful and
morose. The words that he addressed to his great-
grandson when giving him his blessing convey an echo of those
Death of troubled times :
Louis XIV.   " You will be a great King ; do not imitate
me in my taste for building, nor in my taste for war. . . . Try
to lighten the burden of your people, as I, unhappily, have not
been able to do."

These moving and humane words had in them something
of the prophetic. In 1715 a new era was beginning. The
King was to retain his divine prestige for nearly a century in spite of everything, but the nation around him
was adopting a new life. The history of the eighteenth
century is the history of the disorganization of the ancient
monarchy, to end at last in revolution. Imperceptibly, the
modern spirit grew, developed, and assumed more tangible
shapes. Soon a lamentable ruin was all that remained of
the ancient edifice ; our Acropolis was destroyed, and like
that of Athens it became but a shrine for pilgrims where
some might come to mourn the vanity of human things,
others to raise the song of victory. Chamfort triumphantly
recalled the saying of a courtier in 1715 : " After the death
of a Louis XIV anything may be expected ; the greatest
calamities may occur."

3

The great King's successor was five and a half years old ;
he was the son of the Duc de Bourgogne and Marie Adelaïde
The Royal of Savoy, whose wit and charm had cheered and
Family. solaced the last years of Louis XIV. At his
birth, on February 5, 1710, Louis XV had seemed far enough
from the throne. His great-grandfather, his grandfather (the
great Dauphin), his father and his elder brother (the Duc de
Bretagne) were still living, four barriers in his way to the
throne. In two years all had gone, and the only representative
of the direct Bourbon line was a feeble orphan. Both the State
and the King needed a guardian. Until the heir to the throne
should attain his majority the country would have to be
governed by a Regent. Louis XIV, in his will, appointed two
persons to perform this duty : his nephew, Philippe, Duc
d'Orléans, son of Monsieur and Elisabeth Charlotte, Princess
Palatine, and his legitimized son, the Duc du Maine. The
former was to have the title of Regent, but he was to be at
the mercy of the latter who alone was " charged with watching
over the safety, preservation and education of the King during
his minority."

These princes represented two rival parties. The Duc du
Maine, brought up by Madame de Maintenon, was the Benjamin
The Duc of Louis XIV. The edict of August 2, 1714, by
du Maine. recognizing the legitimized children of Louis XIV
and their descendants as equal to the princes of the blood-
royal had " put the finishing touch to the hereditary greatness "
of M. du Maine. This paternal weakness encouraged the
flattery of place-seekers, and grouped around the Duke such
people as the Marshal de Villeroy and President de Mesmes,
to say nothing of those who awaited events before knowing to
which side they should give their allegiance.

M. du Maine was not lacking in intelligence, but he had a
tendency towards avarice and one weakness that is fatal among
Frenchmen—cowardice. At the siege of Namur, in 1695,
M. d'Elbeuf asked him before a number of officers where he
would be stationed in the approaching campaign. When the
Duke asked the reason for this question, M. d'Elbeuf replied
" Because with you one's life is safe."

The Duke made a bad use of his intelligence ; he took

especial pleasure in false and tortuous ways. In appearance, his face was sufficiently prepossessing, but he had little resemblance to his majestic father ; he was small of stature, deformed and lame, and he had " an ungainly walk." Philippe d'Orléans, on the contrary, was popular : both from his frank, open, and amiable character and from the retirement in which his uncle had kept him. He had wished for a military command, but in spite of the brilliance of his first engagements at Leuze in 1691, at Steinkerque, where he was wounded, in 1692, and at Nerwinde in 1693, he had difficulty in obtaining permission to take part in the Italian campaign of 1706. There, owing to the folly of La Feuillade and de Marsin, who would not listen to him, he was present at the defeat of Turin where he conducted himself with courage and was seriously wounded. During the years 1707 and 1708 he was in Spain defending the interests of Philip V. As master of the situation he showed a considerable talent both in administration and generalship ; the towns of Valencia, Saragossa, Lerida, and Tortosa surrendered to him. His popularity increased to the point of overshadowing that of the King of Spain himself. Unpleasant rumours were spread about him ; it was reported that he wished to seize the crown of Castille. These calumnies brought him into disgrace, and for a while he was condemned to obscurity ; but he profited thereby in acquiring a closer knowledge of men. During this period he had to struggle against far more formidable enemies than those he had conquered. Certain courtiers, led by M. du Maine, accused him of having poisoned the Duc and Duchess de Bourgogne, stating as evidence that he studied chemistry in his leisure hours. Then, again, he gave Louis XIV cause to be angry with him ; he conducted himself with culpable frivolity and neglected his wife, a legitimized daughter of Louis XIV and a sister of M. du Maine, to whom the King had married him against his will in 1692.

It is not surprising that Louis XIV followed the dictates of his heart and gave his nephew a phantom regency for the benefit of M. du Maine. No doubt the great King would have liked to go still further, but he could not take from the Duc d'Orléans the title of first prince of the blood-royal or its accompanying rights. Louis knew, however, that wills are fragile. He knew that those of Henri IV and Louis XIII had been disregarded ; he foresaw the difficulties which were certain to arise and he said to Philippe : "I have made what I have considered to be the wisest disposition ; but one cannot foresee everything, and if there is any point which is not satisfactory, it will be changed." For an intelligent prince who was desirous of securing his position this verbal testament was a sufficient programme. Saint-Simon is deceived in thinking that the nephew of Louis XIV was taken unawares. It was not so, for the *coup d'Etat* was prepared with as much skill as discretion. The Duc d' Orléans made certain of a great part of the army and of the Parlement of Paris before the death of the King. He was sure of the support of his cousin and ally, George I of England, with whom he had started a political correspondence in 1714. This newly made monarch had a particular reason for not wishing to see the Duc du Maine master of the kingdom of France ; he had justifiable fears that the latter would support the Pretender, James Stuart, son of James II, and would thus menace both the peace of Europe and the throne which he occupied, more or less as an usurper.

The Duc d'Orléans had also in his favour his brilliant military exploits, his ready eloquence, and his generosity. He The Duc flattered himself on his resemblance to Henri IV d'Orleans. and studied to increase " this resemblance in the vices of that prince as in his virtues." But when put to the proof, he could not continue long in the same direction, for he had no spirit of perseverance. He was impulsive ; if he stopped to reflect he became so undecided that he could not be induced to make up his mind at all. Madame Palatine wrote a cele-brated description of her son in the form of an apology, in which she frankly showed his vulnerable points. He is, said the princess, like the child to whose baptism the fairies had been invited : one willed him a beautiful form, another eloquence, the third a talent for the arts, the fourth an aptitude for physical exercises, the fifth martial glory, the sixth courage. But they had forgotten to invite the seventh fairy : " I cannot take back from the child," she said, " what my sisters have given him, but during his entire life I will be against him, so that all these favours will be useless to him." This seventh fairy was indolence, and the laxity which made the prince *blasé* and bored and led him into his worst errors. Yet the six other fairies did not abandon their protégé; they often came to his aid.

At the decisive moments, on the eve of and on the day after the death of Louis XIV, Philippe d'Orléans was entirely master **The King's** of himself and scored a brilliant success over the **Will** Duc du Maine. On September 2, the Parlement **disregarded.** of Paris, charged with opening and executing the royal testament, decided first of all that the Regency should go to the Duc d'Orléans " by right of birth." In return the prince, by an adroit move, revoked the edicts of 1667 and 1673 which had taken all political authority from the Parlement; in his speech he emphasized his liberality. " Whatever my right," he said, " to aspire to the Regency, I dare assure you, gentlemen, that I shall merit it by my zeal in the service of the King, and by my love of the public welfare, *with the aid, above all, of your advice and wise admonition.*" The victory was won. The Duc du Maine took fright, as was his wont on a field of battle, and appealed to the court to decide " what he was to be " ; he hoped that they would not leave him an empty title. At these words, the Duc d'Orléans declared the clauses of the testament which had just been opened to be monstrous. Was it possible that he, the Regent, should be under the orders of a prince who would be master of everything, of the King, of Paris, and consequently of the State ? He wished to be freed of this tutelage, to have the free disposition of pardon, employment, place and benefice ; then summing up all in a phrase borrowed from *Télémaque,* recalling the noble traditions of the Duc de Bourgogne, he added : " I wish to be independent that I may do good, and I am willing to be bound in whatever way you please so that I may not do evil." There was loud applause. The Duc du Maine saw that the game was lost and abandoned the contest, merely stipulating that he should have the superintendence of the education of Louis XV.

" Willingly," said the Regent, " that does not matter so much."

The voting was in accordance with the wishes of Philippe d'Orléans ; no vestige of authority was left to the Duc du

Maine. Everything was in the hands of the Regent, who had the right to surround himself with persons chosen by himself, and to arrange the form of the government as he thought fit. The direction of affairs, however, was vested in a Council of Regency, who were to decide according to the vote of the majority, while in the case of an equal division the Regent was to have the casting vote.

Thus, Louis's nephew, with the strength of his prestige, annulled the dispositions of his uncle by means of the very magistrates who had been commissioned to uphold them; at the same time he had restored the Parlement to its rightful position, which had been disregarded for many years. This was the first liberal measure of the Regent, though it was not absolutely disinterested. None the less he gave an impetus to the power of that Assembly which was to play so leading a part during the whole eighteenth century. The precautions which were taken for the safety of the Duke were unnecessary; there was no need to have recourse to the armed force which was stationed at the Palais de Justice in readiness to support him. As he left the Sainte-Chapelle there were repeated cries of " Vive le Roi, Vive le Régent ! " On the same evening he returned to Versailles, where he received the congratulations of the court.

The powers with which he had just been vested were confirmed at the *lit de justice* held on September 12. There is an *The new* interesting picture at Versailles painted by *King's* Dumesnil which shows the minutest details of *lit de justice.* the ceremony : the great chamber, or *chambre doré*, with its royal decoration of blue hangings ornamented with golden fleurs-de-lis ; in one corner, on a daïs, Louis XV is seated, still so fragile that he was obliged to have his governess, the Duchesse de Ventadour, with him ; the Duc de Tresmes, Governor of Paris, had carried the King from his carriage to the throne, a woman kneels at his feet to watch over his weakness—symbolical of his whole reign, for Louis XV was for ever surrounded by women and courtiers.

It was a large assembly ; the King was supported by the Grand Chamberlain, peers spiritual and temporal, princes of the blood-royal, governors and lieutenants-general of provinces, the chancellor, the chief president, the chief justice and the councillors

8

of the Parlement. There are two portraits of the child-King also at Versailles, one by Rigaud and the other by Ranc. In spite of the official character of these state portraits they show the whole charm of his youth, grace, and beauty. They depict faithfully the Louis XV whom Madame Palatine has described, with large, black eyes, long curling lashes, fresh complexion, tiny mouth, quantities of long, dark hair, and a straight and well-formed figure. The painters have reproduced these attributes marvellously, Rigaud with the masterly touch of an assured artist, and Ranc with that scrupulous attention to detail which in him took the place of genius.

P. D. Martin's picture, also at Versailles, shows us the front of the Sainte-Chapelle, from which the King has just come after the *lit de justice*. Louis XV, once more carried by the Duc de Tresmes, is on the top of the flight of steps, escorted by the Regent, the Duc de Bourbon and the princes of the blood-royal. The square was crowded with people wishing to see the King. The French and the Swiss guards could hardly move amongst the enthusiastic crowd that cheered the new monarch. The cannon of the Bastille was fired and the town was *en fête*. An officer of the bodyguard distributed money to the people from time to time on the journey from Paris to Vincennes where, in accordance with Louis XIV's express desire, his descendant and successor was to live, that he might be in " the fresh air." Following an ancient custom, birds were set free in the court of the palace, symbolical of the deliverance of prisoners ; the Regent, not contented with the symbol alone, ordered the doors of Vincennes, the Bastille, the Conciergerie, Saint-Eloi and For-l'Evêque to be opened, liberating most of the prisoners, particularly the Jansenists. Thus the new reign began under the best auspices. The Regent contented himself with exiling Père le Tellier, the confessor of Louis XIV, and he softened the voluntary retreat into which Madame de Maintenon had retired. The young King kept for a long time the popularity Popularity of of which he received the first proof on that day. Louis XV. Ready sympathy was naturally given to this charming child, the only remaining representative of a great family which had been smitten by successive blows at the hand of death.

9

THE EIGHTEENTH CENTURY

DESCENDANTS OF LOUIS XIV

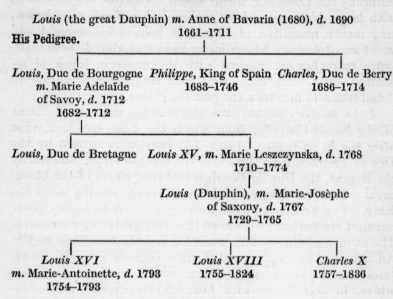

Louis XIV m. Maria-Theresa of Austria (1660), *d.* 1683
1638–1715

Louis (the great Dauphin) *m.* Anne of Bavaria (1680), *d.* 1690

His Pedigree.   1661–1711

Louis, Duc de Bourgogne *Philippe,* King of Spain *Charles,* Duc de Berry
m. Marie Adelaïde   1683–1746   1686–1714
of Savoy, *d.* 1712
1682–1712

Louis, Duc de Bretagne *Louis XV, m.* Marie Leszczynska, *d.* 1768
1710–1774

Louis (Dauphin), *m.* Marie-Josèphe
of Saxony, *d.* 1767
1729–1765

Louis XVI   *Louis XVIII*   *Charles X*
m. Marie-Antoinette, *d.* 1793   1755–1824   1757–1836
1754–1793

DESCENDANTS OF LOUIS XIV

(Legitimized Princes)

Louis XIV

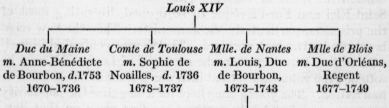

Duc du Maine   *Comte de Toulouse* *Mlle. de Nantes* *Mlle de Blois*
m. Anne-Bénédicte *m.* Sophie de   *m.* Louis, Duc *m.* Duc d'Orléans,
de Bourbon, *d.*1753 Noailles, *d.* 1736 de Bourbon,   Regent
1670–1736   1678–1737   1673–1743   1677–1749

Louis, Duc de Bourbon
Prime Minister under Louis XV
1692–1740

COMMENCEMENT OF REGENCY

HOUSE OF ORLEANS

Philippe, Duc d'Orléans (brother of Louis XIV)
m. 1. Henrietta of England, *d*. 1670.
   2. Elisabeth Charlotte, Princess Palatine, *d*. 1722
By his second marriage
|
Philippe, Regent (1674–1723)
|
Louis, Duc d'Orleans (1703–1752)
|
Louis Philippe, Duc d'Orleans (1725–1785)
|
Louis Philippe, Egalité (1747–1793)
|
Louis Philippe I, King of the French (1773–1850)

PRINCIPAL SOURCES. Archives of the Ministry for Foreign Affairs, memoirs and documents, France, 139 ; *Mémoire* of Le Dran on the Regency ; Spanheim, *Relation de la Cour de France en* 1690, 1 vol., Paris, 1882 ; *Mémoires* of Saint-Simon ; *Journaux* of Buvat, Monais, Barbier ; *Correspondence* of Madame Palatine, Duchesse d'Orléans ; *Mémoires sur la Régence*, 3 vols., The Hague, 1737 ; Toussaint, *Anecdotes curieuses de la Cour de France* (first edition with real names of the celebrated *Mémoires secrets pour servir à l'histoire de Perse*), Paris, 1905 ; Lemontey, *Histoire de la Régence*, Paris, 1832 ; Rocquain, *L'Esprit révolutionnaire avant la Révolution*, 1 vol., Paris, 1878 ; Nolhac and Pérate, *Le musée de Versailles*, 1 vol., Paris, 1896.

CHAPTER II

THE EDUCATION OF LOUIS XV
1715-1722

The Minority of Louis XV. The Duchesse de Ventadour Gover-
ness to the young prince. Letters of Madame Palatine and of
Madame de Ventadour. Visit of Peter the Great. Marshal
Villeroy, the King's Governor. His portrait (Saint-Simon, Span-
heim, Rigaud). Reception of Mehemet Effendi, Ambassador
from the Grand Turk. "The people is yours." Dismissal of
Louis' Governor. Fleury. Louis and the Papal Nuncio.
Responsibilities of the Bishop of Fréjus. The Duc de Charost
appointed to succeed Villeroy. The Return from the Coronation.
Lessons in the Art of Governing.

THE Regency was to last until February 22, 1723, when
the King officially attained his majority. At the
age of thirteen, Louis was to become absolute master
of France, though naturally he would remain under the guidance
of his chief minister. His minority was not troubled by sedition
Minority of   as that of Louis XIV had been. During the early
Louis XV.   years a considerable party was formed, which
seemed ready to grant liberty to the Parlements, to Jansenists,
to members of the reformed religions, and to those subject to
" taille " ; blessings were to flow spontaneously over the country.

The ambition of Philip V of Spain, who asserted his rights to
the regency as the grandson of Louis XIV, and the speculations
of Law the Scotsman momentarily disturbed the prevailing
calm, but there was no other excitement during that period.
However, the Regency did not keep its promises, but in the end
reverted to the policy of the preceding reign. The nephew
of the Great King, owing to his indolent character and to the
necessity, which statesmen find so pressing, of giving way to
private interests, never completed his purpose ; the seventh
fairy brought him ill luck.

12

But before these events are dealt with, we must introduce some of the personalities, who, in addition to the Regent, were charged with superintending the education of the young monarch. It is important to know how they acquitted themselves of their task, what their influence was, and how far they were responsible for the results obtained. In this way we shall better understand the strictures passed by history upon Louis XV, who gave evidence of his character at an early age.

In accordance with the settled custom, the King was at first placed in the charge of women. His Governess was the **The Duchesse** Duchesse de Ventadour, Charlotte de la Motte **de Ventadour.** Houdancourt, late lady-in-waiting to Madame Palatine. She was now elderly; but there had been a time when in her youth and beauty she had had a brief but brilliant career, and rumour had been busy about her. In 1715 she had become extremely pious, and she maintained the tradition of the court of Louis XIV and Madame de Maintenon in all its rigorous austerity.

She performed her duties to the best of her lights and imagined that she was acting wisely in flattering her pupil and in telling him that he was a being apart, to whom nothing was comparable. In return the child loved his Governess alone, and gave the Duchess, whom he called his " dear mamma " all the affection of which his heart was capable. He was small and delicate; consequently he was never crossed or contradicted and was allowed to do whatever he pleased. Thus he was badly brought up and began to give indications of what he was to be throughout his life, obstinate, self-opinionated, and proud, taking dislikes to people for no apparent reason, only breaking his usual taciturnity to make some offensive remark. One day when Monseigneur de Coislin, Bishop of Metz, came to present his homage, Louis cried, " Ah, mon Dieu! how ugly he is ! " The bishop turned on his heel remarking, " What a badly brought up little boy ! "

Occasionally, he was merely playful. On one occasion he asked M. de la Vrillière who he was and the courtier replied, " Your Secretary of State." The King at once requested him to enter his study and for work gave him nuts to shell.

13

His childish pranks were overlooked; every one showed complete devotion to him, young as he was, as Madame Palatine said. She herself treated him as a spoilt child, remarking: " I am not in his good graces, but it does not disturb me, for by the time he is old enough to reign, I shall be no more of this world and I shall not be dependent on his caprices."

Letters of Madame Palatine and Madame de Ventadour.

There is a letter from Madame de Ventadour to Madame de Maintenon, which proves that the Governess at least foresaw the future character of this being who was so sad and morose in his childhood, and seemed to bear the burden of the troubles which had afflicted his family. " He is a child," she wrote, " who must be taken care of; he is not naturally gay and great pleasures will be harmful to him, for he will abandon himself to them too much. They wish him to display the same disposition on all occasions; and you know, Madame, how intolerable such restraint is at any time of life. You will laugh at me when I tell you that he has the vapours; yet it is true; he had them in his cradle. The result is his mournful air and the constant necessity of rousing him. One can do anything with him if one speaks without passion."

It is difficult to undertake the defence of Louis XV; but before he is condemned, an allowance must be made for his education at the hands of flatterers; it must be remembered that he was always surrounded by strangers, and, as he himself said, that he had lost his parents before he could realize his loss. All these are extenuating circumstances from a psychological point of view. Shakespeare, with his great human knowledge, has noticed this particular agent in the deformation of character; when he introduces unnatural people they are always orphans; thus Regan and Goneril, the odious daughters of King Lear, had never known a mother's smile.

Madame de Ventadour retained her position until 1717, when Louis, who was now seven years old, was placed in the charge of men. The ceremony which took place on this occasion was conducted with great pomp, in accordance with custom. The Regent and the whole Court repaired to the Tuileries in brilliant equipages; the King was disrobed in the sight of all, that every one might witness the good state of his health ; then he was dressed in new clothes and handed over to his governors and preceptors. The officers who were to serve him were presented, even including a Swiss boy " aged six and a half, the son of the Swiss attendant of Marshal de Villeroy, clothed in black in the fashion of the Swiss Guard, holding in his hand a halberd with silver blade and ebony shaft."

About this time, the Czar, Peter the Great, came on a visit to the King ; the visit was political but the result was negative.

Visit of Peter the Great. The Regent rejected the advances of the Russian Emperor, not wishing to ally himself with an enemy of England ; he also declined the proposals for the marriage of the young King made by the Czar. Peter had a daughter, Elizabeth Petrovna, who was of the same age as Louis, and he dreamt for the moment of placing her on the throne of France.

This event excited the well-known curiosity of Parisians ; for a month and a half the Czar was extremely popular. As he passed through the streets with his half-barbarous appearance, his restless gaze, his simple tastes and dark clothes, forming a contrast to the fastidiousness of the French Court, the Parisians were delighted. He showed an interest in the people, in the workmen, and in the philanthropic institutions, disdaining anything which was merely pleasure. The luxury of the French surprised him greatly. He even said that this luxury would be the ruin of the country. Peter received a visit from the King, and embraced him several times. He lifted him in his arms until he was on a level with him, caressed him often and seemed charmed with his grace and his handsome face.

To revert to the education of Louis XV. The Governor appointed was Marshal de Villeroy ; he had been nominated

Marshal de Villeroy, the King's Governor. by Louis XIV himself, who said of him in his will : " By his good conduct, his probity and his talents he has seemed to merit the honour of this mark of our esteem and confidence."

Villeroy was incapable of giving Louis any serious guidance. He had often been unfortunate on the field of battle and was in reality little more than a courtier sated by royal favours, owing all to the chance circumstance that he had been brought up with Louis XIV. In his latest capacity as Governor his attitude was servile, and he attached little importance to anything but futilities. He was seventy-three years of age, but retained all the fine airs of the old Court ; tall, well made, and of pleasant appearance, he remains essentially magnificent, a very prince of dandies. Saint-Simon says of him : " He was the kind of man who is created for the especial purpose of presiding over a ball, of being judge at a tournament, and, if he had the voice, of singing at the opera in the part of king or hero ; essentially fitted to set the fashions, but good for nothing else." His judgment may seem severe, but it is confirmed by Spanheim, the discreet ambassador whose descriptions of the Court of Louis XIV are so interesting. His verdict on the subject of the Marshal was : " His views are restricted and his discernment dull, and if we may judge his capacity by the event, he is the sort of officer who finds himself better suited to the ballroom than to the field of battle. Magnificence is his mania, but magnificence with a suspicion of bad taste ; there is always something of the flunkey (*Mascarille*) about him." The portrait of Ménippe in la Bruyère is a complete portrait of the Marshal : " Ménippe is the bird decked in divers plumes which do not belong to him . . . a man who is tolerable for a quarter of an hour at a time, but after that degenerates, loses the little lustre that a little memory may give him, and reveals the sow's ear." The Marshal was not popular and intercourse with him was insupportable ; it was impossible to endure this man who sought applause and whose sole topics were mere reflections of fashion and the trite formulas of polite speech. In spite of the pomp of an official portrait, Rigaud's picture in the Musée de Caen has faithfully shown the self-satisfied air which was the principal feature of Villeroy's physiognomy.

When Louis XIV was very young he had danced ballets in public with girls from the opera ; Villeroy " a worshipper of the late King even in trifles," desired that Louis XV should follow his example ; he merely succeeded in disgusting the child with such exhibitions, which he held in abhorrence for the rest of his life.

In another way, Villeroy showed the trifling pre-occupations which seem to have been his sole concern. In March 1721, Mehemet Effendi, the ambassador of the Sublime Porte, was presented to Louis. The scene as described by the Sultan's envoy himself was delightful :

Mehemet Effendi, Ambassador from Turkey.

" As soon as the prince saw me, he turned to me and I approached him. Friendly discussions on divers matters were the subject of our conversation. He was delighted to examine our clothes and our poignards one after another. The Marshal (Villeroy) asked me :

" ' What is your opinion of our King's beauty ? '

" ' God be praised,' I replied, ' and may He preserve him from evil ! '

" ' He is only eleven years and four months old, and is not his figure well proportioned ? Notice especially that his hair is his own.'

" In saying this he turned the King round, and I looked at his hyacinthine locks as I caressed him. They were like smooth strands of gold and reached down to his waist.

" ' His carriage too is particularly fine,' went on the Governor and at the same time he said to the King : ' Take a few steps.'

" Louis XV walked to the centre of the room with the majestic step of a partridge and returned.

" ' Walk a little quicker,' added the Marshal, ' so that we may see how lightly you run.'

" Immediately the King began to run speedily. The Governor then asked me if I found him amiable.

" ' May the All-powerful God who has created so beautiful a creature bless him,' I rejoined."

On each festival of Saint-Louis, the Marshal said to his pupil in the presence of the multitude which thronged around the Tuileries : " See ! my master, see all this people, this gathering ! All is yours ! " He seemed to forget that the lessons given to the King's father, the Duc de Bourgogne, had been very different. The grandson of Louis XIV had been taught that the people did not belong to the King, but the King to the people, that he might make them happy by the equity, wisdom, and mildness of his

" The People belong to You ! "

government. Villeroy had not read *Télémaque* and was too much of a courtier to admire Fénelon. He forgot the words which Massillon, a few months previously, had addressed to Louis himself before the whole Court : " Never, Sire, may you efface from your memory the wise maxims which that great prince (Louis XIV) bequeathed to you in his last moments as a heritage more precious than the Crown. He exhorted you to lighten the burden of your people. *Be their father and you will be doubly their master.*"

The Regent was exasperated by the old man who so little understood his duties ; consequently he resolved that as in August 1718, he had abolished the rights of the Duc du Maine to the crown and the superintendence of the royal education, so he would get rid of the influence of Villeroy. He had other grievances against the Marshal. Villeroy had spread slanderous reports, accusing Louis XIV's nephew of having poisoned the Duc and Duchesse de Bourgogne. Even under the Regency he had affected to take precautions, " full of the blackest motives of self-interest, which angered such as were honest, and amused others, but which impressed the people and the fools and had the double effect of renewing the wicked reports which he had so carefully engendered against the Duc d'Orléans, and of making it appear that the safety and life of the King were dependent on the care and vigilance of so faithful and attached a Governor." *

When Louis, in July 1721, was sick and kept his bed for five days, scandal again reported that he was being poisoned and Villeroy did not hesitate to allow suspicion to rest on the Duc d'Orléans. More than ever he posed as the protector and guardian angel of France. It was easy to lay a trap for Villeroy. The Marshal was extremely jealous of his prerogatives and did not allow any one to speak to the King unless he himself was present.

On Sunday, August 9, 1722, at Versailles, the Regent submitted some business to the King in the presence of the Governor, and afterwards he requested Louis to pass into his inner apart-
Dismissal of Villeroy. ment, where he had something to say to him in private. Villeroy objected to this, but the Duc held to his point. The King, he said, was so nearly of the age

* Saint-Simon.

18

when he would govern for himself, that it was time for the trustee of his whole power to inform him of matters which could only be explained to him in private. The Marshal was indignant and replied that he would not allow his Royal Highness to speak to the King in private. Whereupon the Regent regarded him fixedly, made a profound reverence to Louis and left the room, since he did not wish, out of respect for the King's youth, to reply to Villeroy as he deserved. On the next day the Marshal went to see the Duc in order to make an explanation ; but the Marquis de la Fare, captain of the Regent's guards, stopped him and demanded his sword ; at the same time the Comte d'Artagnan, captain of the grey musketeers, approached Villeroy. He was hustled into a sedan chair, shut in, and carried through one of the windows which opened into the garden ; then he was taken down the staircase of the Orangery to a coach and six. The captain got in beside Villeroy ; in front were an officer and a gentleman in ordinary ; twenty musketeers surrounded the carriage ; they left at full speed for the castle of Villeroy in Brie, situated eight leagues from Paris, where the exile arrived in about three hours.

This arrest caused a thousand rumours ; it was insinuated that the King would not live long, that he would be poisoned and the Regent would become Seneschal of the kingdom. Villeroy's complaints were so loud that an official manifesto was published for the purpose of satisfying the public. This document asserted that the Marshal "wished to assume a royal authority, in order to oppose the Regency, as though the royal power could be divided. But for these indiscretions, which do not affect the probity of the Marshal, we could still have the pleasure of seeing him near the King ; but good intentions are not sufficient in important officials ; they must know how to behave with tact."

Louis was extremely displeased. He had a certain affection for this "grand-papa" who satisfied all his whims. He wept bitterly, and the more so because his tutor, Fleury, Bishop of Fréjus, left the court on the same day ; the latter retired voluntarily to Bâville to stay with the Lamoignons, as soon as he learnt of the Marshal's exile, since he considered himself indebted to him. He was hastily recalled, and the Duc d'Orléans received him with favour; he assured him that it was to spare his feelings that he had not been informed of the secret arrest of Villeroy; he explained the reason for the exile "the more freely, because Fleury hated the Marshal, his pride and jealousies and caprices, and secretly rejoiced at his dismissal and at the prospect of having the King to himself." This is Saint-Simon's account, but perhaps it should be modified if what Bernis says is true. According to the latter, the Regent said to Fleury with his usual somewhat crude frankness: "You have lost your friend, but you will be master of the house! (*tripot*)." Did Orléans foresee the lofty destiny which awaited the Bishop? Anyhow, Fleury yielded to his arguments, and although he had to submit to the violent reproaches of the Marshal, he shared his hatred with the Duc de Charost, Villeroy's successor designate, with the Regent, and also with the Abbé Dubois, whose influence was not wanting on this occasion, since he saw in the Marshal an enemy to his English policy.

Fleury performed his functions conscientiously; he was capable and he did not forget a single one of his duties, as Villars testifies. It is true that Bernis gives an amusing description of the King putting his instructor's grey hairs into curl-papers, and Argenson affirms that Quintus Curtius remained open at the same page for six months while, instead of working, Fleury amused the child by playing with cards. But in the National Library there are whole copy books filled with Louis' work corrected in Fleury's handwriting, and these are clear proof of his industry. The King had lessons in writing, Latin, and French history every day, while three days a week he studied geography, for which he showed a pronounced taste, astronomy, drawing, mathematics, and botany; he remembered this last even later in his life, since he laid out a garden at Trianon where the horticulturist, Claude Richard, taught him how to graft. The gardener was put into communication with Linnaeus and sent him on behalf of his Most Christian Majesty, some strawberry seeds: "To the most celebrated and most noble M. de Linné, Knight of the Pole Star, chief physician to the King, professor of medicine and botany at Upsala, associate member of the Academy of Paris." Louis, as Buvat relates,

Cardinal Fleury.

made great progress in all these studies, with the help of such able specialists as Guillaume Delisle, the greatest geographer of his age, and Chevalier, the eminent mathematician. Even the name of his writing master has been preserved and a small engraving was published in his honour, showing him beside his pupil, while Fleury and Madame de Ventadour superintend his work ; underneath is written the following verse :

> En trois heures de temps le Roy sçait bien écrire ;
> Par un secret nouveau, que toute le monde admire,
> A lui seul Dom Duchène, enfant de Besançon
> Sceut faire ce prodige en moins de six leçons.*

Military studies were not neglected, this branch being under the direction of Lieutenant-General Puységur and the engineer, Hermann.

In every case Louis distinguished himself by the excellence of his memory and the comparative quickness of his intellect. **Louis XV and the Papal Nuncio.** One day he inquired of the Papal Nuncio, Bentivoglio : " Monsieur le Nonce, how many Popes have there been up to the present ? " The prelate hesitated. " You do not know the number of popes ? Why, I know how many monarchs there have been in France before me." Whereupon he named his predecessors one after the other in chronological order.

Fleury also instructed Louis in religious doctrine, but he did not carry his self-sacrifice far enough to recommend his pupil to read a book which might have taught him how to govern wisely ; he had no more appreciation for the principles of Fénelon than had Villeroy. " I was imprudent enough," wrote Voltaire, " to inquire one day of the Cardinal de Fleury, whether he had made the King read Fénelon's *Télémaque*. He replied that he made him read better works, and has never forgiven me."

His particular care was to develop in his pupil a taste for order and economy ; he was celebrated for his avarice and as Prime Minister he managed the finances of the State as if he had

---

* In three hours the King learns how to write ; by a secret method admired of all, with him alone could Dom Duchène, son of Besançon, work this miracle in less than six lessons.

to deal with the small acounts of a middle-class establishment, though it must be admitted that he made it a rule only to divert to his own profit enough to maintain a modest suite and a frugal table. He is a curious example of the advancement of plebeians, which was more common than might be imagined under the *ancien régime*. He was the son of a tax-collector of Lodève, and had risen in the world thanks to his handsome appearance, his ability, and his ambition ; he was appointed Bishop of Fréjus in 1698. He owed the position of trust in which he was now placed to the great King who had nominated him in his will. Such were the beginnings of a brilliant career based on the affection which the instructor was able to inspire in his royal pupil. But, to repeat the just criticism of a historian, Fleury did not seek to make Louis a king, he sought to ensure the place of Prime Minister for himself ; and it is a fact that he was more successful in that direction and must, as well as Villeroy, be held partly responsible for the troubles which were in store for France during the new reign.

The Duc de Charost, the Marshal's successor, is best known by the letter which Villeroy addressed to him on learning of his appointment. "I cannot rejoice," he wrote, "that they have given you the place of Governor, because I held this charge at the hand of the late King, to whom I promised that I would never abandon His Majesty. When I see that it is out of my power to keep so noble a promise given to a great king on his deathbed, I am unable to identify myself with a preferment which deprives me of that honour and forces me to break my word." This is the letter of the magnificent *grand seigneur* we know ; but it also shows us that Villeroy knew at least how to complain with tact and dignity.

His successor was recommended by the connexion he had formerly had with the circle of the Duc de Bourgogne, with Villeroy's Beauvilliers, Chevreuse and Fénelon, and as early successor, as 1712 he had been marked out to fulfil the the Duc function ; consequently the Regent's choice was de Charost. justified. But the Duc de Charost had no better knowledge of business than the Marshal, and his attainments were not of the highest order. However, it must be realized that Louis was now twelve years old and the mischief was already done. All his life the prince was to bear the traces of the worthless instruction of his first Governor. Gradually studies were abandoned, and riding, as a prelude to the exploits of the chase, so dear to the Bourbons, superseded everything in the education of the young monarch. The Duc de Charost merely had to figure in two ceremonies ; the one private—the first Communion on September 15, 1722 ; the other surrounded by royal pomp—the coronation at Reims on October 25, 1722. After this ceremony it was noticed that Louis spoke a great deal; he often said, " I will." Mathieu Marais recounts that " he makes fun of M. de Charost and M. de Fréjus. On one occasion he ordered every one to leave the room ; when M. de Fréjus remained, he told him that the order applied to him as well as to the others. He rides often, shoots well, and is devoted to play, even playing early in the morning before mass."

The only studies which remained to him were studies in administration and politics, over which the Regent himself presided. The subjects for the King's instruction were drawn up by able specialists : Le Dran, chief of the Department of Foreign Affairs ; Briquet, first Secretary for War ; Fagon and Ormesson, the Intendants of Finance. Louis was taught how to govern ; it remained for him to take advantage of the instruction, dull as it may have been, and to realize his position ; but that depended more on his heart than his intelligence. Before we see how he acquitted himself of his task, it will be as well to review the state in which France was left to him by the Regent and the Duc de Bourbon.

Lessons in the art of Government.

PRINCIPAL SOURCES. Most of the works mentioned at the end of the previous chapter. La Bruyère, *Caractères* ; *Mémoires* of the Marquis d'Argenson, of Bernis and of the Duc de Richelieu ; Duclos, *Mémoires secrets de la Régence* ; Massillon, *Petit Carême* ; Albert Vandal, *Louis XV et Elisabeth de Russie*, 1 vol., Paris, 1882 ; Druon, *Histoire de l'éducation des Princes dans la maison des Bourbons de France*, 2 vols., Paris, 1897 ; Comte de Fleury, *Louis XV intime*, 1 vol., Paris, 1899 ; Casimir Stryienski, *Le Gendre de Louis XV*, 1 vol., Paris, 1904.

CHAPTER III

THE SYSTEM
1715–1720

The Councils. A good-natured Prince. The Public Debt.
Marshal de Noailles. The Chambre de Justice. Lenormand in
the Pillory. Bethelot de Pléneuf. John Law. His youth.
His financial system. Founding of the Bank. Law appointed
Controller-General. Les *mères*, les *filles* et les *petites-filles*. The
Rue Quincampoix. The Parvenus. The Comte de Horn.
Popular anger against Law. Exile of the Parlement. Flight of
Law. His destitution. Results of the bankruptcy. The *Philip-
piques* of Lagrange-Chancel. The plague at Marseilles.

THE Regent transformed the administration, taking his
inspiration from the Duc de Bourgogne and Fénelon ;
he instituted groups of councillors to replace the
Secretaries of State. In addition to the Council of the Regency,
over which he presided, with the princes of the blood-royal and
The Councils. certain dukes and peers as his colleagues, he
created seven councils to deal with war, finance, navy, foreign
affairs, home affairs, matters of conscience or ecclesiastical
affairs, and commerce. This new administration afforded him
the disposal of numerous appointments, besides giving satisfaction to his supporters, and seemed advantageous from the
point of view of the public ; decisions were now taken not on
the discretion of a single individual, but after due debate by
several people, many of whom, although holding inferior
positions, were able by their intelligence to be of great use to
the chief councillors. The Abbé de Saint-Pierre, the friend of
perpetual peace, in his *Discours sur la Polysynodie*, has shown
how much is to be gained by such an organization. But it
could not last. It was soon apparent that Louis XIV had
been wise in excluding the great nobles from a share in the
government ; when they returned to power at the commence-
24

ment of the Regency, they showed themselves incapable of forgetting their own interests, privileges and futile pretensions, incapable also of taking a serious view of their duties as statesmen. The Councils were abolished in September 1718, a step which was justified by the disturbance, slowness, and indecision that had resulted in public affairs, in spite of the enthusiasm with which the innovation had been received. Chancellor d'Aguesseau, in his harangue at Martinmas, 1715, said in justification of the Duc d'Orléans : " Mediocre intellects may fear the Councils, the greater minds are among those who value them most highly ; in their self-reliance they are not afraid to seem to be governed by those whom in reality they govern, and disdaining the false honour of ruling by virtue of their rank, they reign more gloriously by the transcendency of their ability." There was general relief on the return to the old system ; the Secretaries of State were re-established after this unsuccessful experiment, which on the whole did honour to the liberal sentiments of Philippe d'Orléans.

Monarchic power regained its full strength ; but a rebellious spirit spread over the intellectual world ; the Regent himself **A good-** authorized the publication of *Télémaque ;* the **natured Prince.** *Mémoires* of the Cardinal de Retz were published in 1717, at a time when philosophers like Fontenelle, humorists like Montesquieu, and ambitious men like Voltaire began to show hitherto unheard-of audacity, and made themselves the mouthpieces of moral, religious, literary and political liberty. They thought aloud, relying on the good-nature of a prince who in his heart agreed with them, while preserving an outward respect for tradition. When the Duc d'Orléans went to Mass he took a volume of Rabelais disguised as a prayer-book ; when he exiled the Parlement, he softened the exile by furnishing sufficient money for the necessities and even the pleasures of the members in retirement at Pontoise ; this town became a pleasant place, where folks dined well in company with people of quality who came daily from Paris ; the road to Pontoise was as much frequented as that to Versailles, and as Duclos wittily remarked, it probably would not have been impossible to take the Regent himself there.

The Duc d'Orléans, as we have seen, was under a serious obligation to the Parlement ; he had accordingly given a certain **The National** share of authority to that Assembly, until he **Debt.** began to realize that the royal power would be compromised by the attempt of the delegates to assume the part of fathers of the people. This was one of the reasons which induced the prince to treat them with severity ; another reason was the opposition that the Assembly made to his financial reforms. The most oppressive heritage left by Louis XIV was the National Debt—it had risen to 90,000,000 livres, representing practically the arrears of four years. At the head of the Council of Finance was the Marshal de Villeroy, who was there by virtue of his office of Governor. With Villeroy was Adrien-Maurice, Marshal de Noailles. Saint-Simon has drawn his portrait with a pen dipped in gall ; he could never pardon Noailles for having married Françoise d'Aubigné, Madame de Maintenon's niece ; moreover, he was politically opposed to him.

It is certain that Noailles was not a great man, but to represent him as a " demon," a " replica of the serpent which tempted **Marshal de** Eve," was somewhat of an exaggeration. The **Noailles.** Marshal had had the confidence of Louis XIV ; he had been intrusted with the monarch's most precious documents, among others his *Réflexions sur le Métier de Roi ;* and he continued, like a true Nestor of the monarchy, to act as counsellor to Louis XV until the reversal of the alliances in 1756, which destroyed French traditions, and made it impossible for an old servant to follow the new direction of affairs.

Under the Regency, Noailles was conspicuous for his opposition to the declaration of bankruptcy proposed by Saint-Simon, which was to free Louis XV from the debts incurred by his great-grandfather. " France would never have recovered from the blow," said Noailles, in a minute addressed to the Duc d'Orléans ; " for, besides the extreme injustice of such an action, the injury caused both to commerce and to public credit would be prejudicial to us both in the eyes of foreigners and of subjects of the realm ; one may truthfully say that the only fruit we could gather from it would be shame and eternal disgrace." The Marshal triumphed, but he was less successful, when, following the example of Sully and Richelieu, he resorted to a *Chambre de Justice* in order to compel the financiers—the contractors stigmatized by Lesages in his *Turcaret* (1709)—to restore the illegal profits extorted from the public pocket and from the taxpayer. The inquiry was to extend as far back as 1689, twenty-seven years before, while the edict was so vaguely worded that no one could be certain of its application. The result was that people who had originally praised its severity were soon brought to tremble for their own safety.

This Court was installed at the Grands-Augustins and continued its functions for about a year; it did a great deal of harm **The Chambre** and little good; as Saint-Simon remarked: **de Justice.** " the harm consisted in the notorious subterfuges, the concealments, the flights and the total discredit of officials to which it gave rise; the little or nothing of good in the large returns of taxation which were made and the pernicious means employed to obtain them." The nation became tired of the prosecutions which caused commerce to flag, and gave rise to scenes like the one of which Buvat has recorded the details. One Lenormand was condemned to pay twenty thousand livres as damages to the Community of Arts and Crafts for his exactions, and a hundred thousand livres to the King. He was compelled to do penance for his conduct at the door of the church of Notre-Dame, at the Augustins and at the Halle; finally, he was condemned to the galleys for life, after being exposed in the pillory, where, with bare feet and head, clad only in his shirt, and holding a lighted torch in his hand, he had to submit to the insults of the people. A placard bearing in large letters " Robber of the People " was attached to the unfortunate man's chest and excited the gibes of the multitude.

The financiers were hunted out; some of them surrendered to the summons; others, like Berthelot de Pléneuf, father of the Marquise de Prie, placed the frontier between them and their pursuers, but all were deprived of their goods, often justly. Berthelot de Pléneuf especially had a heavy load on his conscience. He had been a provision contractor, and had not contented himself with the enormous profits he was enabled to make, but had robbed the public funds, his method being to allow the soldiers in the army hospitals to die of hunger, while

27

entering their keep in his bogus account-books; when the unfortunate men died he represented them as living and drew the money for their support. But while Lenormand was subjected to needless insults, the more adroit Berthelot de Pléneuf was able to return to France in 1719, and was appointed extraordinary Treasurer-General for war. Surely this crying injustice warrants the strictures of Saint-Simon against this Chambre de Justice, which went as far so to pronounce the death-sentence on Paparel and others. On this occasion the Regent exercised his right of pardon, and commuted the penalty; he desired to see retribution fall on the pockets of those who had robbed the people, and thought them sufficiently punished by the loss of their ill-gotten gains. The very severity of its judgments condemned this tribunal, which was also called the *Chambre Ardente!* The Chancellor, in the speech he made on the occasion of its abrogation, very justly said : " You are aware that even remedies may become evils when they last too long. . . The people easily change from excessive hate to excessive compassion ; they like the spectacle of speedy and severe chastisement, but their mood does not last, and once the first outburst of indignation against the guilty dies down, they almost come to believe them innocent, when they see them long in misery."

What was necessary was to recover the money hidden in the strong boxes in France and abroad, and to re-establish the monetary circulation ; so far the Chambre de Justice succeeded. A satirical engraving, *The Squeezer of the King's Sponges*, shows us the victims of the Chambre de Justice vomiting streams of gold ; it is ornamented by the following legend :

> Ces sangsues icy pressoirez
> Sont les pirates de la France
> Qui regorgent les flots dorez
> De nos trésors, en abondance.*

The time had now come to consider seriously a reorganization of the finances ; in this matter the Duc de Noailles gave John Law. up his place nominally to Argenson, but in reality to a foreigner, John Law, of Lauriston, who was to have an

---

* The leeches here squeezed are the robbers of France, vomiting in abundance the golden streams of our Treasure.

important effect on the Regent's conduct of affairs. Philippe, intelligent as he was, relied on others ; he was a man of swift determinations, but owing to his lack of energy, he was quickly discouraged. He was feeble and jaded by pleasure and allowed himself to be influenced. In the early success of the *System* he found a sort of justification for his attitude and a direct advantage, inasmuch as it enabled him to appear generous and prodigal to all. Unfortunately he could not foresee that the private interest of the reckless financier would make him forget the interests of the kingdom.

Law came from Scotland. Through his mother, Jean Campbell, he was descended from the Dukes of Argyll. He was born in 1671, and at his birth his father was carrying on the business of goldsmith and banker at Edinburgh. Law received a good education, and while still young showed a pronounced taste for scientific study. He came into the management of his father's fortune early in his life, and made use of it in order to see the world, scorning to follow the lucrative career to which he owed his wealth.

Tall, handsome, and pleasing of appearance, he had all the gifts which are necessary to success. London was his first stage, and there his success was remarkable, and his expenditure enormous. But in spite of his ample income, and his winnings at the gaming table, winnings which were perfectly honest and due to his extraordinary talent for figures, Law was soon overwhelmed with debts which were paid by his mother. As the result of a sword duel in which he killed his adversary, he was condemned to death ; he was pardoned and confined to prison, whence he escaped to sea.

He arrived on the Continent and waited his opportunity ; his head was full of projects, but he was still too young to have had sufficient experience. In Holland he studied the system of the famous bank of Amsterdam ; then he returned to Scotland, hoping that he would be able to put into practice his system of credit, founded on the creation of a new currency—banknotes and paper money, much as they exist to-day.

Law has often been represented as an adventurer, but in reality he was a pioneer, and, in some degree, the ancestor of the modern financier ; the majority of his ideas have found a place in modern banking. His mistake lay in his belief that the prosperity of a nation depended on the quantity of currency, and that this quantity could be increased at discretion, whereas the establishment of banks should be the result of prosperity. To borrow an "illustration" from Thiers who has given so clear an account of the famous System : "Supposing," says the great economist, " one were to cover a desert island with all the gold of the Americas or all the paper of the Bank of England, one could not immediately cause the growth of roads, canals, cultivation, factories, in fact, industry." Law failed, but his initial error was to a certain extent aggravated by the fever of speculation and jobbing which affected every class, from the greatest nobles, like the Prince de Conti or the Duc de la Force, to the lower orders and the lackeys.

Law's fellow-countrymen would not listen to him ; so he again left the shores of Scotland and went first to Brussels and then to Paris. He made the acquaintance of the future Regent, who was struck by the novelty of his ideas and received him warmly. Louis XIV would not allow " this Huguenot " to be mentioned in his presence. In the interval Law won at the gaming-tables, and the nobles of the Court lost enormous sums to him ; in consequence he was suspected, and was ordered to quit Paris within twenty-four hours. He was next seen in Italy, at Genoa, Venice, and Turin, where he lent money to the Duc de Vendôme, who was always his staunch protector ; he had interviews with Victor Amadeus, King of Sicily and Duke of Savoy, and with the Emperor Charles VI, but he was always rebuffed, and returned to Scotland with a fortune of eighty thousand pounds. This sum he sent over into France, hoping eventually to find that country favourable to the realization of his system. When Louis XIV died, and the royal power was in the hands of the Duc d'Orléans, the finances were in a deplorable condition, and Law's time had come.

The Regent was already on his side, but for a long time he was kept in suspense. However, on October 24, 1715, he made **Law's Bank.** the first exposition of his principles to the Council ; all the revenues of the King were to be paid into his Bank ; those to whom money was due from the State were only to receive paper money from the royal Treasury (consisting of notes for ten, one hundred and one thousand crowns) for which they could immediately receive the value by going to the Bank ; no one was bound to keep them or to receive them commercially ; but Law demonstrated that every one would be content to have the notes instead of coin " because of the ease with which payments could be made in paper, and the certainty of receiving payment for them whenever it was desired," adding "that it would be impossible to have more notes than coin, since notes could only be issued in proportion to the coin, and thus the expenses of remittance, the risks of carriage, of transport from one town to another, and the multiplication of clerks, would be avoided."

Law had not yet won his case ; the Bank was not established until some months later by the edict of May 2, 1716. The popularity of the establishment is well known ; the curious flocked there in crowds ; this new house of credit, established first in the old Hôtel de Mesmes, in the Rue Sainte-Avoye, and later at the Hôtel Mazarin, in the Rue Vivienne, now the Bibliothèque Nationale, offered a novel spectacle. People entered a vast hall divided into counting-houses in which gold and silver abounded ; in exchange for a note they received coin ; but later they came to exchange coin for notes, which were popular since they were found so convenient for business transactions. In less than a year the bitterest enemies of the Scottish financier were convinced, for the results which he had foretold seemed for the most part to be realized. In April 1717, the Bank opened branches in the provinces. At first notes were only issued to the extent of six million francs ; fifty or sixty millions might have been issued without shaking the public confidences in the least. Everything was going well, but Law was impatient, and so were the people he had enriched. Following this prosperous venture other speculations were tried—with disastrous effects. The Bank was declared the Royal Bank on May 4, 1718 ; Law became master of the public revenues, on the one hand encouraging, by means of a stock commonly called Mississippi Stock, the colonial trade, in which he was assisted by great companies, on the other hand taking over the whole farming of the revenue, including that of tobacco, the privilege of coining money, and the collection of taxes. After his conversion to Catholicism, which was brought about by the Abbé Tencin, he was appointed Controller-General.

Law
Controller-
General.

He was all-powerful, and according to a picturesque expression of Saint-Simon, he possessed in his paper a tap of finance which he allowed to run on any who would. His son was invited to dance in the King's ballet; but owing to smallpox he missed the honour. Even a duchess courted Law, one of them so far forgetting herself as to kiss his hand. Every stratagem was tried to obtain an interview with him; one lady ordered her carriage to be driven past the Scotsman's house, and when she arrived there she was heard to shout to the coachman, " Upset, you fool, upset ! " The coachman obeyed; the financier hastened to her assistance, and the lady admitted the accident had been designed to procure an interview with him. He was for ever in demand, and besieged by petitioners. " Law," says Saint-Simon, " saw them force his doors, enter from the garden through the windows, or tumble down the chimney into his room." Madame Palatine also recounts that her son, the Regent, required a duchess to attend his daughter, the Princess of Modena, and a courtier said to him, " If you wish, sir, to have your choice of duchesses, send to Madame Law; you will find them all collected there."

There was nothing derogatory on the part of the great noblemen in mixing in the affairs of the Bank and the companies, since the Duc d'Orléans himself had decreed it. Matters came to such a pass that the fictitious value of the paper in 1719 represented eighty times the coin in circulation in the kingdom, for the jobbers succeeded in raising the value of every kind of stock issued by the Royal Bank. These stocks were called first the *mères*, then the *filles*, and the *petites-filles* (mothers, daughters, and grand-daughters); these last could only be bought at the price of four *mères* and one *fille*, because of the successive premiums.

The Bourse was established in the Rue Quincampoix, where the crowd was so great that horses and carriages could not be The Rue Quin- allowed there, and guards were placed at either campoix. end of the street, while drummers and men with bells were stationed to announce the opening of business at seven in the morning, and to clear the premises in the evening. The madness which prevailed was without parallel; it was even difficult to guard the entry of the narrow street on Sundays and holidays. Paris was filled with strangers attracted by the desire for gain; in 1719, it held 250,000 more people than in preceding years. Rooms had to be built above the attics to accommodate them. The end, however, was approaching. The bank was on a solid foundation, the Mississippi scheme was merely a chimera " a continual catch (*tour de passe passe*) to attract the money of some and give it to others; it was absolutely certain that in the end these stocks would fail, since there was neither mine nor philosopher's stone, and that the few would find themselves enriched at the expense of the total ruin of the greater number; and this is what happened."*

Panic seized the speculators, shareholders wished to realize. The Prince de Conti sent three wagons to the bank, and they returned full of coin in exchange for his " paper." The till was soon empty. The authorities had recourse to extreme measures. No one was allowed to have in his house more than five hundred francs in specie or to wear diamonds. The following was a rhyme sung in the streets of Paris at this time :

> Lundi, j'achetai des actions
> Mardi, je gagnai des millions
> Mercredi, j'ornai mon ménage
> Jeudi, je pris un equipage
> Vendredi, je m'en fus au bal
> Et Samedi, à l'hôpital.†

Positions were reversed, servants were enriched, while noblemen put their houses up for sale.

One lackey gained enough to buy a carriage; when the carriage was brought to him he forgot he was the master and mounted behind. His servant exclaimed, " Oh !
The Parvenus. là ! Monsieur, the carriage is yours ! " " Ah ! true ! " he said, " I did not remember."

Some ladies of quality saw a finely dressed woman, whom none of them knew, descend from a smart carriage, and sent to ask the coachman who she was. " She is a lady," he replied grinning, " who has fallen into this carriage from the fourth

* Saint-Simon.
† Monday, I bought shares ; Tuesday, I won millions ; Wednesday, I furnished my house ; Thursday, I bought a carriage ; Friday, I was at the ball ; and Saturday at the poorhouse.

storey." She was just a parvenu like Madame Béjon's servant. Madame Béjon and her daughter saw their cook in a box at the opera ; they could not believe their eyes ; " It is Marie, our cook " said they. The young people in the amphitheatre took up the cry, " Marie the Cook ! Marie the Cook ! " Whereupon the *cordon-bleu* rose and addressed her former mistress : " Yes, madame, I am Marie, the cook ; I have made money at the Rue Quincampoix ; I am fond of fine clothes ; I have bought pretty dresses and I have paid for them ; can you say the same for yours ? "

The comedy is amusing, but there were also tragedies. A young Comte de Horn, of a noble Flanders house, allied to many **The Comte** of the princely families of Europe, murdered a **de Horn.** clerk of the Bank at the " Epée de Bois " Inn in the Rue de Venise, near the Rue Quincampoix ; he had lost a great deal of money at the fair of Saint-Germain and recouped himself by robbing the clerk. Hoping to conceal his crime he ran, bloodstained as he was, to the house of the Police Commissary, and affirmed that an attempt had been made to kill him. The Commissary replied, " You come here, monsieur, all covered with blood, yet you are not wounded, I shall arrest you." He had two accomplices who were smitten with remorse and confessed. Judgment was pronounced without delay. The relatives of the culprit made efforts, not to save his life, but to secure that he should not be executed in public, but should be beheaded privately in the prison. The Regent was inflexible. Doubtless it cost him an effort to do violence to his own kindness of heart, but the fact that he had not yielded made him popular. He told his mother that when the Comte de Horn was broken on the wheel people said : " If anything is done against our Regent, personally, he pardons all, but if anything is done against ourselves, he is not to be trifled with, but gives us justice as is seen in the case of this Comte de Horn." In recounting this the Duke's eyes were moist.

The agitation in Paris was extreme ; on July 17, 1720, the crowd before the Bank in the Rue Vivienne, all seeking their **Popular fury** money, was so great that sixteen people were **against Law.** stifled. Law ventured outside, and as he passed the little market of Quinze-Vingts, a woman threw herself before the door of his carriage and demanded her husband who had just been killed. As pale as death, he went on foot to the Palais Royal where he found refuge and remained for several days under the protection of the Duc d'Orléans. The carriage went home; the crowd believing that the financier was returning, flung stones at the vehicle and the coachman was wounded:

> " Messieurs, Messieurs, grande nouvelle,
> Le carosse de Law est réduite en canelle ! " *

said the President de Mesmes, at the Duchesse du Maine's, in the tragic tones he assumed in the theatre of Sceaux. His colleagues asked about the man himself. " He was not inside." " So much the worse," was the reply.

On the same day there was a sharp struggle between the Parlement and the Regency, the former refusing to register an **The Parlement** edict purporting to grant fresh monopolies to the **exiled.** Mississippi company; consequently *lettres de cachet* were issued to each president and councillor of the Parlement, ordering them to quit Paris within forty-eight hours and retire to Pontoise. Little excitement was caused by this event, as the financial disaster eclipsed everything. The musketeers had been summoned, but they were not needed, and remained in the halls of the Palais drinking and amusing themselves with the trial of a cat, with pleadings and formal condemnation, reviving the scenes of *Les Plaideurs*.

Law was obliged to take to flight to escape the hatred of the Parisians who, after damaging his carriage, broke the windows **Flight of Law.** of his house. He was guarded on his departure, and he went away to die in Venice in 1729 in misery and destitution. When he took his leave of the Regent he said to him, " Monseigneur, I have made some great mistakes; I have made them because I am mortal; but in my conduct you will find neither malice nor roguery." He wrote in exile to the Duc de Bourbon: " Æsop was a model of probity; yet the courtiers accused him of possessing treasures in a coffer which he often visited; all they found in it was a coat he had had before he had gained the prince's favour. If I had saved my

* Gentlemen ! Great news ! Law's coach is reduced to splinters.

coat, I would not change my place with those who are in the first positions; but I am naked; they seem to expect me to exist with nothing, and to pay my debts without having any funds." Law never recovered the coat he claimed. He justified the remark of La Bruyère: "If the financier fails the courtiers say of him: he is a bourgeois, a nobody, an ill-bred person; if he succeeds, they ask him for his daughter."

By a curious irony of fate, at the very moment of the bankruptcy, the Regent was presented with a vignette placed at the head of the dedicatory epistle of the third edition of the *Dictionnaire de Bayle*. It showed his portrait, after Rigaud, supported by Mercury, while Minerva pointed it out for universal admiration. On the left was portrayed France, sorrowful and afflicted, bearing an empty cornucopia from which some pieces of money had fallen; on the right the Royal Bank, triumphant, with genii bearing a conch full of gold, and near them a small negro with a map of the Mississippi, the source of all this wealth! Eulogy had turned to satire, and the public was amused to read the following words of the academician, La Motte, who wrote the dedicatory epistle: "Your justice and your goodness have enabled you to find, for the payment of the debts of the State and the bestowal of fresh treasures, the mighty resources which astonish the nations, and of which they would be jealous, but that your own equity, and that which they may expect from our young monarch, who is being schooled in your example, re-assures them as to your might." This dithyramb arrived at a truly opportune moment! The Regent, who was a man of wit, did not keep the copy in his library.

Everything was not lost in this disaster. Though Law has left the memory of a financier at bay, crazed by speculation, it must not be forgotten, that as Controller-General he made wise reforms, diminished the taxes, lightened the burden which weighed on the people, and even anticipated Turgot in an attempt to facilitate the distribution of corn. He prepared the way for the economists, and supplied an example of the power of credit.

But the immediate consequences of the bankruptcy were disastrous; to the lucky Mississippians, favoured by fortune

THE SYSTEM

and not their own efforts, it meant an unnatural life, a life of luxury and pleasure, of fêtes often degenerating into orgies which, equally with the suppers given by the Regent and his *roués*, lowered the moral standard of the nation. Men sought after riches as before they had sought after glory and honour, and, in this wild pursuit, the different classes began to forget their respective traditions.

The financial problem was not solved. Matters were placed in the hands of the Pâris brothers, who were bankers to the State for many years. Then a return was made to the system of Farmers-General, who leased the collection of taxes. But during the whole of the eighteenth century, the public debt was far in excess of the receipts and the financial embarrassment was extreme.

In 1720—the inauspicious year of the Regency—the cele-
The Philip- brated *Philippiques* appeared, in which Lagrange-
piques of Chancel, a hired satirist, perverted history and
Lagrange- dragged Philippe d'Orléans in the mud with
Chancel. ridiculous exaggeration.

A more serious scourge fell on Provence, and Marseilles especially ; for a whole year a pestilence desolated that fair
The Plague at country. The occasion gave birth to deeds of
Marseilles. great devotion. Monseigneur de Belzunce, at the head of his clergy, showed an example of heroism rivalling that of Carlo Borromeo at Milan. He was supported by the sheriffs, Estelle and Moustier, and by the Chevalier de Roze. Many saw in this calamity a divine visitation.

PRINCIPAL SOURCES. Fénelon, *Ecrits politiques, Télémaque* ; President Hénault, *Mémoires* ; Memoirs and correspondence previously quoted ; *Correspondance de Louis XV et du Maréchal de Noailles*, edited by Camille Rousset (2 vols., Paris, 1869) ; Thiers, *Histoire de Law* (1 vol., Paris, n.d.)

CHAPTER IV

THE TWO CARDINALS
1716–1723

Dubois. The second marriage of Philip V of Spain. Elizabeth
Farnese. Alberoni. His treaty with England. George I and
the Regent. Dubois' mission to Holland. Stanhope. The Pitt
diamond. The Triple Alliance Dubois in London. Alberoni
and the Sicilian Expedition. The Intrigues of the Duchesse
du Maine and the Prince de Cellamare. War declared against
Spain. Alberoni's plans. His dismissal. The Quadruple
Alliance. The Spanish marriages. Mariannita. Dubois at
his zenith. Watteau.

THE Regent had another satellite, the Abbé Dubois;
a man of the greatest ambition, he directed foreign
affairs from behind the scenes, with more skill but with
no less daring than Law had shown in the management of
finance. He was the son of a doctor at Brive-la-Gaillarde, and
came to Paris at the expense of a nobleman, for
Dubois. he had no private means. Entrusted with the
education of Philippe d'Orléans at a salary of five hundred
crowns, he gradually won for himself a place in the sun. He
reaped the reward of services performed for his pupil, often of
an ignoble nature, by becoming his most powerful minister,
and finally he was to receive the highest ecclesiastical prize,
the cardinal's purple.

On September 2, 1715, the day on which the Duke was
proclaimed Regent, he went to see his mother at Versailles.
She embraced him tenderly and said : " I do not intend to
interfere in anything, there is only one thing that I wish, and
that is that the Abbé Dubois may have no share in the future
government. He is the greatest knave and the most notorious
rascal in the world ; he would do anything to advance himself

38

in the slightest degree, and would sell his master and the State
to serve his smallest interest." The Regent promised all the
princess asked, but his promises were but empty words.

Dubois' reign was about to begin, and in certain respects
it was to be a glorious reign. Knave he may have been, but he
was also a skilful politician. The Regent foresaw that this
bugbear of Madame Palatine, Saint-Simon, and after them, of
Michelet, could be of service to him. Events were to justify
his confidence in his old tutor. We shall see Dubois at grips
with Spain, where a Bourbon was King, the grandson of Louis
XIV, and with England, whose interests were closely allied to
those of France, and to those of the Regent especially.

Philip V had officially renounced his rights to the crown
of his ancestors, and might have been satisfied with his throne
in Spain; but his whole policy was directed towards obtaining
the ultimate succession to Louis XV, if not for himself, at least
for his descendants. His minister Grimaldo had written thus
in May 1714, in anticipation of the King's death: " If the
Dauphin (Louis XV) should die, his Catholic Majesty, who has
never dreamed of possessing the two crowns himself, would
wish to give that of France to one of his sons, while himself keeping the crown of Spain."

Philip V had lost his first wife, Marie-Louise of Savoy, sister
of the Duchesse de Bourgogne, on February 14, 1714, and had
Second Marriage of Philip V of Spain. married again. The new Queen was twenty-two
years of age. Her first act was the courageous
one of dismissing the Princesse des Ursins, the
all powerful *camerera mayor*, thus indicating that
she would submit to no yoke. Elizabeth Farnese brought with
her into Spain all the energy of a descendant of Charles the
Fifth, and all the pride of a woman whom fortune has placed
in a position beyond her hopes.

She travelled over land from Parma, receiving homage by
the way, along the Ligurian coast and through the south of
France. The stages of her journey were short, in spite of her
husband's impatience. The judgment passed on her was everywhere the same, that she was not beautiful, that she was deeply
pitted with small-pox, but that her demeanour was lofty and
that she could be extremely gracious when she pleased. " Heart

of a Lombard, spirit of a Florentine, her will was very strong,"
said the Prince of Monaco. The Duc de Saint-Aignan, who was
sent by Louis XIV to greet her on her entry into Provence,
wrote : "Her will is very pronounced . . . but I believe
there will be some means of ruling her ; if this is so, it will be
done by those of her household who know how to please her."
Saint-Aignan foresaw Alberoni, who, as was known later,
planned the dismissal of the Princesse des Ursins. Philip's
ambitions were strengthened by the influence of Elizabeth and
her confidant.

Alberoni's career is singularly like that of Dubois. Like
him he was of humble origin. He was the son of a gardener of

Alberoni. Placentia and "had assumed the gown, by becoming an abbé, to enable him to reach heights
which would have been inaccessible to his smock." He was able to
secure the favour of the Duke of Parma, who discovered his capa-
bility, and appointed him to represent him at the court of Madrid.
Like Dubois, he succeeded in making an unique position for
himself ; and this was assured when he had brought about the
marriage of Elizabeth Farnese, his master's niece, with the
King of Spain. Also, like Dubois he became a Cardinal, and
the same indignation was expressed when it was known that
he had been admitted to the Sacred College.

He had enormous influence over the mind of the princess
whom he had made Queen, and through her over the King,
who allowed himself to be easily led. He inspired all Philip's
policy during the early years of the Regency. He urged the
King to the conquest of Italy, and he instilled in the mind of
Elizabeth that consistent hatred of France, which, in spite of
subsequent *rapprochements,* even survived his fall.

He courted England with the object of dealing a mortal
blow at France. At his instigation, Philip, on November 14,
His Treaty 1715, signed a treaty under which the King of
with England. Great Britain was accorded greater privileges in
America than had ever been given to France, a treaty so
advantageous, "that the Dutch ambassador at Madrid showed
his joy as though it meant the ruin of French commerce." But
the English did not accept the alliance proposed by Alberoni,
and to the great surprise of Madrid, George I and the Emperor

concluded a treaty in May 1716, to guarantee each other's territories; the Emperor was Philip's irreconcilable enemy, and had been an unsuccessful competitor for the Castillian succession. The King of Spain was punished for having broken with France and for his estrangement from the elder Bourbon line.

It is surely not to the discredit of the Regent that he upset the plans of Alberoni, assured himself in his turn of the friendship of England, and re-established peace, which was threatened by the schemes of a skilful intriguer whose fault was that his vision was too vast. Had Alberoni the true qualities of a statesman? He said of himself: " My temperament is lively, and the little pot boils quickly." On his own showing, he had not the self-possession which is necessary to secure diplomatic victories; his designs were ambitious, but he always failed—owing to his temperament and his lack of tact and prudence.

As a matter of fact, England was playing with Spain. She had no interest in supporting Philip in his attempt to secure the throne of France.

George I and the Regent were able to be mutually useful. It must not be forgotten that they were very close relatives. George I and On their mothers' side they were descended from the Regent. the Stuarts; the grandmother of the one, and the great-grandmother of the other was Elizabeth, Charles I's sister, the unfortunate Queen of Bohemia, who was deposed and exiled at the beginning of the Thirty Years War. The two cousins had exchanged courteous and even affectionate letters before September 1, 1715. They cultivated one another in anticipation of the future. George needed the King of France to keep away the Pretender, the son of James II, whose throne he had taken, while on his side the Duc d'Orléans relied on the King of England to keep Spain in order. There was a compact between them, though there was some hesitation on either side. The Regent temporized. In his anxiety to settle his numerous daughters, he thought of marrying Mademoiselle de Valois, afterwards the Duchess of Modena, to the Chevalier de Saint-Georges; consequently he secretly supported the Pretender; while George I allowed Alberoni to burn himself in picking chestnuts from the fire. In spite of these complications

41

the first *entente cordiale* was concluded and cemented by both real and personal interests. The understanding was useful to the House of Orléans, whose ultimate triumph in the event of Louis' death the Regent was determined to secure. George also gained the support he needed to assure his position as a usurper. In fact, the whole policy of this period was founded on open egotism ; whether at Versailles, London, or Madrid, the interests considered were dynastic and not national.

But during this struggle the diplomats performed marvels, and Dubois, after considerable difficulty and sacrifice, extricated the Regent from the imbroglio in which he found himself between England, discontented at his equivocal conduct, Spain, in open hostility to France, and the faction of the legitimized princes, who in their present eclipse expected everything from the intervention of Philip V. These three problems were solved at practically the same time, thanks to Dubois, who had been given full powers to treat.

The future Cardinal could trust only himself with the conduct of these delicate negotiations. In June 1716, he went to Holland in the strictest incognito, under the **Dubois' Mission to Holland.** assumed name of Saint-Albin. His disguise consisted of a whole wardrobe of different costumes and perruques. He was accompanied by a single secretary, the Sieur de Sourdeval, who passed as his master. This mission, which was to end in the Triple and Quadruple Alliances, had at the outset the appearance of comedy, and seemed to have been entrusted to Dorante and Pasquin.

Dubois arrived at the Hague on July 5, and waited for the arrival of George I, who was to land at a secret spot, on a visit to his dominion of Hanover. He bore a letter from the Regent, couched as follows : " Should the Abbé Dubois, who is in Holland on his private affairs, be there when His Majesty passes, and should the opportunity be given him to have the honour to convey the sentiments he is aware that I feel for the person of Your Majesty and for union between France and England, I pray Your Majesty to have confidence in him and to be persuaded that he cannot exaggerate my respect and esteem for Your Majesty."

After waiting for a fortnight Dubois heard of the King's

arrival, and sent a note to the minister Stanhope, in which he said : " I could not, my lord, resist the temptation to take advantage of your passage through Holland that I might do myself the honour of embracing you. I am at the Hague, unknown to anyone and incognito. I ask you to keep my secret, and to be so good as to let me know where and when it would be convenient for me to meet you and converse with you without interruption. I hope you will grant this favour in remembrance of the friendship with which you have honoured me, and the sincere interest I take in all that concerns you." The Abbé saw Stanhope on July 21, and was able to reassure him as to the Regent's attitude, declaring that he had abandoned all idea of assisting James II's son. After three interviews Dubois hurriedly returned to Paris to seek instructions. A week later he left again for Hanover, where, in the meantime, an agreement had been drawn up, embodying Stanhope's conditions, which, after some discussion, were accepted.

The English minister had been the mainspring of these transactions ; he was a skilled diplomat, who was actively concerned in most of the important events of his time; his **Stanhope.** policy is summed up by his phrase : " I hope to make the English lose the habit of considering the French their natural enemies." He had known the Regent in Spain, and Dubois in Paris. It suited him to encourage a bold policy, since he realized the advantage to be derived therefrom, a purely moral advantage, for during the negotiations, he was compelled to refuse a bribe from Dubois, who offered him 600,000 livres. The only present that was accepted was sixty casks of the best Champagne and Burgundy, which were sent to the English Court. Saint-Simon accused Dubois of having sold himself to the English, but he could hardly have accepted and offered a gratuity at the same time. His cupidity is well known, but on this occasion it is only just to refute the calumnies of the memoir-writer. One of Dubois' historians, M. Wiesener, after careful research in the Record Office in London, has been unable to find any trace of money given to Dubois. There **The Pitt** remains the question of the diamond which was **Diamond.** bought from Stanhope's father-in-law, Pitt, for 2,500,000 francs—the famous " Regent " diamond, now in the

Louvre. Here again it was necessary to win over the English, or rather the small but powerful party in the House of Commons, which was then opposed to an alliance with France. It is possible that Dubois received a commission from Pitt, but this is a pure conjecture founded on a presumption from the known character of the man.

The Triple Alliance between France, England and Holland, was signed on January 4, 1717, in all the sunshine of a "true, **The Triple** firm, and inviolable peace." The conditions **Alliance.** were that "the person who had taken the title of Prince of Wales, during the life of the late King James II, and, after his death, that of King of Great Britain," should be for ever expelled from French territory, and should be obliged to live "on the other side of the Alps." England had no wish to see a repetition of the unsuccessful attempt which the Pretender had just made on English territory, and therefore had made up her mind to crush the Jacobite party completely. The canal at Mardick, begun by Louis XIV to replace the port at Dunkirk, and then demolished in accordance with the Treaty of Utrecht, was to be abandoned, and to be used only as a conduit for water to irrigate the country, or for the commercial service of that part of the Netherlands ; and the boats to be used for this purpose were not to be larger than sixteen feet in width. The clauses of the Treaty of Utrecht relative to the succession of the Protestant line in Great Britain were maintained, as were those that dealt with the succession to the French crown, whereby the Spanish Bourbons were excluded. As a concession to Holland, France agreed to abolish her import duty of four sous in the pound on Dutch goods.

George I and the Regent thus assured their dynasties, while Holland improved her commercial position. France, it is true, sacrificed the Mardick canal, but in so doing she conformed to the spirit of the Treaty of Utrecht, and it would have meant certain war if she had not yielded. The policy of Dubois and the Regent has been severely criticized; new ideas in defiance of tradition are not readily accepted, and no one likes to swim against the stream, but it is possible to defend this policy in view of the attitude of Spain. For this natural ally of France was now her enemy, while George I had for a long time favoured the idea of an alliance with her. Before the death of Louis XIV he wrote to Stair, his representative at Paris : " We think it expedient to command you, very particularly, to try by all the means in your power to maintain an intimate and confidential connexion with our brother the Duke of Orleans. You will encourage him to trust us and our kingdoms to provide him, should the occasion arise, with the most effective assistance." Eighteen months had barely gone by since then and George was victorious : he had made it appear that he was furthering the interests of his future ally, while he had really assured his own—a triumph of diplomatic ability.

Yet the interests of France, the " real good " of the people, had not been neglected. At the end of 1716, Dubois said to the Regent : " It is certain that this alliance will decide the fate of Europe for a long time and will give France a superiority which she could acquire by no other means. That being so, I believe it to be beyond price, and were I master I would rather lose thirty millions than have it fail." In answer to this declaration the Regent wrote personally : " I agree with you in all this." The day that the Treaty was signed, Stanhope said to Dubois : " Your journey to The Hague, Sir, has saved much bloodshed and there are many nations that unwittingly owe their peace to you."

But Dubois had every intention of profiting by the conclusion of the Triple Alliance. When it was signed, he hastened to assure his position ! " I consider myself happy," he wrote to the Duc d'Orléans, " to have been honoured with your commands in a matter so essential to your welfare, and I am more grateful to you for having given me this proof of the honour of your confidence *than if you had made me a cardinal.*" This was the first hint ; meanwhile, Dubois obtained a list of vacant benefices, and with absolute shamelessness, appropriated a number of remunerative dignities. Among others, he granted himself the Abbey of Alquier, with a revenue of 25,000 *livres,* and sat as Councillor of State for Foreign Affairs. His assumption of office was marked by the abandonment of the Councils ; the old forms were revived, and Dubois was assured of being absolute master of his own department.

For the future Dubois was no longer a comedian in a low
Dutch inn, but a splendid ambassador, living in great style

Dubois in London. in London. He definitely crowned his policy by
the signature of the Quadruple Alliance on August
2, 1718. He persuaded the Emperor Charles VI to renounce
his hope of reuniting the crowns of Spain and Hungary, and
thus made any new usurpation improbable. Philip V, for his
part, obtained the Emperor's promise to cede the Duchy of
Parma to his son, Don Carlos. But the King of Spain agreed
to the conditions reluctantly.

Whilst Dubois was negotiating with the English Court,
Alberoni, who had become a Cardinal on July 12, 1717, was
using the money, raised by papal authority from the clergy
of Spain and the Indies for the *Cruzada* against the infidels,
to strengthen Philip's navy. He attacked Sardinia and hoped
to retake Sicily, which had been given to the Duke of Savoy
by the Treaty of Utrecht. This second armada was entirely
destroyed by the English Admiral Byng, on August 17, 1718,
off Syracuse and Cape Passaro.

A less sanguinary defeat also awaited the Cardinal in the
discovery of the intrigues carried on by the Spanish Ambassador

The Cellamare Conspiracy. at Paris, the Prince of Cellamare, at his instigation. His object had been to persuade the legiti-
mized princes, who were discontented with the obscure position
they occupied under the Regency, to support his master's
claims. The pompous though popular word conspiracy is too
strong an expression to use for so childish a plot, an absurd
conception of the feather-brained Duchesse du Maine, who
found a cure for her neurasthenia in weaving these imbroglios.

But the Government insisted on treating the " conspirators "
as criminals, and in taking them seriously, although they knew
well enough that a handful of madmen do not constitute a
party. The Comte de Laval who, on the pretext of his relation-
ship to Louis XIV, had worn mourning at that king's death, was
seeking only to advertise himself. The Marquis de Pompadour,
whose name was afterwards so celebrated, joined this venture
in the mere hope of retrieving his fortunes, shattered by a new
Government to which he was opposed. These two had been
charged by Madame du Maine, one with the negotiations with

Spain, and the other with the correspondence with the provinces. Cellamare himself has testified to the insignificance of the little Duchess' following and to the ineptitude of their plans. When he received Alberoni's instructions not to quit Paris until all the mines had been fired, he wittily remarked : " Mines without powder." The Duchesse du Maine was sent to the Château of Dijon ; the Duke, in spite of the fact that he was not in his wife's confidence and had kept aloof from the plot, was taken to the fortress of Doullens, and the subordinates were lodged in the Bastille, Vincennes, and other places. But they were all pardoned soon afterwards, the confessions of the culprits being the only condition demanded for their liberty. His status as ambassador made Cellamare inviolable ; he was retained for a short time at Blois, and then escorted over the Spanish frontier.

Dubois naturally made use of this pretended conspiracy to induce the Regent to declare war on Spain, and to support the policy of England. If, at this moment, Philip had joined the Quadruple Alliance, thus abandoning his pretensions and securing for his son the Italian duchies denied him by the Treaty of Utrecht, there would have been no need to resort to extremities. But nothing could check the obstinacy of Alberoni, and it was necessary to give that Cardinal a lesson.

On January 9, 1719, the rupture between France and Spain was complete. The French forces were led by the Marshal Duke of Berwick, who had formerly won battles for the grandson of Louis XIV. Hostilities broke out in the spring, on April 20. They resulted in a series of reverses for Philip's naval and military forces ; the arsenals of Pasajes and Santoña were burnt ; Fontarabia and San Sebastian were captured. The Spanish King came to realize how chimerical was the advice to which he had listened.

War between France and Spain.

All Alberoni's schemes were foundering ; yet how vast were the projects which filled his overcharged imagination ! In March 1719, he attempted to assist the Stuart Pretender, but the fleet which set sail for Scotland was scattered by a tempest. In June he made Philip propose the dismemberment of France and England, promising to reserve one throne for the Duc d'Orléans and another for James. After thus upsetting the

map of Europe in the depths of his palace, Philip wrote to
Orléans on June 12, 1719 : "These are the conditions which
will restore public calm, the balance of power in Europe, peace
and gratification in Spain and France, and the honour of our
august House, so often slighted by England, while the latter
will learn from personal experience the meaning of partition,
the more justly, since she has arranged the same for all Europe.
The lustre of the House of France will shine the brighter by the
addition of a fresh crown on the head of a prince of that august
family." To this letter the Duc d'Orléans made no reply.

Alberoni next turned his attention to the provinces of
France, particularly Brittany ; he made use of an agitation
started by the Breton States-General and encouraged by a
group of gentlemen favourable to the Spanish cause, who
acted with the Cardinal's connivance and were independent of the
Duchesse du Maine. An extraordinary commission called
a Chambre Royale was appointed by letters patent on October
3, 1719, to try the rebels ; four were beheaded, among them
the Marquis de Pontcallec, and sixteen others fled either to
Madrid or Parma, and were condemned by default.

Before this, Alberoni had endeavoured to secure an alliance
with Turkey, when that country was signing the peace of
Passarowitz with the Emperor ; and had derived fresh hopes
from Charles XII of Sweden at the very time the latter fell in
the trenches before Frederikshall.

It is not permissible for a minister to be always at fault
in the situations he creates, nor to be thus persecuted by fortune.
Dismissal of   One by one all the dreams of Alberoni faded ;
Alberoni.   the plots he wove against the King of England
and the Emperor in the north and east, the vain schemes he
prepared against the Regent, all vanished in smoke. He had
revealed the possibilities of his energetic but erratic temperament. The Spanish King's eyes were opened. Philip dismissed the Cardinal like a servant, commanding him to leave
Madrid in eight days and never to appear before him again.
This happened in December 1719, and the relief in Europe
was general. Dubois wrote to Stanhope : "The King and
Queen of Spain have at length had resolution enough to dismiss
the ministry and to drive Cardinal Alberoni out of Spain. . . .

One cannot think of this event, my lord, without realizing how much is due to Your Excellency for the value of the projects that you have made, and for the justice of the means used to bring them about. The slight temporary anxiety and expenditure involved have saved us *from the infinite misfortunes that a general war might have caused.*"

In an unpublished letter of December 11, 1719, now in the Archives at Naples, Elizabeth Farnese wrote to the Duke of Parma : "God be praised ! the Cardinal departs to-morrow ; but keep an eye on him, for he is capable of anything ; his brain is diabolical—*un cervello diabolico.*"

Alberoni himself realized that he was an obstacle in the way of European peace. On December 6, he admitted to his friend Rocca : "You will learn what has happened from the Marquis Annibale Scotti. It was the smallest sacrifice that could be made to give peace to Europe." Was this resignation, pride, or irony ? Anything may be read between the lines.

Alberoni lived until 1752. Before his death, at the age of eighty-eight he had the pleasure of seeing Don Carlos and Don Philip, the sons of Philip V and Elizabeth Farnese, in possession of the Kingdom of Naples and the Duchy of Parma, and an Italy partially delivered from Austrian rule—a pleasure which must have had some bitterness in it, since he himself had nothing to do with the result.

In spite of his defeat, the King of Spain endeavoured to exact sacrifices from the conqueror ; he seemed to wish to The Quadruple recompense himself for the dismissal of Alberoni Alliance. by demanding, as a condition to the signature of the treaty, the restitution of the territory occupied by the belligerents, and the recognition of the rights of his son Don Carlos to the succession of Parma and Tuscany, without Imperial investiture. Philip was disarmed by the very excess of his claims. He finally acceded to the Quadruple Alliance on January 20, 1720. His accession was ratified at The Hague on May 20 ; Sicily reverted to the Emperor, and the Duke of Savoy, late King of Sicily, became King of Sardinia. The King of Spain again renounced the Crown of France, and submitted to the Emperor's will as to the establishment of Don Carlos in Italy.

Shortly afterwards, the friendly relations between the Regent and Philip V were sealed by proposals of marriage. It seemed **The Spanish** that there was to be a return of happy days for **Marriages.** the two Houses, and that the most cherished dynastic ambitions were to be satisfied. In 1721, Louis XV was affianced to Anna-Maria-Victoria, his first cousin, daughter of the King of Spain and Elizabeth Farnese. The King was in his fourteenth year, the Infanta in her fifth, so that this arrangement was a little premature, and some time would have to elapse before the marriage could be celebrated ; but the Regent decided that there should be an exchange of princesses in order to establish his own daughters. One of them, Mlle. de Montpensier, as the wife of Louis I, was to be Queen of Spain for a few months ; * another, Mlle. de Beaujolais, was affianced to Don Carlos. Mariannita, as her mother called her, made her solemn entry into Paris on March 2, 1722, amid popular rejoicings. She was thought charming, spirited, comparatively pretty, " fair, pink, and white." While she was at Chartres, on the previous day, the Cardinal de Rohan, Grand Almoner of France, and Madame de Soubise came to see her. As a joke the Infanta was told that the Cardinal was very ugly, more so even than the Bishop of Bazas, of whom she was afraid. When she saw, on the contrary, how handsome M. de Rohan was (he was called the *Belle Eminence*) she remained quiet, but at dinner, half an hour later, she made a mischievous remark : " Madame de Soubise must be whipped, for she has lied." On March 24, a superb firework display was held on the Seine ; a fête given by the Duke of Ossona, the Spanish Ambassador. Louis XV and Anna-Maria-Victoria watched from a box constructed at the Louvre. As the King said nothing, the Infanta often pulled his sleeve and asked him : " Monsieur, do you not think it beautiful ? " He replied : " Yes," whereupon she waved her hands excitedly to those around and cried : " He has spoken to me ! He has spoken to me ! " The contrast, between this " tiny (*mirmidone*) Infanta " as the songs called her, and the young King

* In January 1724, Philip abdicated in favour of the Prince of Asturias who reigned under the name of Louis I and died in the month of July following. Philip then re-assumed the crown.

beside her, melancholy and taciturn, was striking. Artists have handed down to us the characteristics of Mariannita, and the graceful portrait of her by Belle is one of the most charming pictures at Versailles. She is here depicted smiling, with a crown of flowers, a crown doomed to fade, symbolical of the little princess' destiny in France.

President Hénault described these matrimonial arrangements rather harshly, but he must come very near the truth when he says in his *Mémoires:* " The Regent after hasty deliberation said to his companions : I understand the motives of Spain; but the present need is that my regency should be peaceful and I consent to the Infanta's coming. Why did he not add that his ambitions were the same as the King of Spain's, though their rights were in conflict, and that counting on the strength of Philip's renunciations, he had no need to desire heirs for the King too soon ! "

What a brilliant future for all these princesses, and failing them for their parents ! These marriages were expected to accomplish what policy and war had failed to achieve.

All was now calm after the troubles caused by Law's system and the dreams of Alberoni. On the disappearance **Apogee of** of his rival Dubois could satisfy all his ambitions. **Dubois.** On June 9, 1720, he was consecrated Archbishop of Cambrai ; on July 16, 1721, he obtained the Cardinal's hat ; on December 4, he was received into the Académie Française ; on August 22, 1722, he was appointed Prime Minister. It would take too long to recount, as the chronicler Saint-Simon and the historian Lémontey have done, all the intrigues involved in this triumphal progress. It is sufficient to recall that, in order to become a prelate and to occupy the chair of Fénelon, Dubois had to be ordained priest, and that to secure the purple he put in motion the King of England, a Lutheran, the Pretender, a Catholic, the Courts of Madrid and Vienna, the Oratorians and the Molinists, directing the most irreconcilable enemies towards the same goal, and squandering eight million francs of French gold ! His cause was only won by his making the Parlement accept the famous Bull *Unigenitus* of 1713, condemning the hundred and one propositions taken from the book of Père Quesnel the Oratorian

(*Réflexions sur le Nouveau Testament*), which had excited so much dispute. At the commencement of the Regency the Duc d'Orléans had strongly opposed this submission, from a desire to prove himself liberal and to support the Jansenists, who believed in Père Quesnel. But he could do nothing against this fevered desire for the hat, which has been compared to the papal mania of some influential cardinals.

Dubois did not long enjoy his remarkable position ; he died on August 10, 1723 ; while on December 2, in the same year his master the Regent was carried off by an attack of apoplexy at the Château of Versailles.

Both of them had faults which history has mercilessly and justly criticized. But they left behind them an accomplished task, though their work is unpopular with certain historians even to this day, and though it was to be endangered in the entire reversal of Dubois' policy by his successor, the Cardinal de Fleury.

Many people consider the Regency to have been a mere succession of suppers, masquerades, and balls at the Opéra —" a little wit and much debauchery," said Voltaire. But the Regent, who had entirely changed the old pompous court etiquette of Louis XIV, did his share of serious work. This Don Juan did not forget that he had public duties to fulfil. He was as temperate in his statesmanship as he was intemperate in his private life. He deserves a better fate than the perpetuation of all the slanders and legends levelled against him.

A great poet lived at that time. In his *Embarquement pour Cythère*, he synthesizes a *fête galante* during the Regency with **Watteau.** amazing artistic taste, audacity, and brilliance of colour. If we are to rely on such æsthetic testimony we must try only to see the beautiful side of this pagan episode. Watteau, beloved of the gods, died young ; yet we owe him a debt for discovering the poetry of love and discreetly veiling the bacchanals of that licentious period.

PRINCIPAL SOURCES. Archives of Naples, fascio 56 ; *Lettere confidenziali di E. Farnese al Duca di Parma.* Documents lent us by Glauco Lombardi ; *Mémoires* of the Marshal, Duke of Berwick, of Mme. de Staal, and of Président Hénault ; *Lettres intimes d'Alberoni à Rocca,* published by E. Bourgeois, 1 vol., Paris, 1892 ; Dumont, *Corps diplo-*

matique VIII ; Voltaire, *Siècle de Louis XV* ; Michelet, *Histoire de France* ; Aubertin, *L'Esprit public au XVIII siècle*, 1 vol., 1872 ; A. Baudrillart, *Philippe V et la Cour de France*, vol. ii., 1890 ; Wiesener, *Le Régent, l'Abbé Dubois et les Anglais*, 3 vols., 1891 ; Glasson, *Le Parlement de Paris*, 2 vols., Paris, 1901 ; Bliard, *Dubois, cardinal et premier ministre*, 2 vols., 1902.

SECOND PART

THE DUC DE BOURBON AND CARDINAL DE FLEURY

CHAPTER V

THE KING'S MARRIAGE
1723–1725

The Court at the Regent's death. Fleury's patience. The Duc de Bourbon and the Marquise de Prie. The new government. Its unpopularity. Results of the abdication of Philip V. The marriage of the Regent's son. The Infanta sent away. The candidates for the French throne. The sisters of Monsieur le Duc. The overtures of Catherine I. Marie Leszczynska. Her life at Wissembourg. Correspondence between the Marquise de Prie and Stanislas. The *Polonaise*. Talk of a mésalliance. A parody of the *Ecole des Femmes*. The vengeance of Spain. The marriage celebrated at Fontainebleau. Stanislas Leszczynski's advice to the Queen of France.

AFTER the death of Dubois, the Duc d'Orléans, whose Regency came to an end with Louis' majority, had accepted the office of Prime Minister, which thus became vacant once more, on December 2, 1723. His successor was The Court at appointed the same evening. Louis-Henri de the Regent's Bourbon, called Monsieur le Duc, was at Ver-Death. sailles when Philippe died. He had no difficulty in gaining the approval of the King and Fleury. The Bishop supported the prince's candidature, Louis made a sign of assent, and the new minister immediately took the oath of his office. This great-grandson of the great Condé did not owe his promotion to his intelligence or his capacity, but he was the only member of the Royal Family in a position to take up the post. The two legitimized brothers, the Duc du Maine and the Comte de Toulouse, were out of favour; the former and his wife were distrusted; while the latter was said to be too honest a man to make a good minister.

There were other princes of the blood-royal, but nearly all were born after 1700 and were too young to be serious rivals to the Duc de Bourbon. There was Louis, Duc de Chartres, the only son of the Regent, who showed an inclination to expiate his father's excesses by living a life of piety. There were the two younger brothers of the new minister, the Comte de Charolais, a rough, ill-tempered man, and the Comte de Clermont. There were the Prince de Dombes and the Comte d'Eu, sons of the Duc du Maine ; lastly, there was the Prince de Conti, who was of the youngest branch of the Bourbon-Condés, born in 1695, and married to a sister of Monsieur le Duc. But neither husband nor wife was popular at Court.

The only man of real consequence was Fleury ; but the preceptor of Louis XV was one of those who are patient in their ambitions. He knew that his time would come, for the sincere affection with which he had inspired his royal pupil was a guarantee for the future.

The Duc de Bourbon was born in 1692 and was therefore thirty-one when he came into power. In his early youth he was **The Duc de** rather good-looking, but one of his eyes had been **Bourbon.** put out by the Duc de Berri while hunting, and this disfigured him. By degrees he lost his figure and became as thin as a lath. Being too tall, he began to stoop, his stork-like legs could hardly support his body, and his eyes were so red that the good eye could hardly be distinguished from the blind one ; in fact, he was " hardly of a prepossessing appearance." This description of him is taken from Madame Palatine and Toussaint. His temper was short and suspicious ; he would have been unpopular even without the bitter feeling felt towards him by the many victims of Law's System, by which he had been enriched. His large fortune enabled him to live in great style. He loved rare and precious things, and helped to make Chantilly a Château worthy of a great nobleman. As a minister he proved to be shallow and ignorant, and none were surprised. He had little credit with the King and never transacted business with him in private, a condition imposed on him by the Bishop of Fréjus, when he agreed to propose the Duke's appointment to Louis. His weak character made him a puppet in the hands of a young woman, the Marquise de Prie, daughter of Berthelot de Pléneuf, the farmer of the revenues whose good name was compromised at the time of the Chambre de Justice. The Duke inaugurated the period of feminine interference in affairs of State. He was a contrast to the Regent, who divided his life into two distinct parts, never allowed pleasure to interfere with politics, and always kept the secrets of the government with jealous reserve. Philippe d'Orléans had followed his mother's advice when she wrote in 1715 : "I have resolved not to interfere. Between ourselves, France has, to her detriment, been too long governed by women " (she was thinking of her great enemy, Madame de Maintenon). "I wish my example to be useful to my son, that he may let no woman lead him."

The Marquise de Prie, Agnès Berthelot de Pléneuf, was twenty-five years old in 1725. She was an attractive person-
The Marquise ality; she had shone as ambassadress at Turin
de Prie. and immediately on her return to France she had distinguished herself by her genius for intrigue. She had plotted against Le Blanc, Minister for War, against the Belle-Isles, and against her own mother. She was now to have wider scope for her activities, for she was to govern the State and gain great profit thereby, though gain was indeed a secondary consideration to her, and she would have been contented with a modest fortune provided she had power. But all her ambitions were realized ; her term of power resulted in a large revenue for herself at the expense of France.

Président Hénault has drawn a charming pen-portrait of the Marquise. " She was of a slender build and above medium height ; she had the form and the air of a nymph, a delicate face, pretty cheeks, a well-made nose, and ash-coloured hair. Her eyes were slightly almond-shaped but bright and gay ; as a whole her face was refined and distinguished. Nature had endowed her with all the gifts essential to the art of coquetry ; her voice was light like her form ; she was very musical and played the harpsichord extremely well. . . ." The Marquis d'Argenson describes her as " even more graceful than beautiful " with " a ready wit on all subjects. . . ." These portraits tell us more about the beautiful sorceress than Vanloo's picture in which the Marquise is represented holding a bird, a symbol of the attraction of this captivating creature. The allusion in the verses underneath is sufficiently obvious :

> Sur votre belle main, ce captif enchanté
> De l'aile méprisant le secours et l'usage,
> Content de badiner, de pousser son ramage,
> N'a pas, pour être heureux, besoin de liberté.
> Le cœur, né libre, Iris, n'a de plus chère envie,
> Que d'atteindre au plus tôt le temps de s'engager ;
> Est-il coulé se temps si doux, mais trop léger,
> Ah ! que la liberté nous pèse dans la vie ! *

And when Trémolières describes Monsieur le Duc and Madame de Prie in the characters of Rinaldo and Armida, he confirms Vanloo's graceful allegory.

The Marquise has been compared to Agnès, but she had nothing of the *ingénue* except a feigned candour and a pretended *naïveté* ; her grace, her youth, her nymph-like form of which Saint-Simon also speaks, her modest air, her mind which appeared so cultivated, her experience of the world and foreign courts, all these attributes were deceptive. Clever and artful, she knew that it was essential to keep the Duke in the mistaken belief that he was able and independent. She pretended to interfere with nothing and to wait until affairs were communicated to her. She chose Pâris-Duverney, Law's adversary, as intermediary between herself and the Prime Minister. She made him Minister of Finance. Pâris-Duverney reversed Law's System ; he did away with paper money and sought to lower the price of provisions by decreasing the value of specie. He lowered the value of the louis d'or from twenty-seven livres to fourteen, and caused strikes by trying to introduce a fixed scale of wages and prices in spite of economic laws and the relations of supply and demand. Président Hénault asserts that Pâris advised the Duke after consultation with the Marquise, while that clever person, to keep up the illusion, even contradicted the Duke when he consulted her. He never ceased to admire the intelligence with which she grasped questions that he believed her to be handling for the first time. The known astuteness of

---

* On your fair hand the enchanted captive scorns to use its wings to fly away ; it is content to sport and warble ; for happiness it needs not liberty. Iris, the freeborn heart has no more fond desire than to seek the opportunity to enslave itself. Has it passed, this hour so pleasant, but too fleeting ? Ah ! how oppressive is a life of liberty !

Madame de Prie makes this subterfuge very probable. With the aid of two secretaries she manipulated all decisions, adding recommendations with her own hand to the petitions presented to the Prime Minister.

Such were the masters of the kingdom : a false Agnès and a foolish and narrow-minded nobleman ; and their policy was purely egotistical. The most important event of their administration was Louis' marriage, a very daring enterprise. The Duc de Bourbon further distinguished himself at the beginning of his ministry by some fiscal reforms, among which we find a decrease in the duties on corn and dairy produce coming into Paris ; by improvements on the Saint-Quentin canal from the Somme to the Oise, and the institution of a ballot to decide who should serve in the militia of 60,000 soldiers, which later performed such splendid services in the wars of the eighteenth century. But his inexperience and his despotic nature caused him to introduce some very unpopular measures, such as the persecution of the Protestants and Jansenists whom the Regency had left in peace, the mendicancy laws which condemned old offenders to the galleys, and the tax on the fiftieth of all the revenues of the kingdom which was decreed for ten years. This tax gave rise to the following witty verses :

> Prince, quelle misère extrême !
> Vous imposez le cinquantième
> Quand vous nous savez sans argent !
> Pour votre maudit ministère,
> Le cinquantième du bon sens
> Vous serez bien plus nécessaire.*

Happily, no foreign complication arose to reveal the weakness of the Government. But the Duc de Bourbon had a lucky escape when Mariannita was sent home, for Spain in her anger nearly fired the powder.

In 1722 Noailles had said : " The marriage of the Infanta will end as Law's System did." The Marshal was exiled as **The Infanta sent back to Spain.** a reward for his prophecy, but events proved that he was right. On April 5, 1725, Philip's daughter left the Louvre and the garden which still bears her name, without saying good-bye to the King, and

* Prince, how extreme is our misery ! You impose the " fiftieth " when you know we have no money ! For your wretched ministry a " fiftieth " of good sense would be far more necessary.

went back to Spain in charge of the Duchesse de Tallard, never to return. They had sufficient tact to tell the poor Infanta that " her parents wanted to see her."

After the Regent's death there had been countless intrigues directed towards undoing all he had done and against the House of Orléans, whose power excited the jealousy of the House of Condé. Henri de Bourbon could not support the idea that the crown of Spain should be the appanage of a rival family. But when Philip abdicated on January 14, 1724, in favour of his son, the Prince of Asturias, who became King under the title of Louis I, Louise-Elisabeth, the daughter of the Duc d'Orléans, became Queen. Moreover, on July 13, 1724, the Regent's son married Marie Jeanne, Princess of Baden, who was destined to assure the succession by giving birth to a prince in May 12, 1725. If Louis XV were to die without an heir, the French throne would pass to the descendants of the younger branch. The Prime Minister had many sisters to establish, and he hoped to profit by his position and benefit his family by raising Mlle. de Sens or Mlle. de Vermandois to the throne. He secretly pursued this purpose, and suddenly the young King's health gave cause for some anxiety, which for political reasons was exaggerated. On February 18, 1725, he awoke with a fever and was ill all day ; towards evening he began to improve, but while the doctors were busy at his bedside the two factions at Court held councils so as to be prepared for anything which might happen. The Dowager Duchesse d'Orléans summoned her son and his partisans, while Monsieur le Duc and the Marquise de Prie conferred with Marshal de Villars, the Minister of War, and Morville, the Secretary of State.

It had already been decided that the Infanta should be sent home before this alarm, as it was thought that her **Candidates** youth would interpose too long a time before **for the** the marriage could take place. The King's **King's hand.** illness hastened new matrimonial schemes. The Duc de Bourbon was haunted by the recollection of the death of Louis, the young King of Spain, and wished to assure the future. The choice fell on a princess whose character and position would leave Madame de Prie free to govern the kingdom as she pleased. There were ninety-nine candidates for the

King's hand, 25 Catholics, 3 Anglicans, 13 Calvinists, 55 Lutherans and 3 Greeks. Inquiries were made in all the European courts where there were marriageable princesses, from Lisbon to St. Petersburg and from London to Athens. This long list was reduced to seventeen names and then to five; these were: Anne, daughter of the Prince of Wales, aged fifteen; her sister, Amelia Sophia Eleanor, aged thirteen; Mlle. de Vermandois, aged twenty-one, and Mlle. de Sens, aged nineteen, both sisters of Monsieur le Duc; and lastly, Marie, aged twenty-one, the daughter of the dethroned King of Poland, Stanislas Leszczynski (which is the correct way of spelling the name). The objection to the candidature of the two English princesses was their religion; it was feared that they might remain Protestant at heart like Elizabeth Charlotte, Monsieur's second wife, the mother of the Regent. Nor did George I really approve of the union. The candidates were thus reduced to three, and Henri de Bourbon naturally wished to support the candidature of one of his sisters; possibly also he desired to avenge himself upon the Regent's son for refusing to marry Mlle. de Vermandois; but Madame de Prie eventually carried the day. From the Marquise's point of view Marie Leszczynska seemed a perfect queen. She thought that the daughter of Stanislas, who was poor and simple, would not forget the person to whom she owed her throne, and that she would thus retain her influence.

A story was started based on supposed overtures made to Mlle. de Vermandois in her convent at Fontevrault near Chinon, whither she had retired from the world without taking any religious vows. Among others who have repeated the details of this story are Voltaire and Soulavie. It was said that the Dowager Duchesse de Bourbon and the Marquise de Prie visited Mlle. de Vermandois, and that the Marquise was disguised when she went into the princess' presence, in order to make a sensation. The conversation was brought round to Madame de Prie, whereupon Mlle. de Vermandois changed her tone and spoke openly and with copious invectives against "the wicked creature" who was the cause of her brother's unpopularity. The Marquise listened to this discourse without flinching but, on leaving the room cried: "You shall not be Queen of France!"

Either this scene was entirely invented by the Orleans faction, or it was the fabrication of the Lorraine group. The latter were closely allied to the Palais-Royal, because Princess Elizabeth (daughter of Duke Leopold), who had been one of the rejected seventeen candidates, was the first cousin of the young Duc d'Orléans.

The real reason for the rejection of two Bourbon-Condé princesses was that Monsieur le Duc's sisters did not suit **Intervention of** Madame de Prie. Among the pretexts given **Catherine of** were these: the King could not marry a subject; **Russia.** and the Dowager Duchesse de Bourbon, a legitimized daughter of Louis XIV, would have had too great an influence over her son and daughter. One thing certain is that the Marquise, having at last found her ideal queen, held to her choice and was determined to have her own way. Catherine, widow of Peter the Great, personally intervened with the object of maintaining her husband's policy. She wished to ally herself with Louis XV by giving him her daughter Elizabeth; but she was too late. The siege was over. No political consideration could affect Madame de Prie's desire to see Marie Leszczynska on the throne.

How strange was the destiny of this poor daughter of a fallen king! In retirement with her father and mother at Wissembourg in a house put at the disposal of her family by Philip Michael Weber, Councillor of the Elector Palatine, she led an uncertain existence divided between piety and charity. Stanislas had been dispossessed of his kingdom by Augustus II, Elector of Saxony, and by the favour of the Regent he had found a refuge in this small Alsatian town. With some difficulty he contrived to live and keep up some appearance of a court in company with seven or eight gentlemen who were faithful to their late King in his misfortune. His sole support came from the charity of the monarchs of Europe. The Duc d'Orléans gave him a pension which was not regularly paid, and assistance came also from Spain, Sweden, and Lorraine. He had pledged his wife's jewels with a Frankfort merchant and but for Marie's unexpected good fortune he would never have been able to redeem them. Very few people came to visit this Castle of Indigence; but Stanislas was friendly with the Cardinal de

64

Rohan-Soubise (Armand Gaston Maximilien), Bishop of Strasburg, who liked to receive him in his beautiful residence at Saverne, with the Andlau family, and Lieutenant-General the Comte du Bourg, commanding at Strasburg, who was the " confidant of all the troubles " of the unhappy prince.

Marie's future gave him much anxiety. When the Duc de Bourbon became a widower in 1720, he proposed, through the **Marie** Chevalier de Vauchoux, his diplomatic agent, **Leszczynska.** to give him his daughter in marriage ; but Anne of Bavaria, Princess Palatine, widow of the great Condé's son, was still living, and opposed her grandson's marriage in an almost insulting manner. Equally fruitless were Stanislas' overtures to others such as Prince Ludwig Georg of Baden, brother of the Duchesse d'Orléans, and the Comte de Charolais. There was one candidate for Marie's hand, a gentleman in command of a regiment of cavalry at Wissembourg named Le Tellier de Courtenvaux (then Chevalier de Louvois and later Comte d'Estrées) ; but Stanislas insisted that Courtenvaux must become a duke and peer of France, and since he was unable to secure this favour he was obliged to retire. At this point the Regent died. Madame de Prie was well aware of events at Wissembourg, and thanks to her genius for intrigue she saw how she might derive benefit from the situation. She **Correspondence** was in communication with the Chevalier de **between** Vauchoux, and since the beginning of 1724 had **Madame** been carrying on a correspondence with the sur-**de Prie and** prised but greatly flattered Stanislas. The Mar-**Stanislas.** quise, under the cover of letters of pure courtesy, made her investigations without revealing her designs. Monsieur le Duc continued to hesitate. The alarm given by Louis' illness conquered his last scruples and finally on March 31, 1725, he wrote to ask Stanislas in the name of Louis XV for the hand of his daughter in marriage. This letter arrived at Wissembourg on April 2. The scene has often been described. The ex-King of Poland assembled his wife and daughter, told them to kneel down, and addressed a prayer of thanksgiving to God without any explanation.

" Ah ! my father," said Marie, " then you are recalled to the throne of Poland ? "

"No, Heaven is far more favourable to us," said Stanislas; "you are Queen of France."

The news was not published until a month later when the Infanta had arrived in Spain. Then a list of the ladies who were to form part of the future Queen's household was circulated, and wits who knew Latin compared this household with the temple at Rome which bore the inscription: DEO IGNOTO, *to the unknown god.*

On April 5 Marais records in his *Journal* the rumours of the town and deals with the Princess Marie at some length; he speaks of the difference in their ages (she was twenty-one and the King fifteen), and says that she is well-made and well brought up. Then he mentions the other candidates, explaining why they could not be chosen, and concludes with the following **"The Polish** words: "So the Polish woman must be chosen **Woman."** and we must have a Queen whose name ends in *ski.* A few months ago people complained of the Duc d'Orléans because he had married a princess of Baden, who was not considered to have come from a sufficiently illustrious family, and now we are to accept as Queen one who is even less exalted."

On May 27, when Mariannita had arrived in Spain and was with her parents, the King announced his marriage in these terms: "I am marrying the Princess of Poland. This princess, who was born on the 23rd of June, 1703, is the only daughter of Stanislas Leszczynski, Count of Leszno, formerly Starost of Adelnau, then Palatine of Posnania, and finally elected King of Poland in the month of July 1704, and of Catherine Opalinska, daughter of the Castellan of Posnania, who are both coming to live in the Château of Saint-Germain-en-Laye with King Stanislas' mother, Anne Jablonowska." After this Marais published a diatribe against this marriage which depressed the Court "as if some one had told them that the King was having an apoplectic fit." He said that French hearts could not love Poles, those Gascons of the North and ultra-republicans. He foresaw "a terrible war" in which all Europe would be leagued against France. "Perhaps nothing will happen," he said in conclusion; "everything is in the hands of the Lord of Hosts." There was some excitement, but it subsided when the people saw the graciousness of the *demoiselle* Leszczynska, as she was irreverently called; the Queen was the Queen, and every one bowed before the crown which adorned her brow.

The various Courts kept a diplomatic silence. The King of Sardinia alone, as grandfather of Louis XV, made a useless remonstrance to this "mésalliance," founding his opposition on calumnious reports which accused Marie of bodily defects, alleging that she was epileptic, that two of her fingers were webbed, and that she had scrofula. The Regent's sister, Elisabeth-Charlotte de Lorraine, was also much annoyed at not having been able to secure her daughter's claims. She poured out her heart in her letters to the Marquise d'Aulède saying: "If the late King could see what is happening to France, I think he would be surprised. . . . It seems to me that més-alliances are very much in fashion . . . since they have now even reached the sacred person of the King; I shall say no more. . . . In marrying her he will do a very novel thing, for he will be, I think, the first of our Kings to marry a simple *demoiselle*. . . . Everyone laughs at it. . . ."

Voltaire himself, who later was so subservient to the Queen and flattered her as he never failed to flatter the favourites of the moment, allowed himself to write to the wife of the Président de Bernières : "The marriage of Louis XV is detrimental to poor Voltaire. They do not speak of paying any pensions, or even of keeping them up; but they are going to have a new tax to buy **Parody on the** lace and stuffs for the *demoiselle Leszczynska*." **Ecole des** Pamphleteers entered the field. The most signi-**Femmes.** ficant of their satires was a parody on the *Ecole des Femmes* in which the Marquise de Prie says to the Queen :

> Notre roi vous épouse et, cent fois la journée,
> Vous devez bénir l'heur de votre destinée.
> Contemplez la bassesse ou vous avez été,
> Et du prince qui m'aime admirez la bouté,
> Qui, de l'état obscur de simple demoiselle,
> Sur le trône des lys par mon choix vous appelle . . .
> Nous ne prétendons pas, en vous déclarant reine,
> Que sur lui, ni sur moi, vous soyez souveraine ;
> Vous gouterez en paix les plaisirs les plus doux ;
> Les affaires d'Etat n'iront point jusqu'à vous . . . *

---

* Our King is marrying you, and a hundred times a day you must bless the fortune of your fate. Think on the lowliness of your former

Marie was spared nothing. They reminded her of the proposed marriage with Courtenvaux and the rejection of the Infanta—

> Preuve certaine
> Qu'à rompre ûn autre hymen on n'àurá pàs de peine*

if she was not entirely in subjection to her " real master " the Duc de Bourbon.

" The ' affair ' has become public and therefore those who wished to frustrate it are disconcerted," wrote the Duc de Bourbon to Stanislas on the day of the proclamation. He also wrote a very skilful letter to the future Queen in which he did not fear to allude to the marriage that had been proposed between Marie and himself : " Permit me," he said at the end of his letter, " to say here that your Majesty is under all the more obligation to me, because I cannot think without regret that I sacrificed to you a hope on which all the happiness of my life depended. But the respect which I owe to a princess who will always be my Queen and Mistress, does not permit me to say more on this subject."

The King's marriage had no political significance; this was the great mistake to be laid to the charge of Madame

Spanish Vengeance. de Prie and the Chief Minister. It was not displeasing to the Court of Spain, but Philip, nevertheless, had serious cause for irritation. The overtures that Monsieur le Duc had made to the English Court proved that George I had known of the rejection of the Infanta before himself, and he felt bitterly this affront which excited the most violent anger. The immediate result was the departure of Louise-Elisabeth of Orléans, widow of Louis I, who became Dowager Queen of Spain at the age of sixteen, and of her sister, Mlle. de Beaujolais, affianced to Don Carlos ; they were sent from Spain in such haste that at Bayonne they had to

estate, and admire the generosity of the prince who loves me. For, from the humble state of a simple gentlewoman, through my choice he calls you to the throne of lilies. We do not pretend that in declaring you queen, you are to be sovereign over him or me ; in peace you will taste the choicest pleasures ; affairs of State will not affect you.

* A certain proof that it would not be difficult to break off another marriage.

await an escort to attend them on their journey. Thus ended the brilliant hopes that their father had conceived for their future in Spain.

But the Court had no time to trouble about these princesses. It was busy preparing for the ceremonies at Strasbourg and Fontainebleau and could speak only of Marie Leszczynska. Every one listened eagerly to any details of her faults or her qualities, especially the former.

She was not beautiful, but her face was full of expression and possessed that undeniable charm which increased with **Portraits of** age—a characteristic well brought out in the **the Queen.** striking portrait by La Tour, painted twenty years later, which now hangs as fresh as ever in the Louvre. Those who knew her at Wissembourg said she looked like a *bourgeoise* and that her disposition seemed sullen to those who saw her every day. But it is impossible to believe that the great portrait-painter of St. Quentin, so faithful in portraying both the soul and the outward form of his models, could be absolutely misleading. He shows us a woman, clothed it is true, like some rich private individual, but gracious and refined, with intelligent eyes and a smile full of indulgent kindness.

At Versailles there is a great state portrait either by Gobert or Belle, painted at the time of the marriage, in which the Queen is shown holding a large bunch of lilies and followed by a page in Polish costume. The studied stiffness and forced smile of the central figure denote an inferior artist obviously attempting to imitate Santerre's portrait of the Duchesse de Bourgogne.

Then there are the written descriptions. First of all that of Sieur Lozillière, called the Chevalier de Méré, a tool of Madame de Prie, who was sent to Wissembourg and afterwards to several of the German courts in order to allay suspicion. Lozillière has a natural tendency towards eulogy. He did not forget any detail of her appearance, from her good complexion (fresh water in summer and snow in winter provided Marie's whole make-up) to her sweet and pleasant voice. He finishes with these words : " Without being beautiful, this princess is lovable for her wit, goodness and behaviour ; she is a combination of all the virtues." Such is the natural refuge of anyone who has to speak of a bride who lacks beauty. It must be admitted that according to all the contemporary writers the future Queen was not the equal in looks of "the handsomest young man in the kingdom." Marie with her heavy shoulders and her breadth of body made the slender youth of Louis XV the more noticeable.

"I agree that she is ugly," wrote the Duc d'Antin to Morville, "but she pleases me above everything that I can express." The intriguers were very active. Scandal-mongers passed their tales from mouth to mouth, until the Queen was made out to be an absolute monster.

> On dit qu'elle est hideuse,
> Mais cela ne fait rien,
> Car elle est vertueuse,
> Et très fille de bièn ! *

Monsieur de Conflans, who was sent to tell the King of the celebration of the marriage at Strasburg, gave a just account of her. Villars says, "He reassured us about the Queen, who, as he tells us, is certainly amiable, not beautiful, but far removed from the ugliness which is generally attributed to her."

The whole Court met at the capital of Alsace on August 15 ; the Duc d'Antin, Ambassador Extraordinary to Stanislas, accompanied by the Comte de Beauvais and the Marquis de Dreux, Grand Master of the Ceremonies, Mlle. de Clermont, Superintendent of the Queen's Household, and with her the ladies of the Palace, amongst whom was the Marquise de Prie, who had not forgotten herself.

Stanislas, on his part, did his best to make some show of royalty to honour the occasion, aided by his relative and general factotum the Count of Tarlo, and Baron of Meszek, Marshal of the Palace. The Comtesse de Linange acted as Lady of Honour to Marie. With some difficulty and finally through the good offices of the Marshal du Bourg, six pages were mustered. The Duc d'Orléans was the most important person present ; he was to marry the Queen by proxy, this honour being given to him because he was first prince of the blood-royal ; but there

---

* They say she is hideous, but that matters naught, for she is virtuous and very good.

was a certain irony in this chance which made the son the instrument for the undoing of his father's work.

The Cardinal Bishop de Rohan, surrounded by his clergy, received the procession at the door of the Cathedral. Marie entered the church between her father and mother; in front of her went the Duc d'Orléans and two ambassadors. The prelate gave a dignified address before the mass and the nuptial benediction. The roar of cannon and a *Te Deum* concluded the ceremony.

The Queen dined in public, "served by officers of the King, her husband," then she returned to the Cathedral for the Procession of the Vow of Louis XIII. There were popular fêtes in the afternoon and in the evening a wonderful firework display, while food and wine was distributed at the public fountains.

Madame de Prie did not waste her time in Strasburg; she gave Stanislas a letter from Monsieur le Duc, which said : "Your Majesty has shown me so much kindness that I have thought you might allow me to take the liberty of instructing you on many of the things which are happening in the country ; but as prudence forbids me to write them and as I can trust Madame de Prie's discretion, I have charged her to inform your Majesty and to hide nothing, believing that there are many things our future Queen would be glad to know." The nets were spread and the traps all ready ; Madame de Prie, no doubt, spoke with as much eloquence as ability. She brought presents to the Queen and talked of her own exalted position with an incredible want of tact. She even offered her chemises, not hesitating thus to humiliate the poor daughter of Stanislas, who accepted them with a smile. . . .

On August 17 Marie set out for Fontainebleau. The weather she experienced was execrable ; it never ceased to rain during the whole journey. Several times the Queen's coach stuck fast in the mud. The crops were injured by the floods, and the summer of 1725 was remembered as a time when the evils of nature were made worse by the maladministration of Monsieur le Duc. Bread was so scarce that there were riots both in Paris and the provinces, and the bakers' shops were pillaged. The Prime Minister and the favourite were accused of speculating in corn and of making large profits out of the people's distress.

Faithful to her reputation, Marie distributed alms at each halt. The fifteen thousand livres sent her for largesse were soon exhausted. Everywhere she went she was fêted, and heard highly coloured addresses. Her good sense and tact prevented her from losing her head, as is shown by the charming letter to her father, quoted by the Abbé Proyart : " There is nothing that these good French people will not do to divert me. They say the prettiest things in the world ; but no one tells me that you are near me. Perhaps they will tell me so later, for I am journeying in fairyland, and am indeed under a magic sway. I pass through transformations every instant, and each seems more brilliant than the one before. At one place I have the virtues of an angel ; at another the sight of me makes people happy ; yesterday I was the wonder of the world ; to-day I am a star of benign import. Every one does his best to deify me, and to-morrow, doubtless, I shall be higher than the immortals. To break the spell, I put my hand up to my head ; and then, my dearest papa, I find her whom you love, and who loves you too so tenderly, your dear Maruchna."

The young wife who could write these lines must have had wit as well as heart. Very soon she appeared wearisome and ill-humoured. Doubtless her new surroundings changed her character, but she was still lovable to those who could gain her affection and conquer her shyness.

The meeting between husband and wife took place near Moret, at a spot which has still retained the name of The Queen's **Marriage of Louis XV and Marie Leszczynska.** Crossways (*Carrefour de la Reine*). A small monument was erected to commemorate the event. Louis was kept waiting for some time owing to the badness of the roads, which made the progress of the coaches extremely difficult. It was sometimes necessary to attach more than thirty horses to Marie's coach to drag it out of the ruts. Barbier relates that all the King's Household was smothered in mud. A carpet and flooring were placed on the ground. The queen alighted and was about to fall on her knees, but Louis allowed her to make no more than a formal obeisance ; then he raised and embraced her with an ardour that had never before been seen in him. He entered the coach with the Duchesse d'Orléans, and accompanied his wife to Moret, where he remained for half an hour talking to her with extreme affability. Marie spent the night in this little town, and the next day, September 5, she reached Fontainebleau at about ten o'clock in the morning. The marriage was celebrated in the chapel of the palace. The scene was magnificent, everywhere was the glitter of embroidered dresses, robes covered with precious stones and hangings ornamented with golden fleurs-de-lis. The procession was announced by trumpets, fifes and drums ; it started from the King's Great Chamber, crossed the Gallery of Francis I, and arrived at the Staircase of Honour, which was lined by the Hundred Swiss. Louis came first, a picture of youthful grace, preceded by the princes of the blood, the Comtes de Charolais and de Clermont and the Prince de Conti ; then came the Queen escorted by the Duc de Bourbon and the Duc d'Orléans ; she wore a violet train, lined with ermine, which was borne by the Dowager Duchesse de Bourbon, the Princesse de Conti, and Mlle. de Charolais. She was followed by the Duchesse d'Orléans, Mlle. de Clermont, and Mlle. de la Roche-sur-Yon, sister of the Prince de Conti. Attending the various royalties came the dignitaries of the Court, officers and knights of the Holy Ghost, maids-of-honour, heralds at arms, Scotch guards, and bodyguards with their shining arms.

The Cardinal de Rohan, Grand Almoner of France, again officiated and gave the address. At Strasburg he had drawn a touching picture of the vicissitudes of Stanislas and had spoken his praises ; on this occasion he addressed himself particularly to Louis, exalting the greatness of his ancestors, and finally he presented him with a wife whom God had made after His own heart, " a virtuons and prudent woman." The nuptial benediction was given, and while medals struck in honour of the occasion were being distributed, music burst forth, and hymns of thanksgiving filled the vaulted roof of the chapel.

The procession returned again to the royal apartments. After dinner the Duc de Mortemart presented the Queen with a velvet casket embroidered with gold containing " the splendid trifles which are called the *corbeille* (wedding gifts)." The

Queen distributed them to her household, saying " This is the first time that I have been able to make presents."

The day ended with a display given by the court actors ; plays of Molière were selected so that no one might be offended. The result was that Voltaire, who had prepared an entertainment, decided that the *Amphitryon* and the *Médecin malgré lui* were not a suitable choice ; he criticized everything even to the display of fireworks given at about half-past eleven after supper, " with many rockets and little originality " ; he saw nothing in the festivities but noise, crowds, uproar, and tumult. A few days later all seemed fair to him. Adrienne Lecouvreur played his *Marianne*. Madame de Prie presented him to the Queen, and she spoke to him of his *Henriade*, as yet unpublished, and called him " my poor Voltaire." A pension was granted to him, and he quitted the ranks of the rhymers who resorted to Fontainebleau and assailed the young bride with " Pindaric odes, sonnets, epistles and epithalamia." It must be admitted that Voltaire was right and that these starveling poets must have seemed to Marie "a band of court jesters." They called the King Alcides or Adonis, the Queen was changed into Astræa, Cypris, Diana, or even Flora—an excellent rhyme for Aurora ! The whole fashionable mythology was resuscitated. Voltaire dedicated *Marianne* to the daughter of Stanislas, and was himself unable to avoid comparing her to the ancient goddesses :

> Du trône redouté que vous rendez aimable,
> Jetez sur cet écrit un coup d'œil favorable ;
> Daignez m'encourager d'un seul de vos regards,
> Et songez que Pallas, cette auguste déesse,
> Dont vous avez le port, la bonté, la sagesse,
> Est la divinité qui préside aux Beaux-Arts ! *

These uninspired and unpoetic verses were the best with which the Queen was afflicted !

In all probability she read nothing but the celebrated *Conseils* written by her father, which began with the scrip-

* From your dread throne, that you make so gracious, cast on these lines a favourable glance, deign to encourage me with a single look, and remember that Pallas, the august goddess whose bearing and grace and wisdom you have, is the divinity who presides over the Arts.

tural reminiscence : "Hearken, my daughter, behold and give
ear. Forget thy people and thy father's house. . . ." Stanislas

Advice of King Stanislas to his Daughter. warned his daughter of the dangers she would encounter at the Court, such as grandeur and prosperity and flattery ; he enlarged upon these three subjects with emotion, showing all the tender affection he felt for his daughter. " Prosperity," he said, " is the more dangerous in that it is practically unknown to you ; since infancy you have participated so fully in my adversities that, as you are aware, there is nothing like the experience of misfortune to guard us from abusing our happiness." Flattery inspires him to some wise precepts : " You must realize that you will be surrounded by those who will vie with one another to pay court to you ; there will be no one who will not be prepared to obey you, to sacrifice his goods, his life, for your service, but there will be no one who will tell you the truth, or who will not think that if he did so he would displease you and risk his fortunes. Though you are surrounded by those who are devotedly attached to you and are most attentive in your service, yet, on this point, you are left to yourself, and have nothing to rely on but your own good sense and reason."

Stanislas sought for some one on whom she might rely. He found only the King and him " who is the depositary of all his wishes," meaning Monsieur le Duc, to whom the Queen was under " an infinite obligation." This was the real danger to avoid. But fortune blinded the King of Poland ; he could not foresee that the queen was to shed her first tears simply because she had too much confidence in the Duc de Bourbon.

PRINCIPAL SOURCES. National Archives, Carton K. 139, 140 ; Foreign Affairs, France, 314 ; Bibl. Sainte-Geneviève, MS. 2197.
Journal Historique ou Fastes du règne de Louis XV, Paris, 1766 ; *Mémoires* of Villars and Luynes ; *Souvenirs du Comte de Tressan*, Versailles, 1897 ; Voltaire, *Correspondence, Epîtres* ; Moufle d'Angerville, *Vie privée de Louis XV*, 4 vols., London, 1781 ; Abbé Proyart, *Vie de Marie Leckzinska*, 1794 ; Paul de Raynal, *Le Mariage d'un Roi*, Paris, 1887 ; Marquise de Réaulx, *Le roi Stanislas et Marie Leczinska*, Paris, 1895 ; P. Boyé, *Stanislas Leszczynski et le troisiéme traité de Vienne*, Nancy, 1898 ; P. de Nolhac, *Louis XV et Marie Leczinska*, Paris, 1902 ; H. Thirion, *Madame de Prie*, Paris, 1905.

CHAPTER VI

A PALACE REVOLUTION
1725–1726

Stanislas at Fontainebleau. The honeymoon. Louis' character.
Intrigues of Madame de Prie. Interview between Monsieur le
Duc and the King. Departure of Fleury. Marshal de Villars'
advice to the Queen. Public complaints against the Ministry.
Dismissal of the Duc de Bourbon. The King's dissimulation.
The Duc exiled to Chantilly. The madness of " Orestes."
Illness of the King and Queen. Coldness of Louis. Cardinal
de Fleury.

ON the day after the wedding, to the great joy of the
Queen, her parents arrived to take up their residence,
not indeed at Saint-Germain, but at the Château de
Chambord. Stanislas spent three days with his daughter " in
raptures," then some weeks at Bourron until his new residence
should be furnished.

Louis and Marie spent the whole autumn at Fontainebleau.
Their perfect harmony promised well for the future. The
The King was transformed ; he was high-spirited,
Honeymoon. a pleasant companion and lover. The Queen
found her husband comparing her to Blanche of Castille.
When anyone wished him to admire a lady of the Court,
Louis replied : " The Queen is still more beautiful ! " But these
were merely the illusions and the words of a young husband ;
the King's enthusiasm was only an instinctive recognition
that he owed to Marie an existence to which he had hitherto
been a stranger, and the first emotions of a new life.
Louis' heart and mind were incapable of other and nobler
sentiments. It has often been said of Stanislas' daughter that
she did not know how to make use of her opportunities, and
that at her age she might have gained a complete influence over
the as yet unformed character of the young King. But she

76

believed she was doing what was right in submitting to the Duc de Bourbon, as if to the King himself. This attitude, which recommended itself to the ingenuousness of the young wife, was the most fatal she could have adopted. Unfortunately, the perceptions of Stanislas were no clearer; he thought that Monsieur le Duc's cajoleries were sincere, and had no suspicion of the intrigues of which his daughter was to be the plaything. As for Louis, would he ever have submitted to the influence of any queen? He was inconstant by nature, and his chief object was to escape the ennui which was already beginning to poison his most brilliant days. "Sire," said Marshal de Villars to him in 1735, "to see a King of France listless and bored at twenty-five is unconscionable. . . . Besides, your affairs are in so good a condition, that it will never be a trouble for your Majesty to **Character of** attend to them. . . ." Words such as these **Louis XV.** had little effect on Louis. His lamentable education had given him neither the taste for serious matters, nor application, nor the energy which had made a great King of Louis XIV. All his life he was idle, a great hunter, and an equally great gambler. He made it his habit never to interfere, and, according to Dufort de Cheverny, he spoke of affairs of State as though some one else were at the head of the kingdom. He displayed the same carelessness in his private life, much to the Queen's distress. In reality it was essential for him to be in bondage to some one, and owing to her timidity and to bad advice, the dominion was not to be Marie's, but that of a politician. Fleury, the King's tutor, in seeming simplicity and modesty, awaited the time when he would be able to profit by the remarkable ascendency he had gained over his pupil. Marie made the unconscious blunder of attacking the one person whom she should have propitiated; she did not realize his unostentatious but immense influence, and so, acting at the instigation of the Prime Minister and Madame de Prie, she displeased Fleury. Madame de Prie continually interfered; she took complete possession of the Queen, allowing her neither to speak nor write to whom she would, and abused her position as lady-in-waiting to enter the royal apartments at all times.

When the Court returned to Versailles, there were preparations on foot for a revolution in the Palace which was to compromise Marie and bring the first clouds, never again to be dispersed.

It will be remembered that Henri de Bourbon was never allowed to see Louis alone; the Bishop of Fréjus even made it his custom on all occasions to enter the King's cabinet half an hour before the Prime Minister. There he did what was called his *work*, which consisted in the distribution of favours, both great and small, such as commands in war and the like, while Monsieur le Duc could dispose of no favours, and saw them all go to creatures of Fleury.

The baffled minister sought to rid himself of this constraint. He made overtures to the Queen, who at first resisted, but afterwards gave way on being informed that it was a question of State secrets. He thought he had found an accomplice. One

Interview between the King and the Duc de Bourbon. evening the Queen contrived an interview between the King and the Duc de Bourbon in her presence; the Duc aired his complaints against Fleury, criticizing both his character and his conduct. The King was annoyed, although he said nothing, but at last his anger broke out.

"Have I displeased your Majesty?" asked the Duke naïvely.

"Yes."

"Your Majesty no longer has a kindly feeling towards me?"

"No."

"M. de Fréjus alone has your Majesty's confidence?"

"Yes."

Thereupon the minister fell on his knees and burst into tears. The Queen also wept, and Louis immediately retired to his apartment in extreme displeasure. Fleury went to see his master and found the apartments closed by order of Monsieur le Duc. On the next day he left the Court and retired to the Convent of the Sulpiciens at Issy. The following day he came back on receiving a letter from the Duc himself soliciting his return to Versailles. The Prime Minister was charged with the performance of this humiliating task by the King, on the advice of Monsieur de Mortemart, First Gentleman of the Bedchamber.

The Duc was doomed, and Fleury only waited his time to get rid of him. The Queen herself was not long in seeing how great a mistake she had made. She tearfully complained to the Marshal de Villars of the change she saw in her husband's affection, attributing that change to the influence and jealousy of the Bishop. The Marshal consoled her to the best of his ability and made some remarks which are useful as revealing the psychology of these incidents : " I believe, Madame, that the King's heart is far removed from what is called love. He has not the feelings towards you that he had ; but do not show any signs of resentment. He must not perceive that you fear the weakening of his affections, lest the many fair eyes which continually ogle him make a desperate attempt to profit by the change." The advice might have been couched in better language, but the sense could not have been improved upon. The Queen did not yet understand, however, and a few weeks later in conversation with Fleury, she again defended those who had been the cause of her trouble.

" What is your complaint against them ? " said Marie, " that you insist so strongly on their removal ? "

" I have no personal feeling against them," replied Fleury, " and if I oppose Monsieur le Duc, it is because of the harm tht Madame de Prie and Pâris-Duverney do to the King."

" But how can I decide to send away these people, one of whom, my private secretary, asks for judgment as to the accusations against him, the other, that strict inquiry should be made into the wrongs attributed to her. I assure you that the disgrace of these people, who satisfy me, will cause me distress."

Marie went on to speak of the coldness of Louis, to which the Bishop drily replied : " It is not my fault."

Meanwhile, the complaints against Henri de Bourbon began to take definite shape. The town came to the help **Dissatisfaction** of the Bishop. Public opinion played Fleury's **of the People.** game and brought matters to a head. The Bishop remained behind the scenes, keeping an outward appearance of friendliness. His proverbial patience was destined to assure his victory, and his long desired succession to the position of prime minister, without the name, indeed, but with all the power.

Reforms were demanded, but never came. The people desired the abolition of heavy taxes representing an annual income to the King of a hundred and eighty million francs, and the reorganization of the administration on more equitable lines. There was need for a better distribution of the revenues from the monopolies—for instance, the tobacco monopoly that had been given over to the Compagnie des Indes—and for new sources fo taxation less onerous to the exhausted and impoverished nation. The King was silent, following, no doubt, the advice of the Bishop of Fréjus. He was affable to Monsieur le Duc, and seemed to have pardoned his errors. At three o'clock on June 11, 1726, he left for Rambouillet with the intention of hunting with the Comte de Toulouse, which he was fond of doing. Before he left he said to the Duc de Bourbon :

" Do not make me wait for supper."

Some hours later the Duc de Charost, who had been let into the secret the day before, asked to speak to Monsieur le Duc, **Dismissal of the Duc de Bourbon.** and handed him a severely worded *lettre de cachet :* " I command you, on pain of punishment for disobedience, to retire to Chantilly, and remain there until further orders. Louis."

The Duke obeyed immediately, though complaining of the harsh manner in which he had been treated.

The King's dissimulation was severely criticized ; it was said to be unlike the conduct of anyone of his age, and to show " a mind at once feeble and petty " ; the influence of Fleury was also plainly discernible. However, Louis never showed frankness and courage in similar circumstances. His defenders explain his invariable line of conduct by his timidity.

The triumph of the Bishop of Fréjus was assured. The Queen also had her *lettre de cachet*, brought to her by Fleury himself : " Madame," said the King, " do not be surprised at the orders I have given. Pay attention to what Monsieur de Fréjus will tell you on my behalf, I pray you and I command you." After this, a correspondence was established between the Bishop and the Queen ; but though they have an appearance of affectionate confidence, these letters prove that Marie was deluded, and that she did not find an echo in him through whom she hoped to keep the heart of the King. Fleury deceived Stanislas also later on.

Reading the exile's letters one might think that the Bishop was really interested in his fate.

The ministers of State, Morville and Maurepas, received similar orders. To celebrate his victory, Fleury confined Pâris-Duverney in the Bastille, sent away his three brothers, and exiled Madame de Prie to her castle of Courbépine in Normandy, where she died a year later. He accepted the resignation of Dodun, Marquis d'Herbault, the Controller-General, who was succeeded by Desforts, and of Breteuil, whose successor was Le Blanc, returned to favour. An order was at once drawn up to revoke the *Cinquantième* tax, and everyone smiled on Monsieur le Duc's enemies. The joy was extreme. The lieutenant of police had to take the most rigorous precautions to prevent the people of Paris from illuminating the town on the day of the departure for Chantilly.

Henri de Bourbon distracted himself by hunting " in the world's fairest residence," but he was " troubled by the natural constraint felt by all who cannot go away, at any rate for any distance." His mother paid him many visits, less to console him than to reproach him continually for not having married Mademoiselle de Sens to the King. Louis was ill in July : Madame la Duchesse took occasion to ask that her son might come to hear the bulletins. To her importunities the King replied that he did not wish to be troubled.

" But, Sire, you overwhelm me with the keenest grief ! Would you drive my son and myself to despair ? Allow him the consolation of seeing you, if it is only for a moment."

" No ! " said the King, and he turned away to put an end to the monologue.

The Duc de Bourbon was restored to favour in 1727, on his second marriage with Charlotte of Hesse-Rheinfels. He died in 1740, leaving no record in history beyond that of his deplorable administration.

A celebrated passage in *Andromaque* was parodied, in which he was made to say :

> Si j'ai reduit la France aux pleurs, à la misère ;
> Si j'ai frappé Le Blanc d'une injuste colère,
> C'est que je voulais être un tyran accompli :
> Hé bien, je suis content et mon sort est rempli . . .

Mais quelle épaisse nuit tout à coup m'environne ?
De Prie, où êtes vous ?   D'où vient que je frissonne ?
Quelle horreur me saisit ?   grâce au ciel j'entrevoi . . .
Dieu ! ce sont les Pâris perdus autour de moi . . .
Viens, ma chère de Prie, à toi je m'abandonne . . .
Je te réserve encor mon cœur à déchirer,
Après t'avoir donné l'État à dévorer.*

The King's illness which had served as a pretext for Madame
la Duchesse to come to Versailles, was only indigestion. He

Illness of the King and Queen.
had had "too many figs and walnuts and too much milk and other things," besides being over-fatigued by hunting. The alarm was, however, great, and upset the Queen to such an extent that she fell into a fever. But according to a letter from Stanislas, there was yet another cause for this illness : "You have heard of the indisposition of the King and Queen. God be thanked it is over. . . . Their sympathetic feelings extend even to the cause of their maladies, which is over-eating. They both had violent indigestion, and the Queen especially, after eating a hundred and eighty oysters, and drinking four glasses of beer. . . . As you will realize, there is a charming touch in the assistance they have lent one another during their indisposition. You will be equally glad when I tell you that their confidence and their tenderness have been strengthened. . . ."

Stanislas was always an optimist, and he was far from understanding that this confidence and this tenderness did not exist. After the first four days, in which the small-pox was feared, Louis went often to see the Queen, but his visits were only for a few minutes, and Villars remarked that " the tenderness did not seem very great " on the King's side. When Marie recovered, Louis spent three-quarters of an hour with his wife, accompanied by the Bishop of Fréjus. This mark of affection did something to repair the pain caused by his coldness, even

* If I have reduced France to tears and misery, if in my unjust anger I struck down Le Blanc, it is because I wished to be a complete tyrant ; ah ! well ! I am content, I have fulfilled my destiny. But what is this dark night which now envelops me ? De Prie, where are you ? Why do I shiver ? What horror seizes me ? Thanks to heaven I have a glimpse of . . . God ! It is Pâris and the rest ruined all round me. . . . Come, my dear de Prie, I abandon myself to you. . . . I have kept my heart for you to rend after having given you the State to devour.

though the presence of Fleury gave it an official air. The King left for Fontainebleau without bidding the Queen good-bye ; it was announced that he would return every Saturday until Marie was well enough to rejoin him, but he did not in fact do so. This was not all, for when the Queen arrived at Fontainebleau at the end of the month, the huntsman in Louis was stronger than the husband, and instead of going to greet his wife, he went after his hounds. The Queen could retain no illusion as to his feelings, but her own love was constant. The courtiers whispered ; for they saw that the young King was indifferent and selfish.

Thus it was that Stanislas' daughter lost all at the fall of Monsieur le Duc ; the revolution in the Palace had turned **Honours for** against its author and his innocent accomplice. **Fleury.** Henri de Bourbon had arranged the marriage in the belief that he could use it to the profit of himself and Madame de Prie ; his only achievement was to ensure the Queen's unhappiness, and her isolation between a husband who was indifferent, and a minister who was absolute master of the King and the destinies of France, and little troubled by the moral tortures under which her heart bled. Having thus become head of the Government, Fleury received from the Pope the highest honour bestowed on prelates ; Cardinal Gualteri's nephew brought him the Cardinal's hat from Rome on November 5, 1726. Henceforth he had precedence of the Dukes in the council, and he was " cousin " to all Christian kings and princes.

PRINCIPAL SOURCES. The same as in the last chapter with the addition of the *Mémoires* de J. N. Dufort, Comte de Cheverny, 2 vols., Paris, 1886.

CHAPTER VII

THE QUEEN'S DOWRY
1727–1737

The Cardinal's associates. His unostentatious life. Reconciliation with Spain. The Treaty of Seville. Don Carlos, Duke of Parma. Death of Augustus II, Elector of Saxony and King of Poland. The candidates for the throne of the Jagellons. English influence. Stanislas, the protégé of France. Departure of Leszczynski for Poland. His election. Counter-election of Augustus III. The "Forsaken" of Danzig. Intervention of the Comte de Plélo. Operations on the Rhine and in Italy. Ridiculously inadequate support sent by Fleury to Stanislas. Death of Plélo. Stanislas in Prussia. French victories. Don Carlos, King of the Two Sicilies. Stanislas becomes Duke of Lorraine. The Cascade of Marly.

CARDINAL DE FLEURY'S only desire was to govern in peace, to effect stringent economies, and to avoid war. On his advent to power he was seventy-two years old; but in spite of his age he was in excellent health, The Cardinal and there was some analogy between his methods and his of treating his own constitution and that of the Collaborators. State. Voltaire was justified in saying that Fleury considered France a strong and robust body which would recover of its own accord.

The Bishop surrounded himself with associates, but he chose men who would place his own capacity in relief and strengthen his position. The best known was Chauvelin, who, in spite of public opposition, was entrusted with two important posts in four days, without having given any proof of his ability. He became Keeper of the Seals in 1727, and immediately undertook the functions of Secretary of State and Minister for Foreign Affairs, in the place of Morville, who decided to retire at the same time as his father, M. d'Armenonville, Chauvelin's predecessor.

84

THE QUEEN'S DOWRY

Fleury was perfectly honest and never abused his high position. He had not the ostentation of a Richelieu, though it **The simplicity** is certain that he had not his talents either ; but **of his life.** after the rule of Dubois, it is only fair to call attention to the integrity of the Cardinal, if but for its novelty. The Court and Paris did not treat him with respect, so extraordinary did this spirit of economy seem. They mocked at his simple life ; the Marquis d'Argenson ridiculed it : " One of the most absurd spectacles is the prelate's *petit-coucher*. All France, from the usual idlers to those who have business, is at his door. His Eminence enters and passes into his cabinet, then the doors are opened and you see the old priest take off his small-clothes and carefully fold them ; an unostentatious dressing-gown is handed him, and then his shift ; he takes a long time combing his four white hairs, discourses, chats, babbles, makes bad jokes interspersed with bland or commonplace remarks. The good man imagines that this is a consolation for the poor folk who press to see him ; he cannot give them a more propitious moment, without interfering with business."

Fault was also found with the niggardly fare of the Cardinal. He was compelled to keep open table, but he only had " four enormous entrées, a dish of roast and four *entremets*." Such was his custom and he would not change it. When the guests were too numerous, the dishes were passed round without the least ceremony. On one occasion the Bishop of Rennes (Vauréal), not finding enough to eat, said to his host :

" *Ma foi*, Monseigneur, however much you try your estate will not equal that of Cardinal Mazarin."

The minister laughed, he considered probity and economy the first of virtues ; a typical phrase he used when he had occasion to defend his finance was : " Silver and gold do not drop like leaves from the trees."

One of Fleury's first objects was to reconcile France and Spain. Ever since the return of the Infanta, Philip and **Reconciliation** Elizabeth had sulked ; they even formed an **with Spain.** alliance with the Emperor, Charles VI, though as Archduke he had claimed to succeed Charles II, and had conducted the war in Catalonia against the combined Franco-Spanish armies.

In 1724 a Congress had been opened at Cambrai, at which the plenipotentiaries of the States who formed the Quadruple Alliance attended, their object being to settle the complicated interests of Spain. But while Mariannita was on the way back to Madrid, Philip recalled his representatives. After the dissolution of the Congress he gave secret instructions to Ripperda, his minister at Vienna, to continue negotiations. As a result four treaties were signed on April 30 and May 1, 1725, three of them with the Emperor and one with the Empire.

The Germans agreed to recognize the hereditary rights of the Infante Don Carlos to the Duchies of Parma, Placentia, **Don Carlos** and Tuscany, in return for the renunciation by **Duke of Parma.** the King of Spain of his claims to Naples and the Two Sicilies. This settlement satisfied Elizabeth Farnese, whose whole skill was concentrated on dynastic claims in favour of her sons, a business in which she displayed the asperity and ill-humour of a virago, threatening and insulting the French ambassadors as if they had been servants.

The remaining treaties confirmed the Quadruple Alliance, guaranteed the Spanish succession as established at Utrecht, recognized the Imperial Pragmatic Sanction, that is to say, acknowledged the right of the Emperor's only daughter to inherit the possessions and powers of her father; assured for Philip the good offices of Charles VI with the King of England to secure the restoration of Gibraltar and Minorca; regulated the commerce between the two countries, according protection to the Ostend Company and so offending the English and Dutch; finally, in case of war, provided for mutual support between the contracting parties. The hereditary enmity between Hapsburg and Bourbon was forgotten.

So strange a political situation caused consternation in Europe. On September 23, 1725, a reply was made by the Treaty of Hanover between France, England and Prussia, to which Sweden and Denmark, and later on Holland, adhered. They were pledged to the maintenance of the Treaty of Utrecht. But Prussia soon detached herself from this league against Vienna, and in company with Russia ranged herself on the side of the Emperor. The Powers who were ultimately to share Poland were preparing for the future. During the whole of the eighteenth century their policy was directed towards the dismemberment of the northern republic.

Such was the position at the disgrace of Monsieur le Duc. The Cardinal saw that it was necessary to bring Philip V to a better frame of mind. It was easy for him to disown all responsibility for the Infanta's return, and having done this, he had recourse to Father Bermudez, the Spanish King's confessor. He wrote a letter on September 1, 1726, in which he insinuated that his Catholic Majesty had renounced his family and his fatherland, and was indifferent to all that was happening in the French Court ; in his postscript he put aside all pretence and said : " It is true that we have formed alliances which are suspected by the Catholic King, but our allies are not our masters, and God grant that it is the same with those of Spain. I trust that you will forgive me for saying this."

A year later a reconciliation was with some difficulty effected; it was brought about by the fall of Ripperda, the daring originator **Treaty of** of the treaties of Vienna, by the Spanish reverse **Paris, 1727.** before Gibraltar, and by Philip's precarious state of health. These causes were quite as effective as Fleury's skill. On May 31, 1727, the Treaty of Paris was signed. By this the Emperor agreed to suspend the concessions given to the Ostend Company for seven years, and to summon a fresh congress with a view to a general peace. Alarmist reports ceased, and the plenipotentiaries, meeting at Soissons, sealed the compact between the two Bourbon branches as a preliminary to the Treaty of Seville. The latter was signed on November 9, 1729, and for the moment reconciled Spain with the members of the Hanoverian alliance. By this treaty Spain was authorized to station six thousand troops in Parma and Tuscany to support the rights of the Infante Don Carlos over the Italian Duchies. The last Farnese died on March 10, 1731, without issue, whereupon the son of Elizabeth became Duke of Parma, and heir-presumptive of the Grand Duke of Tuscany. Calm reigned in Europe until 1733. But on February 1 of that year an event happened which created fresh complications : Augustus II, Elector of Saxony and King of Poland, died of a swelling in the thigh caused by blood poisoning.

His death left the succession to the throne vacant. The new king had to be elected by the Polish nobility assembled in the **Death of** Diet. Among the candidates were the son of **Augustus II** the late King, who was favoured by Austria **of Poland.** and Russia, the young Emmanuel of Portugal, the Prussian candidate, and the Queen's father, Stanislas Leszczynski, who was supported by France, but without much enthusiasm on the part of Fleury. However, the conclusion of this struggle was to be fortunate for France, and after five years of war and negotiations to give her a new province.

The Cardinal was able to compliment himself on having brought a difficult task to a satisfactory conclusion, but the reconciliation with Spain was not particularly successful. Fleury had too blind a confidence in the English minister, Walpole, his great friend, who was paralyzing the commerce and sea-power of France.

He was apprehensive lest the elevation of Stanislas should give Marie a certain amount of influence and diminish his **English** ministerial power ; while if France were to land **Influence.** in Poland from the sea, and thus give the Queen's father effective assistance, he was afraid of what Great Britain might say in her jealousy for her maritime supremacy. Fleury secretly took the advice—one might almost say the orders—of Walpole. Thus he was not only acting against the Polish friends of Leszczynski, but also offending the many Frenchmen who saw in the cause of Stanislas an object worthy of the chivalrous traditions of the nation.

Louis himself intervened at the commencement. Having no suspicion of the purposes of his late tutor he did his duty without reservation. The French Ambassador at Warsaw was the Marquis de Monti, who had no need of moral encouragement as he had already made Stanislas' cause his own. The diplomatist was delighted to receive the promise of a million florins to capture the electors who had been depraved by the election campaign of Augustus II, when money had been flung about in handfuls. Monti was authorized to distribute Cardinals' hats, offices, blue and red ribands, golden jewels, glittering but inexpensive watches, caskets, flagons and patch boxes, to the most loyal of the Polish nobles. Thus far the Cardinal approved.

THE QUEEN'S DOWRY

Louis realized that his father-in-law ought to go to Poland to conduct his electoral battle. "His stay at Chambord," he wrote to Monti, "although possibly advisable for the moment, yet allows discreditable doubts to arise as to the sincerity of the measures I am taking for his restoration. . . . I am aware of the force of your arguments in requesting the presence of King Stanislas. He will leave how and when you suggest. Everything will be ready for his departure at a moment's notice. Until then he will await your final instructions."

Stanislas set out, and monetary support flowed in. Fleury gave him upwards of three million francs, hoping that this sacrifice would keep off war ; for his desire for peace outweighed his care for the coffers of the State.

The affair which was to end in tragedy began with comedy. Leszczynski, attired in garment of pinchina, a coarse woollen material, and wearing a black perruque, left Meudon on August 22, 1733. He reached the frontier in the utmost secrecy and entered Germany, accompanied by the young d'Andlau, son of his friend the Lieutenant of Alsace. One passed as a clerk, the other as a merchant ; their passports were made out in the names of George Bawer and Ernest Bramback. The two travellers arrived at Warsaw on September 8.

Meanwhile, a squadron sailed from Brest towards the Baltic Sea, carrying a French noble, the Comte de Thianges, who vaguely resembled Stanislas. He was dressed in gala costume and wore the cordon of the Holy Ghost in order to make his appearance the more authentic : this stratagem was suggested to Fleury by Walpole.

Received with enthusiasm, Leszczynski was elected King on September 12 amid the acclamations of the electors on the
Stanislas elected King of Poland. field of Wola, near Warsaw. His success was remarkable and induced Narbonne to say : "Posterity will find difficulty in believing that a prince could come to Warsaw from four hundred leagues away and be proclaimed King all in the course of a fortnight." There was great delight at Versailles when a courier named Barthel arrived post-haste with the news of the election after having covered four hundred and twenty leagues in eight days. He reached Versailles between eleven o'clock and mid-

night. The Keeper of the Seals was still at dinner, but the Cardinal was resting, and the King had already retired. When Louis opened the packet and read the missive, he threw himself on the Queen's neck and she embraced him tenderly.

Their joy was not destined to last long. The son of Augustus prepared for vengeance. He was assisted by the Russian army which advanced to threaten Warsaw and was about to effect a junction with the Saxon and Austrian forces. He gained some adherents by distributing gold and buying the fickle electors in his turn. Faced with this invasion of foreign troops and with the desertion of the larger part of his friends, Stanislas fled to Danzig, then a free town under the protection of the Polish Republic, and firmly loyal to its suzerains. Here he found hospitality and valiant defenders.

A new Diet annulled the former one and elected Augustus III on October 25. History repeated itself and the son followed Counter-election of Augustus III. his father's example, dethroning in his turn the ephemeral King, the nominee of French diplomacy, who was thus again driven from his country by the Russians.

Stanislas would not acknowledge himself beaten. He had faith in his star and knew the bravery and devotion of those who had accompanied him, among them Monti and all the flower of the purest Polish nobility, Poniatowski, the hero of the wars of Charles XII, the Primate Theodore Potocki, Prince Frederick Michael Czartoryski, Duke Ossolinski, and Prince George Sapieha. He counted also on the support of France. Fleury decided on war. The Emperor was to be attacked on the Rhine and in Italy in conjunction with the Kings of Sardinia and Spain, but practically nothing was done for him who was justly styled "the forsaken of Danzig."

While the Russians under Lacy were pushing their way to Warsaw, Stanislas' eyes were turned to the sea. His hopes were set on the promised French fleet. But this fleet was delayed at Copenhagen, and Thianges returned to France having played his ridiculous part. "The Commander de Thianges who played the part of king on the flotilla," wrote Marais to President Bouhier, "has arrived in France and deserted the scene. I do not know where he has left the fleet." The French

Ambassador in Denmark, the Comte de Plélo, whose name
is famous, urged La Luzerne, who was in command of the
Intervention squadron, to sail for Danzig; but that officer
of the Comte asserted that he had received secret orders not to
de Plélo. stay more than a night off the town and then
to return with all speed; he made an illusory concession, at
the instance of de Plélo, and left three of his ships in Danish
waters; the *Argonante*, the *Astrée* and the *Méduse*. The
ambassador followed the dictates of his own enthusiasm, but
he had to make excuses for having done his duty! "I have
taken it upon myself," he wrote to the King, "to retain the
vessels here for some days. . . . I am apprehensive lest some
may think it extraordinary that the squadron has not by now
passed Copenhagen, and they may imagine that if it had
appeared off the coast of Poland, its presence alone would have
given great encouragement."

Plélo was severely reprimanded. Generous sentiments were
no longer appreciated at Versailles. The Cardinal contented
himself with writing dispatches, bearing the stamp of the Court,
full of fair words which led to nothing. He had been obliged
to declare war, and Stanislas' injuries had been the cause, but
he maintained an attitude of servility towards the maritime
Powers, and did not allow himself to be disturbed by the misfortunes of the exiled King. He was far from appreciating,
like Marais, "the impulse of glory and the warm ties of kinship."
He would more readily have quoted:

mais que nous chaut que le Nord s'entrepille?

Stanislas thus served as pretext for the operations of armies
on a scene far distant from Danzig. The French, under the
command of Marshal Berwick, conquered Kehl on October 28,
and in Italy entered Milan under Villars; this was the latter's
last campaign; he set forth, in spite of his eighty years,
like a true paladin, and the people remembering his former
exploits, cheered him all along the route. Marie Leszczynska
gave him a cockade, Elizabeth Farnese sent him another at
Lyons, and the Queen of Sardinia pinned a third on him at
Turin. He was able to say: "My hat is decorated by a bevy
of queens, a happy opening to my venture for the three crowns."

The operations could not be decisive during the winter, and the allies of France were chiefly concerned with their own interests. Charles Emmanuel paid little attention to the advice of Villars, assured himself of the Milanese province on December 29, and made no effort to join the Spanish armies beyond the Mincio ; Don Carlos, on his side, directed his troops towards Southern Italy and marched on Naples. The two princes, who were united by treaties, turned their backs on one another and each fought for his own hand. Thus the way was clear for the Imperial forces to fall back on Mantua and the passes of the lower Tyrol.

The whole conduct of this campaign was strange, and it has been described as " a triumph of diplomatic fictions." The Emperor was on the defensive on the Rhine and in Italy, but in Belgium he was neutral. The King of Prussia did not interfere in Poland, and he forbade the passage through his territory of the Russian artillery which wished to attack Danzig ; meanwhile, on the Rhine, in his capacity as Prince of the Holy Roman Empire, he furnished a contingent of six thousand men. George II, as King of England, was also neutral, but as Elector of Hanover he swelled the Imperial forces. Russia, nominally at peace with France, aided Charles VI as auxiliary of Austria. Voltaire called attention to the singularity of the situation, saying to the Abbé de Sade : " The fort of Kehl has been taken ; the Alicante fleet is at Sicily ; and while the wings of the Imperial eagle are being clipped in Italy and Germany, King Stanislas is being more than ever obstructed."

Leszczynski hoped that de Plélo's advice would be followed, and that thirty thousand men would be detached from the army of the Rhine to come to his succour through Saxony, while the Saxon forces were massed in Poland ; but the Cardinal would not listen to reason. The Queen received discouraging letters from her father : " I assure you," said he, " that unless the King occupies Saxony, I shall be compelled to abandon my inheritance and seek again my old homestead, where I shall be your tenant. If, as I am informed, by M. de La Roche (the Cardinal) and M. le Chauve (Chauvelin), treaties and conventions make the invasion of Saxony absolutely impossible, it would be better to end

Stanislas at Danzig.

the matter at once and peaceably than to incur useless expense in further pursuing it ; for I see no other hope of its success." Stanislas began to regret the adventure ; "You are to be envied," he wrote to his wife, Catherine Opalinska, and his daughter, "You are to be envied my dear ones, for being together as you inform me, and for the dinner you have had with mother. I believe I would be willing to fast on bread and water for a whole year to be one of the party."

He could at least depend on the inhabitants of Danzig, who remained faithful to the deposed king even after the coronation of Augustus III in the Cathedral of Wavel at Cracow on January 17, 1734. But the eight hundred defenders of the gallant town could do little against the bombardment which the Russians had commenced. Ten thousand Polish supporters hoped to concentrate in Danzig, but they were soon dispersed on the frontiers of Pomerania. Help from France might still have saved all, but Fleury's abandonment of Stanislas was obvious. Plélo wrote to the Court unceasingly : "Send us a fleet as soon as possible ; we have only ourselves to depend on. I should wish above all that M. Duguay-Trouin should be in command. His name alone is worth a squadron. Moreover, we must have a spirited leader who does not immediately wish to be back again at Brest. . . . Were all Germany and all Italy to be taken from the Emperor it would not enhance our prestige so much as the capture of the King of Poland and the fall of Danzig would shame us and damage our reputation."

While promising a squadron, Fleury only sent one flotilla without stores or ammunition. On their arrival in Denmark, Fleury's illusory support. the men had to be revictualled by the ambassador, who discovered that the soldiers were supplied with but seven rounds a piece ! "Has such a thing ever been seen as that only seven rounds should be served out to men who were going to meet the enemy," he wrote to Chauvelin ; "as for the flints, it is shameful that anyone should dare to supply them." This was not all. The flotilla, equipped as it was, arrived before Danzig on May 11 ; three days later, during the night, the French rejoined their ships and set sail for Copenhagen. La Motte, the commander, had been frightened by the numbers of the enemy and the smallness of his own force ; possibly also he did not take his commission seriously. Modern historians have some reason for thinking that Fleury, after his custom, must have sent the officer secret contradictory instructions. Whatever was the cause, Stanislas was abandoned. "The King of Poland," said Monti, "is plunged in the deepest grief. Consider what my own must be ! The whole town is in tears ; the relief so long expected, which did such honour to the King . . . has set out from France, only to become the laughing-stock of Europe. . . . The Vistula has never seen the French flags. They should never have come if it was but to flee. Condole with me !" Plélo also wrote to the King : " Never, Sire, never have your Majesty's arms suffered so shameful a disgrace."

But the gloom was lightened by one of the fairest acts of heroism in all French history. Plélo reasoned with the **Death of Plélo.** fugitives, telling La Motte that he acted in the name of the King, his master, whose authority he represented. Three other ships were anchored at Copenhagen, and the fleet became almost the squadron that had been desired. On May 20 the ambassador informed the French Court of his decision ; he took over the command and himself led the sailors to battle. "You will only see me again if I am victorious," he wrote to Louis, "or if we survive it will only be in a manner worthy of true Frenchmen and faithful subjects of your Majesty." Addressing Chauvelin he was more explicit : "The resolution I have taken is extraordinary, but the event which causes it is still more so. . . . The shame and infamy of what has happened can only be effaced by a complete victory or by the blood of us all. . . ."

Lastly, he sent a letter to his wife, who knew nothing of his projects : "I should be unworthy of the name of Frenchman and of your love if I did not do my duty on this occasion. My heart is too full to say more. Love, duty, glory, what ills you bring me ! All that there is to do, is to get our people to Danzig . . . thence I shall rejoin you, never to leave you again in this life."

Plélo arrived at Danzig on May 23. Shortly afterwards he led an assault on the enemy's entrenchments. The little force was compelled to retreat under a murderous fire from fifteen thousand Muscovites. The dead body of the ambassador was found covered with wounds at the entrance of the Russian camp.

In the chapel of Saint-Bihi, near Saint-Brieuc, may be seen a memorial inscription marking the spot where this noble heart was laid : " *Sparge lauris sepulchrum, viator, et benedic nomini armorico.* . . . Traveller, strew the tomb with laurels, and praise the Breton name. . . ." This prayer is heard ; no more eloquent proof of the greatness of the sacrifice can be given than the memory this gallant Breton has left.

Events moved rapidly. Stanislas in despair fled from the besieged town and abandoned it to its bitter fate ; he left in the disguise of a peasant, unarmed save for a thorn stick. After braving countless dangers he succeeded in reaching Prussian territory, and arrived at Marienwerder on July 3, on a muddy cart which he drove himself. Danzig capitulated, after a terrible siege lasting one hundred and thirty-five days, and the magistrates were compelled to recognize the election of Augustus III.

The Queen's father found refuge with Frederick William, King of Prussia. He signed his official abdication at Koenigs-

Stanislas in
Prussia.

berg, but the Cardinal hesitated to allow him to re-enter France. Stanislas' letters are full of bitter feeling : " Let the ministers triumph," said he, " as they will ; I will triumph in my turn when by divine assistance and angelic patience I shall arise from my abyss. . . . But now there is a new dagger in my heart, since you tell me of their cruelty in wishing to prevent me from seeing you. I assure you that they will not prove the stronger in this and I will not yield. . . ." He spoke the truth, for during the course of the year (1736), he again saw his beloved Maruchna.

The campaigns continued on the Rhine and in Italy. Here, however, neither troops, supplies, nor ammunition were wanting. Berwick fell before Philippsburg, struck by a cannon ball ; and Villars observed : " That man was always fortunate ! " The Marshal envied his glorious fate ; he himself, completely worn out, died in his bed a little later, on June 17, 1734, at Turin, the town where he was born.

On June 29, 1734, Coigny won the battle of Parma, defeating Mercy, the Imperial general, who was killed with eight thousand of his men. Maillebois captured Modena, but the Prince of Würtemberg, who succeeded Mercy, avenged him by surprising the Comte de Broglie in his tent at Quistello, a reverse which was redeemed by the victory of Guastalla on September 19.

Don Carlos reached Naples in May. His general, the Duke of Montemar, distinguished himself at Bitonto, in Apulia, and **Don Carlos** the Prince crossed over to Sicily, where he secured **King of the** the recognition of the rule of the Spanish Bourbons. **Two Sicilies.** The armies of Charles VI were everywhere defeated ; the Emperor won a kingdom for Saxony, but he lost two others and with them a great part of Italy. It was time to think of peace. Fleury willingly listened to Charles' hints and sent a secret agent to Vienna, Monsieur de la Baune, a gentleman in ordinary of the King's Household. The preliminaries were discussed at length. The Two Sicilies went to Don Carlos ; Parma and Placentia were given back to the House of Austria ; Milan fell to the lot of Charles Emmanuel. Stanislas caused considerable embarrassment. Duke Francis of Lorraine had just been betrothed to the Archduchess Maria Theresa, eldest daughter and heiress of the Emperor, but France could not allow the Duchy to become Austrian. This new diplomatic problem provided a means of settling everything. Lorraine **Stanislas Duke** was to be given to Stanislas for life, and was **of Lorraine.** afterwards to form part of France, and thus become a retrospective dowry for the Queen, who, like Anne of Brittany, would enrich France with a fair and powerful province. In exchange Francis III was to have Tuscany, where Giovanni, the last of the Medici, was about to die without issue. The conditions were signed at Vienna on October 3, 1735, and after interminable conferences with reference to the cession of Lorraine, they were ratified on November 18, 1738. The delicate negotiations were carried through by Chauvelin, but this did not restrain Fleury from sacrificing him to his own English proclivities.

Stanislas was generously provided for ; he received an annual pension of two million livres, but he had no right of taxation in Lorraine. That province became a source of considerable wealth to the French Crown. Stanislas solemnly entered on his rule in 1737. In the future he lived a quiet life of philan-

thropy and patronage, well endowed, but a king without a
kingdom, still dreaming at times of the Polish throne. He was
worn out by struggles for which he was not fitted, and he
found in his affection for Marie some consolation for his political
sorrows. Before everything he was a fond father ; his correspondence gives charming proofs of his sentiments. This hero,
in spite of himself, lives for us as the prince who dearly loved
his Marie.

In his craving for economy the Cardinal had replaced the
magnificent cascade of Marly with grass banks, in order to save
a thousand crowns. One day he was discussing with the Queen
the events which had brought Leszczynski to his satisfactory
retreat :

" Believe me, madame," said he, " the throne of Lorraine
is better for the King, your father, than that of Poland."

" Yes," replied the Queen, " just as a grass-plot is better
than a marble cascade."

Marie Leszczynska was not without wit, but it was her pleasure
to shun the society of courtiers. Consequently she is held to
have been a woman of no importance. It will be apparent later
on why she adopted a secondary role and was content to live
with a few intimate friends, who knew how much sad philosophy
and what resources the " good Queen " had within herself.

PRINCIPAL SOURCES. *Journal historique ou Fastes du règne de Louis
XV*, 1 vol., Paris, 1764 ; *Journal* of Pierre Narbonne, 1 vol., Paris, 1866 ;
Abbé Proyart, *Vie de Marie Leckzinska*, 1 vol., Paris, 1794 ; Rathery,
Le Comte de Plélo, 1 vol., Paris, 1876 ; Farges, *Recueil des Instructions
aux Ambassadeurs (Pologne)*, 2 vols., Paris, 1888 ; Boyé, *Stanislas Lesz-
czinski et le troisième traité de Vienne*, 1 vol., Nancy, 1898. We are indebted to this work for a number of new documents which throw light on
the attitude of Fleury in the War of the Polish succession, and provide
information on the events in Warsaw and Danzig. Lacour-Gayet, *La
Marine militaire de la France sous le régne de Louis XV*, 1 vol., Paris, 1902.

CHAPTER VIII

THE ROYAL FAMILY

Ten births. Portraits of the daughters of Louis XV in the Musée de Versailles. The King's son-in-law. Madame Henriette and the Duc de Chartres. The exiles of Fontevrault. Madame Adélaïde. Madame Victoire. Madame Sophie. The Carmelite of Saint-Denis. The Dauphin and Dauphine. How the Queen spent her days. Idle existence of Louis. The Society of Rambouillet. The three sisters de Nesle.

BETWEEN 1727 and 1737 ten royal children were born. First came twins in 1727, Louise-Elisabeth, the future Duchess of Parma and the only daughter of Louis who married, and Anne-Henriette ; then in 1728 a princess who died young ; in 1729, to the great joy of all France, the Dauphin was born. A second son, the Duc d'Anjou, came into the world in 1730 and only lived three years. Further, there were Adélaïde (1732), Victoire (1733), Sophie (1734), Thérèse-Félicité (1736–1744), and last of all, Louise-Marie (1737), Madame " dernière," who was afterwards Sister Thérèse of Saint-Augustin, Prioress of the Carmel of Saint-Denis.

Ten births.

These princesses may be seen in the Musée de Versailles, in the rooms on the ground floor where they passed the greater part of their lives ; they are there in fitting surroundings, amid scenes on which their fair glances still seem to rest. One might almost imagine they were alive, so skilfully have the painters portrayed the beauty and freshness of their young models. The two eldest are painted by Belle as well-behaved children, looking dainty in their hoods. Adélaïde, in her fifteenth year, is shown by Nattier in a costly rose-coloured dress, shot with white and embroidered with stars, holding a shuttle. But this portrait unquestionably is surpassed in beauty by the portrait of Madame

Portraits of the Princesses.

98

Victoire, in which the artist has shown his full talent. Seldom has he portrayed a smile with more exquisite simplicity, or a face with more radiance and expression. There is unconscious grace in the carriage of her head, a head of amber tints, with large soft eyes, and crowned by a wealth of black hair. A dress of silver and a yellow scarf which the breeze flutters lightly, complete the mellow harmony of this fine portrait. Nattier gives us less happy pictures of Mesdames Sophie and Louise ; in these more artifice was required.

The princesses in life sometimes resembled their portraits and had that smile on their lips, but it was not there always. They spent many monotonous days at Versailles, at Fontaine-bleau, at Choisy, or at Compiègne. These costly changes of residence were their only distractions ; everywhere they were on parade and dressed for ceremony, whether at the King's daily mass, at their dinner, at the taking off of their father's boots, or at their mother's receptions. On one occasion a maid-of-honour complained to Madame Adélaïde that she was dressed and undressed four times a day, and did not get a quarter of an hour to herself.

" Madame," replied Louis' daughter, " you are free to have a week's rest ; but I have to do it all the year through, so you must allow me to keep my pity for myself."

It is the business of painters—for painters of royalty it is their reason for existence—to show us the flattering side of this endless display and finery ; but it is impossible to forget the sadness that is hidden beneath the furbelows. It is pleasant to believe in their deceitful outward appearance, so attractive are the smiling and serene faces of the young girls. Yet it is probable that the princesses have more consideration in the Château of Versailles to-day than they had at the Court of their father. Their biography is but a few lines and the springtime of their lives was dreary ; and for this Louis must be blamed. He really had an affection for his daughters, but he gave them no effective proof of it either by precept or example.

The eldest princess married in 1739 at the age of twelve ; she went to Spain as the bride of the Infante Don Philip, son of Philip V and Elizabeth Farnese ; her departure was a great grief to the whole royal family, though it was a valuable political gage of the good relations between the two crowns.

Louise-Elisabeth's marriage could not have been less satisfactory; Don Philip was the least intelligent man in **The King's** Spain; he was kept in leading strings by his **Son-in-law.** mother and had neither initiative nor will of his own. The unhappy son-in-law of Louis XV had at least the good fortune of possessing an ambitious mother, and a wife who was jealous of his dynastic interests, and to them he owed the Duchy of Parma in 1748. Louise-Elisabeth led a feverish existence; she filled the world with her schemes, moved heaven and earth to gain her ends, went from Madrid to Versailles, from Versailles to Parma, and returned time and again to her father's Court, wearing herself out with fatigue and disappointed hopes. She wanted something better for her husband and her descendants than this " hole " of a Parma, as she called her domain. She dreamed of reigning in Milan, Corsica, Poland, the Netherlands, the Two Sicilies, and even in Spain itself. She had fresh hopes every day, only to be dissipated by circumstances over which she had no control; yet her illusions survived through all. If she could win nothing for herself, she believed she would ensure glorious reigns for her son Ferdinand and her daughters; one of whom became Archduchess of Austria, the other Queen of Spain. She could not foresee the calamities which from one generation to another would destroy the royal fortunes. She could in all sincerity declare that her duty was her first love, and she performed her duty as a princess with unusual energy, perhaps better than her duty as a mother. Also, throughout she remained French at heart.

It is possible that Louise-Elisabeth's example discouraged Louis, and that the hard struggles of the eldest condemned **Madame** her five sisters to celibacy; but it is also true that **Henriette and** the King was indifferent; his family caused him **the Duc** little anxiety. Did he not leave them a kingdom, **de Chartres.** a treasure, and wealth that were unassailable ? For a while he seemed to favour the marriage of the Duc de Chartres, grandson of the Regent, with Madame Henriette. The young prince was much in love, but one day, when he was hunting in the King's company, he thought he had found a favourable moment while their horses were side by side, to make his request to the King: "Sire, I have a great hope. Your Majesty has not rebuked my father for it. . . . I would further the happiness of Madame Henriette, for she would stay in France with Your Majesty. May I still hope?" Louis leaned towards the young prince and sadly pressed his hand twice. It meant a refusal. Was Henriette a victim of the Cardinal's policy as a sworn enemy of the House of Orléans? The Marquis d'Argenson is perhaps a little too certain on this point. Anyhow, the unhappy princess died in 1752, some say of grief, others, with more probability, of a malignant fever which she obstinately refused to have nursed. A phrase of her sister Louise sums up this sweet creature, so sensitive and affectionate, who was cut off in the flower of her age : "Why did they not leave me at Fontevrault? I should never have known Henriette!"

Fontevrault was an abbey, celebrated in the Middle Ages as the sepulchre of the Kings of England. It was eighty **The Exiles at** leagues from Versailles on the borders of Maine **Fontevrault.** and Poitou. Four of Louis' daughters were sent there in 1738. The idea of banishing them was Fleury's; in his passion for economy he asserted that the princesses "encumbered the Château of Versailles and caused expense." Five were to have been exiled, but Adélaïde presented herself to her father on his return from mass ; she kissed his hand, threw herself at his feet and began to weep. The King was touched by the scene—" he wept a little and the Court did the same." Adélaïde remained. But Victoire, Sophie, Thérèse-Félicité (who died there) and Louise, who was not a year old, went to the abbey.

There was no one to protect these innocents; they did not know how to speak or command like their elder sister, whose imperious and masterful nature soon showed itself. Adélaïde had high ideas of the prerogatives of her rank. On one occasion one of her chaplains had the misfortune to pronounce the *Dominus vobiscum* with too little solemnity, and she roundly rated him after the service, reminding him that he was not a bishop and had no right to act as one.

Her beauty quickly faded; she acquired a masculine appearance which was not unsuited to her baritone voice. She **Madame Adélaïde.** had an overwhelming desire to learn everything. She wished to play every musical instrument, from the horn to the Jew's-harp. She learnt Italian, English, the higher mathematics, and watchmaking, without acquiring a very deep knowledge of any of them. All this we learn from the Duc de Luynes and Madame Campan. She endeavoured to interfere in State affairs, but had no influence and could scarcely have had any with a father who said of an unpopular minister : " It is better that he should fall, since there is none but myself to support him."

Madame Adélaïde became soured in her old age, and as aunt of Louis XVI, she was difficult to please. With her sister Victoire she survived to the Revolution, and they both died in exile and poverty at Trieste, one in 1799, the other in 1800.

Thanks to her youthful energy, Adélaïde escaped the convent, while the seclusion of Fontevrault lasted ten years in the case of Madame Victoire, and twelve years in that of Mesdames Sophie and Louise. What did these young girls learn in their distant monastery under the guidance of the Most High and Puissant Dame Claire-Louise de Montmorin de Saint-Hérem ? Madame Campan relates that Madame Louise did not yet know all her letters when she returned to Versailles. This is an exaggeration, for an autograph of the future Carmelite exists dated 1746.

It was no longer a time when king's daughters had philosophers and men of learning for their tutors, when, like Elizabeth of England they understood the classical tongues, and like Marguerite de Valois, sister of Charles IX, could answer the speeches of ambassadors in Latin.

Fontevrault did not change Madame Victoire. She was always essentially a princess and essentially melancholy. She **Madame Victoire.** loved good living—the princesses' fare was marked by great simplicity—she also loved ease. She was asked if she would retire into some Carmelite house like Louise, and her reply was pleasing : " Here is an armchair which corrupts me ! " So saying, she stretched herself with enjoyment in a cosy *bergère*. She was a complete nonentity. The same may be said of Sophie, whose virtues and absurdities Madame Campan records. Sophie always seemed to have fallen from the clouds ; she remained for months without opening her mouth, and she was never seen full face. Victoire and Sophie were the antithesis of Adélaïde. They passively submitted to her tyranny.

Madame Louise. Louise on the other hand revolted, and would not let herself be managed ; she sought refuge at Saint-Denis, and quickly made an independent position for herself. Thus she had influence at court and profited by it to help the Church. She possessed wit and gaiety : the ordinary dower of nuns who entered the Carmelite Houses was six thousand livres ; Madame Louise doubled the amount and said to the Prioress : " I am giving you twelve thousand livres, six for myself and six for my hump." She is known to have had spinal curvature. Until her father's death she obtained numerous favours, but after the accession of Louis XVI, the Court grew tired of her ceaseless demands. " Here is another letter from Louise," Marie-Antoinette would often say to Madame Campan : " she is the most intriguing little Carmelite in the kingdom." " This severe phrase," says a historian, " has the durability and austerity of an antique bronze medal." On that day, Marie-Antoinette forgot the emotion she had experienced in September 1770, on her aunt's taking the veil, when she handed her the scapulary, the mantle and the nun's veil all bedewed with tears. She forgot the impressive ceremony when the princess, before donning the mantle of Sainte-Thérèse, appeared before her household in all the splendours of an apotheosis, covered with pearls and diamonds, whose fires surrounded her with a sort of luminous mist—" truly a king's daughter in her court robe threaded with silver and sprinkled with golden flowers." *

In her youth Madame Louise had loved the pleasures of the chase passionately and on her death-bed her thoughts went back to her existence at court. Her last words were : " To paradise, quick, quick, gallop ! " She thought she was giving orders to her equerry.

* Jules Soury.

Louis saw his daughters for a few minutes practically every day ; to love them was a kind of duty in the King's eyes, and he acquitted himself of the duty conscientiously, but he never thought of treating them as more than pretty dolls. Between the princesses and their mother there was always a certain coldness, due, no doubt, to the isolation in which Marie Leszczynska was left, and to etiquette which the Queen could not break as easily as the King. That Louis' familiarity was a little disconcerting, is shown by the nicknames he gave the princesses : Adélaïde was called *Torche ;* Victoire, who was inclined to be plump, *Coche ;* Sophie, *Graille* (a kind of crow), and Louise, *Chiffe.* This was the fashion of the age. We do not find in the eighteenth century only the pleasing elegance which has come down to us in the pictures of Boucher, in the scented verses of the minor poets and the exquisite chamber decorations. In the letters of the Duchess of Parma, for instance, there are crude expressions and remarks worthy of a trooper. We may have lost the artistic sense of those times, but our language at least is more correct.

The King with his Daughters.

The King used often to descend to Madame Adélaïde's chamber by a private staircase ; he brought down coffee made with his own hands and took it with her—he was fond also of cooking dishes he had prepared, and on days of high festival he used to go and inspect the head cooks and supervise the roast. As soon as the King arrived, Madame Adélaïde pulled the bell to inform Madame Victoire, who, as she rose to go to her sister rang for Madame Sophie, while she in her turn rang for Madame Louise. The latter lived in the most remote room, and being small of stature she could not take long steps ; she had to run as fast as she could and then only arrived in time to embrace her father as he left for the chase. At six o'clock in the evening, the *débotté* * was held, and the princesses publicly visited their father. "Each princess," says Madame de Campan, their reader, " put on an enormous hoop which supported a petticoat trimmed with gold or embroidery ; they fastened a long train round their waists, and hid the *négligé* of the rest of their dress with a large cloak of black taffeta which covered them up to the chin. The gentlemen of the

* The removal of the boots.

Court, ladies-in-waiting, pages, equerries and ushers attended them to the King's presence with large torches. Instantly the whole palace, usually quite deserted, was in motion. The King kissed each princess on the forehead, and the visit was so short that the reading, interrupted by it was often resumed after a quarter of an hour's interval. Mesdames retired to their apartments, undid the ribbons of their petticoats and trains, and again took up their tapestry, and I my reading. . . ."

It was with their brother, the Dauphin, that Mesdames really experienced family life. That Prince was twice married, **The Dauphin's** first of all to Marie-Thérèse-Raphaëlle, Infanta **Family Circle.** of Spain, who left him a widower in 1746, and later to Marie-Josèphe of Saxony, daughter of Stanislas Leszczynski's rival, Augustus III, King of Poland and Elector of Saxony.

Marie-Raphaëlle did not live long enough for any judgment to be formed about her. Marie-Josèphe was a high-minded woman, well educated and loving beautiful things. She soon made a position for herself at Versailles. She had some difficulty in winning the Dauphin's affections, but thanks to Madame Henriette, who loved and supported her, she came to know the joys of wedded life. She was morally strong and a sincere Christian, and won universal esteem. The King had a remarkable affection for her. She had the merit, rare in those days, of looking after her children like a simple *bourgeoise*, and that even before Rousseau had made maternal care the fashion; yet withal she was a princess, and jealous of the prerogatives attached to her title.

The Dauphin was kept in the background by his father. In spite of his distinguished conduct at Fontenoy, he was denied a career in the army, and was given no share in affairs of State. His chief pleasure was to find a quiet corner where he might indulge his taste for study. There, with a considerate and obedient wife, he consoled himself for events which distressed him, in which he was compelled to take part, but which he could not remedy. In this little circle Mesdames also found the inestimable pleasure of intimacy between brother and sister. There they enjoyed an innocent gaiety always in the best taste.

During his lifetime the Dauphin was not understood ; he was thought to be an overgrown boy, apathetic and indifferent. **The Dauphin's** He was very like the Queen, as is shown by their **Character.** two pictures by La Tour in the Louvre. Like Marie, he had wit and a sense of humour ; like her he was also reserved. His conversation was coherent, well-informed, and agreeable ; no one could have shown more tact than he did when giving audiences to ambassadors. He was a considerable judge of character and could express himself concisely. On his death in 1764, the clergy and philosophers, among them Voltaire and Diderot, praised his great qualities. All parties of the public sincerely mourned him. It had been hoped that this prince, who possessed all the virtues of a man, would have also had those of a king. The writings he has left testify to his profound piety ; they contain a series of maxims on laws, administration, and the interests of the State, which display sentiments of justice, humanity, and love for the people.

On one occasion he was leaning over the great balcony of the Château de Bellevue with his eyes fixed on Paris, when one of his friends approached him and said : " Monsieur le Dauphin seems pensive." " I was thinking," he replied, " of the pleasure a sovereign must feel in causing the happiness of so many people."

The Dauphin would doubtless have shown more energy on the throne than did his son Louis XVI, but he could only have delayed the relentless march of events.

The Queen, like the Dauphin, was isolated, but her life was active and her days fully occupied. She was often alone but **The Life of** " she always made good use of her time." Her **the Queen.** mornings were passed in prayers and serious reading ; then, after a short visit to the King, there came recreations, among others painting. The good Queen had never had a master and she was not highly gifted ; her pictures as seen at Trianon and at the Carmel de Sens, have been re-touched by some obliging artist. She also loved music ; she played the guitar, the viol and the harpsichord, and was the first to laugh at her own false notes. At half-past twelve she made her toilet, which was followed by the daily mass and the dinner, at which twelve ladies-in-waiting attended. After dinner she retired to her private apartments and was no longer Queen, but an " ordinary mortal." She did her embroidery, and spoke of her morning's reading, which malicious tongues said she did not always understand. About six o'clock the Court assembled in her apartments, though the attendance was not large ; afterwards every one tried to escape the eternal game of cavagnole at the Duchesse de Luynes', one of the ladies-in-waiting, where Marie Leszczynska spent her evenings and supped. The Dauphin and Dauphine and Mesdames were bound to attend, but in addition there were only the Queen's intimates, President Hénault, Moncrif, all the dowagers, some old gentlemen and some officers of the Gardes, like the Marquis de Razilly, a famous piquet-player. Etiquette was banished from this rather monotonous society. The conversation often flagged, for all ordinary subjects such as intrigues and politics were interdicted. The Queen allowed people to argue with her. Sometimes she was even given a lesson, as the following anecdote related by the Comte de Cheverny will show.

A certain Monsieur de Flamarens, Grand Master of the wolf-hounds, was celebrated for his table accomplishments. **The Queen's** He wagered that he could eat a rabbit after a **Appetite.** large dinner, and won. His achievement was often spoken of, and, at one of her suppers, the Queen who herself ate with " a well sustained appetite," asked the man of the moment, without any notion of giving offence :

" Monsieur de Flamarens, is it true that at Monsieur d'Ardore's (the ambassador of the Two Sicilies) you ate a rabbit in two mouthfuls ? "

" Yes, Madame."

" Then you always have a good appetite, and it is well maintained ? "

" Yes, Madame, and I always pray that Your Majesty may be equally blessed ; I know perfectly well that Your Majesty has this morning eaten *so and so*." He went on to enumerate all that he had seen the Queen eat. Whereupon she was annoyed and left the table saying :

" It serves me right, but I will never speak to him again."

The King lived an idle life. His chief occupations were hunting and trifling—habits which were encouraged by Cardinal **The King's** de Fleury, who only consulted him for form's **idle Life.** sake. His chief care was to avoid being bored, and, such being his attitude, he was easily gulled by his courtiers. With the Queen he was cold and indifferent, even in the early years of their union. Marshal de Villars in his memoirs, notes a characteristic scene in September 1727 : " The King supped with the Queen ; there were very few present, and as he was about to depart for Fontainebleau the next morning, it was whispered that it would be better to leave them alone and every one quitted the room ; but an instant later the King opened the door." Everything proved that the Queen loved him, but was not loved in return.

Louis attended the councils, but if he were indisposed to the slightest extent they were suspended ; hunting, and in winter sledge races, and excessive meals at the Ménagerie followed by balls far into the night, often injured the royal health. These diversions marked a new stage in the King's existence. People began to suggest that some bold woman might easily gain an influence over the young idler. There were ambitious persons endeavouring to be the first in the field and waiting for the right moment ; they encouraged the King's intimates to lay traps for him. There were two factions ; the Chantilly faction headed by Monsieur le Duc and his mother, which had but little influence, and the Rambouillet faction, in which Sophie de Noailles, Comtesse de Toulouse, was most prominent.

Louis delighted to go to Rambouillet to find relaxation from state. The society there was gay ; he felt himself free and **Rambouillet.** showed himself a good conversationalist. The Comte de Toulouse was a kind of great-uncle of the King. Between the interludes, small groups were formed, in which Louis, the owners of the Château and Mlle. de Charolais, a sister of Monsieur le Duc who had quarrelled with him, took part. At these meetings many favours were granted ; in particular, the Comte de Toulouse's son, the Duc de Penthièvre, secured the reversion to the offices and powers of his father. At Rambouillet the idea originated of introducing the King to the Comtesse de Mailly, *née* Mailly-Nesle, one of the Queen's ladies-in-waiting. This lady was discreet and at Versailles had the air of a penitent. There is some reason for comparing her with Mlle. de la Vallière. She was devotedly attached to the King.

Later on, her sister Madame de Vintimille was preferred to her, and she suffered greatly. However, when Madame de Vintimille **The de Nesle** died in 1741, she displayed great self-abnegation **Sisters.** and returned to the King to console him. But the King was overwhelmed by the event, and his grief could not be assuaged. His religious fervour was awakened under the influence of this emotion, the first real emotion of his life, for when he lost his parents and his grandfather he was too young to know what had happened. He returned to the spiritual observances which he had abandoned, and now and then he was heard to express regrets inspired by the purest Christian sentiment. Such moods were rare with him.

Madame de Vintimille bore no resemblance to her sister; she was arrogant, bold, inquisitive, vindictive, fond of power and of inspiring fear, with few friends and little to attract them. Her whole thought was for her own interests, her only aim was to make the best use of the King's favour, and she would have succeeded if she had had the time. She was "a dangerous favourite." Occasionally her intentions were good; she endeavoured to make a soldier of Louis by inducing him to accompany the army. She was hated by the people of Versailles, who were delighted at the news of her death; they called her "an infamous beast." Insulting gibes were hurled after her funeral cortège by the mob.

Another sister of Madame de Mailly was also presented at Court. Her name was Marie-Anne, and she was the widow of the Marquis de la Tournelle. Louis created her Duchesse de Châteauroux, just as Antoinette Poisson, wife of Monsieur le Normand d'Etiolles was created Marquise de Pompadour. Nattier painted Madame de la Tournelle as a victorious Aurora floating on a cloud. This portrait is in the Museum at Marseilles; it was the artist's first success. It is a remarkable psychological study showing, in all her disquieting beauty, her of whom it was said: "Her large blue eyes gave bewitching glances, and all her movements showed infinite grace."

The Duchesse de Châteauroux possessed a natural wit, and though she was quite ignorant, she charmed by the spontaneity **Mme. de** of her conversation. All Madame de Mailly had **Châteauroux.** asked had been a little affection ; Madame de Vintimille died before she had obtained all she coveted ; the future Duchesse, in the words of a chronicler, " made good terms for herself." She asked for the dismissal of her elder sister, and demanded titles and distinctions such as had only once been accorded in the reign of Louis XIV. The King granted all her desires, and her influence became so great that it was feared she would rule as absolute mistress. The Cardinal tried to check this intrigue, but failed. There was a complete revolution at Versailles. Louis did not like governing ; he never entered into discussions, but merely gave his decision. But Madame de la Tournelle busied herself with all that happened both in France and abroad.

" She does not interfere in personal matters," said Louis to Madame de Brancas ; " that would not be worthy of her, but she never ceases talking to me of ministers, the Parlement, and peace ; which makes me wretched. I have often told her she will kill me. Do you know what she replies ? " " So much the better, Sire, a King must be brought to life again and I will revive you."

" I do not understand it," he said. He understood nothing about it, but he was involved in spite of himself. To do her justice, Madame de Châteauroux supported by Noailles and Richelieu, had an excellent influence over Louis. More fortunate than Madame de Vintimille, she induced the monarch to share the campaign in Flanders.

The King's conduct had immediate consequences. His ruinous expenditure burdened the Treasury, and the State fell into the hands of the favourites. From that moment the monarchy was lost ; a vast ground swell was driving it like a disabled vessel against the rocks. But for the present the sky was clear ; neither King nor people saw any threatening signs on the horizon. When Louis escaped from death at Metz he was called Louis the *Well-beloved*, so powerful still were the monarchic traditions which had brought about the unification of the country.

THE ROYAL FAMILY

PRINCIPAL SOURCES. *Mémoires de la Duchesse de Brancas sur Louis XV et Madame de Châteauroux*, Louis Lacour, Paris, 1865 ; *Mémoires* of Madame Campan, 3 vols., Paris, 1823 ; Abbé Proyart, *Vie de Madame Louise de France*, Brussels, 1793 ; Engerand, *Inventaire des tableaux commandés et achetés par la Direction des bâtiments du Roi* (1709–1792), Paris, 1901 ; H. Bonhomme, *Louis XV et sa famille*, Paris, 1873 ; Jules Soury, *Portraits de femmes*, Paris, 1875 ; P. de Nolhac, *Louis XV et Marie Leczinska*, Paris, 1902.

CHAPTER IX

" FOR THE PRUSSIAN KING "
1740–1743

Death of the Emperor Charles VI. The candidates for the Imperial throne. Plans of Frederick II. Louis supports Charles Albert, Elector of Bavaria. The war party. The Comte de Belle-Isle. His designs. The Emperor's election. Frederic victorious in Silesia. Treaty of Nymphenburg. Two French armies cross the Rhine. Surprise of Prague. A letter of Maurice de Saxe. Charles Albert, King of Bohemia. Defection of Frederic II. Voltaire congratulates the King of Prussia. Abandonment of Prague. Death of Cardinal de Fleury. Religious and parliamentary affairs. The Jansenists and the party of Pâris the deacon. Portrait of Fleury by Voltaire.

ON October 20, 1740, the Emperor Charles VI, the last male descendant of Charles V, departed this life at Vienna. He left behind him a depleted treasury and an army weakened by the war of the Polish Succession. **Death of the** The Pragmatic Sanction, his edict giving his **Emperor** inheritance to his daughter Maria Theresa, wife **Charles VI.** of Francis of Lorraine, the Regent's nephew, had been recognized during the Emperor's lifetime by the States of the Empire and by Europe, with the sole exception of Bavaria.

But when it was seen that Charles Albert, the Elector of that Duchy, coveted the Imperial throne of the Hapsburgs, claiming it through his grandmother, a daughter of Ferdinand I and a niece of Charles V, other candidates arose. Firstly, there was Augustus III, Elector of Saxony and King of Poland. He had married Marie-Josèphe daughter of Joseph I, the elder brother of Charles VI and Emperor before him. Next there was Charles Emmanuel III of Sardinia, husband of Elisabeth Thérèse, the sister of Francis of Lorraine ; and lastly, Philip V

112

of Spain, and Frederick II King of Prussia, who had ascended
the throne at twenty-eight years of age on May 31, in the same
year 1740. Each of the two last named desired to profit by
so important an event, the former for one of his sons, the latter
for himself.

Maria Theresa, against whom all this rivalry and covetousness
was arrayed, was twenty-three years of age. She was rather
attractive than beautiful, well educated, intimately conversant
with many languages, pious, simple and home-loving; she
brightened the gloomy court of her father like a delicate flower
blooming in the crevices of an ancient building, to quote the happy
simile of Arneth, one of her biographers. As Queen of Hungary
and Bohemia, she justified the judgment of the English diplomatist, Robinson : " She is so well fitted to reign, that she
already looks upon her father as merely the administrator of
States which belong to her."

Her most redoubtable adversary was Frederick II, a young
sovereign endowed with the character of a conqueror : much
Projects of energy and no scruples. On hearing of the
Frederick the demise of Charles VI he wrote to his friend
Great. Voltaire : " This death upsets my pacific plans,
and I believe we shall be more concerned in the months of June
with gunpowder, soldiers, and entrenchments than with actresses,
ballets, and the theatre. . . . The time has come for the total
change of the old political system. . . . I am overwhelmed with
business. I must get rid of my fever, for I need my machine,
and must draw upon every resource at my command."

In November, Frederick again took up his pen, and this
time confided in Algarotti, a pleasant Italian of his acquaintance : " If you ask me what is happening in Europe, I will
tell you that Saxony is playing at knucklebones ; that Poland
is eating salted beef and rotten cabbage ; the Grand Duke
(Francis of Lorraine, Grand Duke of Tuscany) has a gangrene
in his body and cannot make up his mind to the operation
that would heal him ; France is playing a deep game and watches
her prey ; Holland trembles ; at Rheinsberg we play and
dance. . . ." The picture is amusingly conceived, but the
King of Prussia was covering the scent. If they were dancing
at Rheinsberg, they were also meditating formidable schemes.

The gangrene of the Grand Duke needed a surgeon's knife, and the specialist was none other than Frederick, who intended to annex Silesia and to give a good example to his rival competitors. He appealed to old rights which had been in abeyance for eighty years ; but in fact his troops were ready for action, his finances sound, his confidence firm, and these were his real rights, as he himself declared, though he did not go so far as to admit that he wished to despoil a weak woman. He sent Maria Theresa an ultimatum, and offered to lend his support to the claims of Francis of Lorraine to the Empire, and to pay six million francs in addition, in exchange for Silesia. The young Queen replied that she " defended her subjects and did not sell them." But as a reply, the King of Prussia invaded Austrian territory on December 22, 1740. Frederick needed support and obtained it, blinding his allies and persuading them to co-operate in the bold stroke he proposed to make. It was above all for his benefit that so many victims bled, and that for nearly eight years, central Europe was convulsed.

Louis XV believed it his duty to support the Elector of Bavaria, whose grandmother was the Grande Dauphine, Marie Victoire, the mother of the Duc de Bourgogne. But he had something better to do than to join in a war which was to enrich the King of Prussia by a fair province and to bring nothing to France. The time had come to abandon the ancient struggle with the Hapsburgs, and to be satisfied with the conquests which during the last century had extended the domains of France, and freed her from the pressure of Austria. Cambrai, Besançon and Strasburg were sufficient guarantees ; the recognition of the Pragmatic Sanction, so strangely violated, had strengthened and confirmed the new view of the situation. But Fleury, whom Frederick ironically described as " a great man endowed with so many singular qualities . . . the greatest man that France has had up to now,"—was quite incapable of understanding the advantages to be derived from such a *volte-face*. To do him justice, the prelate was stimulated by the impatience of the young military element, so long inactive, which was anxious to win laurels. Perhaps at bottom there was also a desire to induce Louis to imitate his ancestors in their conduct as kings and soldiers.

Public opinion on this occasion was irresistible and all-powerful. It was one of its first victories; it will be seen whether the victory was a fortunate one.

The spokesman of the young French war party was the grandson of the celebrated Controller Fouquet, Charles Louis **The Comte de** Auguste Fouquet, Comte de Belle-Isle, one of **Belle-Isle.** Madame de Prie's victims. On the day after the Regent's death he had been confined to the Bastille for having been concerned, together with the minister Le Blanc, in a scandal connected with military supplies. He was fifty-six years of age in 1740, and was intelligent, ambitious, and energetic. He knew all the secrets of the Chancelleries, and neglected nothing which could inform him as to the strength and weakness of the various European Powers. He proposed a great scheme to the Cardinal; this was to place the Imperial crown on the head of the Elector of Bavaria, and to seize some of the fairest states of Maria Theresa—as though all the provinces of the Archduchess were up for auction—in order to provide a suitable domain for the Elector, whose possessions were too small to maintain the rank of Emperor. The Cardinal was attracted by the scheme, though he grudged the expense. A hundred thousand men were required for Munich, but he only granted forty thousand; meanwhile, he despatched Belle-Isle, newly promoted to the rank of Field-Marshal, as ambassador extraordinary to the Electoral Diet of Frankfort, where the proud representative of France's interests displayed an almost royal luxury, and astonished the town with his dinners and receptions and retinue. He visited the Electors of Treves, Cologne, Mayence, and Saxony, making liberal payments to their ministers and secretaries; he poured out money like water, and in the end secured the victory of the Elector of Bavaria, who was nominated Emperor on January 24, 1742. **Election of** On January 27, Belle-Isle wrote: " The moment **the Emperor.** the Emperor came to the window of the Town Hall and was shown to the people . . . he was greeted by countless acclamations. I had the honour to be at a window with the Empress, who was incognita. The Emperor at

115

one of these acclamations and outbursts of joy, turned his eyes towards me, and putting his hand to the crown of Charlemagne on his head, he made me a sign, to show that it was to the King of France alone that he owed the glory he was then enjoying."

Important events, which must be recapitulated, had contributed to this success, and first and foremost the victory of **Battle of** the armies of the Prussian King over the Austrians. **Molwitz.** On April 10, 1741, Frederick was almost surprised in his headquarters at Molwitz in Silesia by Field-Marshal Neipperg and was obliged to fly. He owed the ultimate success of that day to Marshal Schwerin. It is asserted that he took refuge in a mill where he passed a night of trepidation. At dawn, Schwerin came to announce the defeat of his enemies, and to bring him to his army, covered, as was maliciously said, with *glory and flour*. However Frederick brought the laugh to his own side, by wittily announcing the news to Voltaire : " They say the Austrians are beaten, and I believe it is true."

Belle-Isle was happy in the diplomatic sphere. On May 18, he signed a treaty at Nymphenburg, the Elector's beautiful **Treaty of** residence in the neighbourhood of Munich. The **Nymphenburg.** participants were France, Spain, and Bavaria, and later Saxony and Sardinia, and they proposed to share Upper Austria, Bohemia, Moravia and the Italian possessions of the Hapsburgs. The Pragmatic Sanction was forgotten. Fleury thought himself justified in what he did by saying that the guarantee was subject to the rights of third parties.

After long discussions Frederick decided on June 7, to conclude an alliance with Louis. He promised to give his support to Charles Albert, and in return he obtained a guarantee for his future possession of Silesia, and for a present dispatch of French troops into Germany. He acted up to the reply he gave to an English ambassador : " Do not talk to me of grandeur of soul ; a prince must only consult his own interests." His manœuvres were astute ; he had entered into negotiation with both North and South, and had accepted the alliance of the one who offered most. " If there is anything to gain by being honest," he said, " we will be honest ; if we must deceive, let us be knaves." All that remained to Maria Theresa was the support of England, but she was able to count on the flimsiness of the coalition which was organized against her. All the allies were concealing their designs and all had ulterior motives. Their shufflings, as Frederick himself said, were the *miracle* which saved the House of Austria.

At this juncture, Maria Theresa was crowned Queen of Hungary and received the oath of her subjects at Presburg on **Coronation of** June 25, 1741, amid the greatest enthusiasm. **Maria Theresa.** "The Queen is grace personified," said one of her admirers, the old diplomatist Robinson : " when she lifted her sword in defiance of the four quarters of the world (for thus the Kings of Hungary swore to defend their people against the enemy from whatever side the danger came), it was easy to see that she neither needed that weapon nor any other to conquer those who entered her presence. The old mantle of St. Stephen became her as well as the richest robes."

This festival preceded some sad to-morrows for the sovereign, and the chances of Louis' *protégé* in his candidature for the Empire were increased. The French were duped by Frederick and crossed the Rhine in the summer of 1741 ; one division, commanded by Marshal de Maillebois, overawed George II, Elector of Hanover and King of Great Britain, compelling him to maintain a neutral attitude to the King of Prussia's advantage and guarding Holland and the Netherlands ; the other division was nominally under the command of Belle-Isle, but the real leader was Marshal de Broglie. This latter was intended to support the Bavarians, of whom Charles Albert was Generalissimo ; in its ranks was Maurice de Saxe, the future victor of Fontenoy, and natural son of Augustus II, Elector of Saxony and King of Poland. He needed nothing but the opportunity to show himself a remarkable general. There were also Lieutenant-Colonel Chevert, a celebrated soldier of fortune, who gained his promotions step by step at a time when they were lavished on birth, and the delicate thinker, Vauvenargues. The Bavarians entered Upper Austria, and on September 10 they were joined by the French, and encamped before Linz on the Danube, three days from Vienna, which they were afraid to besiege. They hoped to have Frederick's assistance, but he was content to play the part of spectator, only showing himself when there was no longer any need of him.

Charles Albert's object was Bohemia, and he directed the Franco-Bavarian army towards Prague. The siege of this **Siege of** town is famous. An ingenious surprise was con-**Prague.** trived by Maurice de Saxe. Besides him there were others who distinguished themselves, the Comte de Broglie, son of the Marshal, and Chevert, who before the assault exchanged the well-known dialogue with a sergeant of the Alsace regiment named Pascal :

" You would like to mount first, comrade ? "

" Yes, colonel."

" When you are on the wall, the sentry will cry 'Wer da ? ' " (Who goes there ?)

" Yes, colonel."

" You will make no reply."

" No, colonel."

" He will fire at you."

" Yes, colonel."

" He will miss you."

" Yes, colonel."

" You will kill him."

" Yes, colonel."

The sentry was not killed ; he took to his heels. The town capitulated on November 25, without a drop of French blood being shed.

The letter which Maurice de Saxe wrote to Belle-Isle, must be quoted ; it is grandiose in spite of the quaint orthography :

" Monsieur . . . vous aves désiré que Prague fût pri et il ait pri ; le gouverneur sait rendus a moy et je vous écri de sa chambre ; je ne saurès au demeurant assez vous faire delloge de la valeur des troupes et surtout de la bonne conduite de M. Chever, lieutenamp-colonel de Bosse (Beauce) ; Je suis un peu occupé à maintenir l'ordre ; se qui n'est pas aissé dans une ville prise l'épée à la main.

" MAURICE DE SAXE." *

* " Monsieur. . . You desired that Prague should be taken and it has been taken ; the Governor has surrendered to me and I am writing from his apartments ; I am indeed unable to eulogize sufficiently the valour

Some days later the gates were solemnly opened to receive Charles Albert. He was escorted to the Hradschin, in the cathedral church, where he was crowned King of Bohemia. It might be said that it was not only the town of Prague and the crown of Bohemia which had been taken by storm, but the Imperial dignity itself.

The news of this event arrived when the Diet of Frankfort was sitting, and ensured the Elector's success. Thus the *protégé* of France became Emperor under the title of Charles VII, and a hard blow was struck at the descendants of Rudolf of Hapsburg, who had held for many generations the orb and sceptre of the Holy Roman Empire. But the insignia fell into feeble hands. Charles Albert was in no way prepared for his new position ; he had neither energy nor initiative, and he had not even the money or the troops necessary to resist the reprisals meditated by the Austrians. Maria Theresa's subjects were fired by the proud attitude of their Queen and were about to make fresh efforts and to avenge the loss of Prague. Khevenhüller crossed the Danube and the Hungarians and the Croats invaded **The Austrians** Bavaria, and reached Munich on the day after **take Munich.** the coronation of Charles VII. The Emperor became a John Lackland. He was at Frankfort with his family without a kingdom in which to exercise his illusory sovereignty. All he now possessed was Prague, his ephemeral capital, while armies led by Francis of Lorraine, his brother Charles Alexander, Lobkowitz, Neipperg, and Koenigseck, blocked his way to Bohemia. The unfortunate Emperor was not spared by the rhymes and lampoons of the time ; the best example was a Latin couplet :

> Aut nihil aut Cæsar, Bavarus dux, esse volebas,
> Et nihil et Cæsar factus utrumque simul.

Which may be translated :

> Cæsar or naught, Bavarian prince, you'd be ;
> Cæsar and naught at once, your destiny.

---

of the troops and especially the conduct of M. Chevert, Lieutenant Colonel of Beauce ; I am somewhat occupied in maintaining order, which is not easy in a town taken sword in hand.—MAURICE DE SAXE."

To this disaster Frederick, the ally of France, had contributed. He profited by Charles' weakness to carry on negotiations with him, by which he secured, not only **Frederick's Defection.** Upper Silesia, but also the County of Glatz, dependencies of the Bohemian crown. He also sounded Vienna ; finally, to give more weight to his arguments, and make some show of keeping his official word, he closed the route to Prague for the Austrian army by the battle of Czazlau on May 17, 1742. " Look to yourselves," he then said to Valori, the French Minister at Berlin : " I have gained my point and am going to make my peace." This was the signal for the negotiations which ended in the Treaty of Berlin on July 27. The treaty guaranteed to the King of Prussia nearly all the territories he coveted and secured the adhesion of the Elector of Saxony. France had been tricked and Belle-Isle could now recognize the vain audacity of plans so easily upset by a young king whose double dealing he had not suspected. France was isolated in Europe, both morally and in fact.

England joined Germany and waited a propitious moment to make her mark in the struggle. The King of Sardinia turned to meet the Spanish troops massed in the north of Italy, and it was apprehended that Elizabeth Farnese, who had been abandoned by Fleury, would join a coalition at the price of an establishment for Don Philip. The Electors of the Rhine deserted France one after another, and even Charles VII followed their example and ceded Bohemia, with the object of regaining a roof under which to hide his mortification. His defection left France small regret, and the memory of a friendship which had heavily burdened her.

Paris was in consternation. Voltaire however, found occasion to congratulate the King of Prussia. His letter **Voltaire congratulates Frederick.** abounds with witticisms and even contains a pun. The following are some of the passages : " The *Saigneur* * of the nations, Frederick the Great, has granted our prayers. . . . I understand that your Majesty has concluded a favourable treaty. That it is favourable to yourself cannot be doubted, for you have trained your mind in political skill. But there is some doubt expressed in Paris

* *i.e.* Blood-letter; this is of course a play on the word " Seigneur."

as to whether it is favourable to us French. One half of our people cries that you have abandoned our troops to the will of the God of war; the other half cries too, but does not know what is the matter. . . . Then you are no longer our ally, Sire ? But you will be the ally of the human race; your desire is that each should peacefully enjoy his rights and his inheritance (a cynical statement, as applied to the despoiler of Silesia) and that troubles should cease; this would be the philosopher's stone of politics; a fit product of your laboratory. Say ' I wish men to be happy ' and they will be. May yours be a successful Opera—a successful comedy. May I be witness of your pleasures and your triumph at Berlin ! "

Frederick replied : " I have little concern for the cries of the Parisians; they are hornets who are always buzzing. . . . If all France condemns me for having made peace, Voltaire the philosopher will never allow himself to be carried away by the crowd." The justification which follows is too gross to quote. Voltaire's letter was intercepted and published; he was forced to disown it under the threat of being sent again to the Bastille.

These two men who hold so important a place in the Eighteenth Century, one in the military annals, the other in the republic of letters, show themselves in an unfavourable light at the commencement of their careers. Frederick twitted those he had deceived; Voltaire clothed the ill-timed homage, which he laid at the feet of his Majesty of Prussia, in philosophic and humanitarian phrases. Both were ignoble; but their pettiness is forgotten in the grandeur of their achievements; here it is indeed the end which justifies the means.

The climax was reached when the French Marshals, Broglie and Belle-Isle, failed to agree as to the orders to be given to the armies; and Fleury accentuated the failure by writing to Koenigseck on July 11, 1742, a letter expressing his regrets and excusing himself for having supported Bavaria, and for having allowed himself to be carried away by such disastrous counsels. A few months earlier, Maria Theresa had tried in vain to soften the Cardinal, and now her only reply was to publish the letter in the Dutch papers. Louis' minister replied to this insult, by summoning to the assistance of the French in Bohemia the troops under Maillebois, who had been quartered in Westphalia since 1741 ; but the junction was not effected.

Broglie retired into Bavaria, being unable to maintain his positions until winter. Belle-Isle evacuated Prague in the **Prague** night of December 16 with fourteen thousand men, **abandoned.** and retired to Egra, which was half way to Munich ; thence he retreated to Frankfort, and informed Charles VII of Frederick's defection, advising him to make terms with the Queen of Hungary. The retreat of Egra was terrible owing to the rigours of the season. To use an expression of Belle-Isle—" nature was forced " ; the troops began to march " at moonrise " in order to climb mountains where soldiers had never before ventured. An echo of the sufferings endured by the French has come down to us in a funeral oration over one of the too numerous victims. In his *Eloge* of his friend, Paul de Seytres, Vauvenargues says : " Mourn, my hapless country, mourn these sad trophies. You are covering all Germany with your gallant soldiers, and you pride yourself on your glory ! . . . Scarce will a remnant of a once flourishing army see your happy fields again. What perils ! I shudder at them. They are fleeing. Hunger and confusion march on their furtive tracks ; night covers them and death follows silently. You say : Is this the army which spread terror before it ? You see that fortune changes ; it is afraid in its turn ; it hastens its flight through woods and snows. It marches incessantly. Sickness, hunger, and fatigue overwhelm our young soldiers. Poor wretches ! We see them laid in the snow and inhumanly deserted. Fires lit on the ice lighten their last moments. The ground is their terrible bed."

A pitiful consolation was found in comparing their mournful achievements with the Retreat of the Ten Thousand. But what advantage did France gain from this sacrifice of men and money ?

At this disastrous period in the fortunes of French arms, came the death of the man, who, in the weakness of his ninety **Death of** years, had allowed himself to be drawn into these **Cardinal Fleury.** barren struggles. On January 29, 1743, the Cardinal-Minister died in his retreat at Issy. The event had been long expected and desired. "At last!" cried the Marquis d'Argenson. "It is certain that our greatest enemy is dead," said Elizabeth Farnese to Don Philip, and she added: "I pardon him with all my heart for the evil he has done us, and may God give peace to his soul!" Louis XV alone had some words of tenderness for "a good friend" and a "good servant" who was "infinitely attached to him."

The history of these two wars for the Polish and Austrian Successions is enough to enable us to judge him in his capacity as Minister for European affairs. But we must not leave the Cardinal without some account of the internal events in which he was concerned.

Louis XIV and Madame de Maintenon had left unsolved a serious problem which placed the Church of France in conflict with the Papacy, Gallican liberty with Roman supremacy. This was the matter of the Constitution or Bull *Unigenitus*. By this celebrated Bull, Clement XI in 1713 denounced the hundred and one propositions contained in the *Augustinus* of Jansenius, and quoted by Père Quesnel the Oratorian in his *Abrégé de la Morale de l'Évangile*. This religious manual was already twenty years old, and no doubts had been raised about it until the Jesuits, hating the Oratorians, and strong in the support of Madame de Maintenon, awakened the susceptibilities of the Papacy.

The Jansenists.

Cardinal de Noailles, Archbishop of Paris, and seven other prelates refused to submit to the demands of Rome and sent a protest to the Holy See. The Regent at first was not disposed to interfere, but, at the time of the intrigues to which Dubois owed his Cardinalate, he intervened without success in favour of the Vatican. The Lateran Council, held in 1725, did not succeed in restoring peace between the rival parties who met there. On one side were the Jansenists, who comprised ecclesiastics and parliamentarians. These were called "Appelants." On the other side were the Molinists and Jesuits, called "Acceptants." In 1727, Fleury summoned the Provincial Council of Embrun which condemned Père Soanem of the Oratoire, Bishop of Senez; this was the starting-point for a general agitation, which was accentuated by the death of the Deacon Pâris in 1727.

François de Pâris was the brother of a Counsellor of the Grand' Chambre, and possessed an income of about ten thousand **The Deacon** livres. He gave liberal alms and lived a simple **Pâris.** and saintly life. Barbier notes that he " only ate vegetables," " slept without covering," and was " a Jansenist in all respects." He was buried at the cemetery of Saint-Médard in the Faubourg Saint-Marcel. Almost immediately his tomb became the resort of the disciples of Jansenius, and an " astonishing number of people " followed them there. The church was some distance from the centre of Paris, and on the way thither might be seen the carriages of many people of fashion, and even bishops and princes of the blood, such as the Comte de Clermont, brother of Monsieur le Duc. Numbers of sick persons went there ; they lay on the tombstone and had convulsions, and some of them went back cured. But these scenes acquired a bad character ; fraud was introduced ; and the real Jansenists were discredited in consequence. The best known of the appellant bishops, the Cardinal de Noailles, after considerable hesitation finally submitted to the papal bull in 1728 ; but the bishops of Troyes, Auxerre and Montpellier, and the Parlements of Paris and the provinces still held out. Fleury had the cemetery of Saint-Médard closed, but the " convulsionnaires " continued their practices in private.

The Parlements on their side made Jansenism a political weapon with which to encroach on the ecclesiastical power and to rouse an opposition sufficient to threaten the royal power under the pretence of asserting Gallican liberties. In 1731, they condemned certain priests of the diocese of Orléans who wished to compel the faithful to range themselves on the side of the "Acceptants." Fleury exiled a number of the magistrates, and their colleagues replied by refusing to sit, but suddenly the King yielded and allowed the most violent decisions of the Grand' Chambre to go unpunished. Hostilities, however, did not abate ; nor did the struggle terminate until 1756, after many conflicts between the same adversaries.

Fleury died without seeing the end of either the European or the religious and parliamentary troubles. The task he left his pupil was a difficult one. The finances were in a fairly prosperous condition, owing to the proverbial economy of the Cardinal, but it was at the expense of the navy and of commerce, which had been badly neglected since the death of Louis XIV. For personal reasons, which, according to Maurepas, he communicated to the King alone, Fleury did not favour the augmentation of the naval forces. It seems that he was afraid of giving offence to the English, who were now about to enter the lists and to show with complete cynicism how blind had been the confidence of their ally.

Voltaire has left a remarkable portrait of the Cardinal. He shows him as " hating all system, because his intellect was **Voltaire's** happily limited ; understanding nothing of finance, **portrait of** and only demanding of his subordinates the **Fleury.** strictest economy ; incapable of being a clerk in an office, but able to govern the State." Voltaire revenged himself for the disdain Fleury had shown when he recommended *Télémaque* to him, and he never cloaked his words with a subtler irony than this.

PRINCIPAL SOURCES. Vauvenargues, *Eloge de Paul Hippolyte Emmanuel de Seytres, Officier au régiment du Roi* ; Frederick II., *Histoire de mons temps—Politische Correspondenz Friedrich's des Grossen* ; *Correspondence de Louis XV et du Maréchal de Noailles*, 2 vols., 1869. Duc de Broglie : *Frédéric II et Marie-Thérèse*, 2 vols., 1882 ; *Frédéric II. et Louis XV*, 2 vols., 1885 ; *Marie-Thérèse impératrice*, 2 vols., 1888. In addition, the various memoirs mentioned for the preceding chapters, and especially those of Barbier, Argenson, Luynes and Noailles.

THIRD PART
LOUIS XV

CHAPTER X

LOUIS THE WELL-BELOVED
1743–1744

The favourites. Belle-Isle. Marshal de Noailles. His advice
followed. Retreat of the army of Bohemia. Intervention of
George II. Dettingen. Noailles' visit to the Emperor. Louis'
decision. Treaties of Worms and Fountainebleau. Attempted
invasion of England. Declaration of war against George II and
Maria Theresa. Louis' departure for Lille. Visits to the frontier
towns. Sieges of Menin, Ypres and Furnes. Treaty with
Frederick II. The King at Metz. The mysterious coaches.
Madame de Châteauroux made the subject of lampoons. News
from Italy. The King's illness. The Queen and whole Court at
Metz. The ill-omened day of August 24. Frederick in Bohemia.
Louis' entry into Paris. Death of Madame de Châteauroux.

"THE Cardinal is dead! Long live the King!" was the
sentiment of the public, and it was confirmed when
Louis announced his intention not to have a chief
minister but to govern by himself.

Yet the position of the King was no more independent
than before. The sole change was that he became subject now
The King's to a fresh and more dangerous tyranny, the
Favourites. tyranny of his favourites. The fate of France
began to be decided in boudoirs, the centres of intrigue and
ambition. There it was that when ministers and generals
saw their favour rise or fall, and diplomatic questions of the
gravest importance solved, they knew that all depended on the
moods or caprices of a woman. In the intervals of choosing a
precious stone or new toy, when the correct spot had been found
for the patch, when the newborn wrinkle had been hidden with
the assistance of some infallible paste, the favourite had leisure
to give her advice on State affairs. Everything, whether
frivolous or serious, was treated as an amusement at a toilet-

table veiled with lace in the woman's hour of triumph, when madrigals and amber-scented trifles were assured of victory, when a smile was the most potent argument. While a guitar twanged or a parrot screamed, amid the hum of conversation, alliances were broken, colonies lost, all Europe convulsed.

This period, which became acute under Madame de Pompadour, was happily preceded by a bright interval; Louis began his part as King conscientiously, and without any illusion as to the difficulties of his task. He worked and studied, and he wrote letters which were seen by his correspondent alone. It is a pleasure to recall this all too short phase when Frenchmen, delighted at the change, were eager to display the most devoted loyalty in return for the attitude of a king, then, indeed, worthy of his ancestors. The Marquis d'Argenson could ask without any irony : " Are we going to have a king ? "

Louis provided himself with a Mentor. For a while it was feared that it would be Marshal de Belle-Isle, who came to **Eclipse of Belle-Isle.** Court to make a survey, "extremely inconvenienced by his sciatica," and only walking " with the support of two men." The Marshal had carried through part of his programme with success ; the Emperor owed his crown to him, and the Grand Duke of Tuscany had been excluded. Was he responsible for the King of Prussia's treason ? No, but he returned to give a disastrous account of the consequences of his over-ambitious projects, and although his breast was covered with the exalted orders of a Prince of the Empire, the Golden Fleece and the Cordon Bleu, he had temporarily lost his prestige ; he retired of his own accord to his estate of Vernon near Gisors. Couplets followed him in his retreat :

> Belle-Isle fameux empirique,
> Grand novateur en politique,
> Homme de guerre sans pratique,
> Dans ses projects vrai frénétique,
> Chargé de la haine publique,
> Porte à Gisors sa sciatique.*

---

* Belle-Isle, the famous empiric, the great political innovator, the inexperienced warrior, insane in his plans, loaded with the public hatred, carries his sciatica to Gisors.

Marshal de Noailles' time had come and he was chosen. Foreseeing the death of Fleury, Louis wrote to this faithful servant **Marshal de** November 1742 : " The late King, my great-**Noailles.** grandfather, whom I desire to imitate as far as possible, counselled me, on his deathbed, to seek advice in all things and to endeavour to know the best, that I might always follow it. I shall be delighted if you will give me yours. I open your mouth, as the Pope does to the cardinals, and I permit you to say whatever your zeal and attachment to my person and kingdom may prompt." Louis was as good as his word, and received from the Marshal sound advice, founded on the actual policy of Louis XIV, whose confidant Noailles had been. Thus the office of Prime Minister was suppressed. The Marshal wrote to the King : " The rule of having neither favourite nor Prime Minister, which your Majesty will read in the directions of your august great-grandfather, was formed, as I have had the honour of learning from the late King himself, as the result of his long experience and great skill, of his profound studies of former governments, and in particular of the ministry of Cardinal Mazarin." In this long memorandum Noailles recalled the examples of Henri III, who was ruled by his favourites to the great detriment of the State, of Henri IV, who would never have other counsellors than his own head and arms, of Louis XIII, whose minority had been so stormy and his reign so troubled. But although the Marshal had not, like Fleury, the title of Prime Minister, he had all the prerogatives.

The pupil seemed to follow his precepts with docility, and the public rejoiced at the change. Barbier said of Louis : " He is accessible, he speaks at Versailles, he administers justice and works with considerable knowledge of his subject. This does not astonish me, for I have long understood that he was intelligent. . . . What does astonish me, so that it almost seems uncanny, is that Cardinal de Fleury should have had such an ascendency over a king more than thirty years old, as to prevent him from displaying all his talents and to dominate him in everything."

The first question which arose was the plight of the French army of Bohemia. The cause of the phantom Emperor,

Charles VII, was lost. It had cost France sufficiently dear, and it had been defended with chivalrous unselfishness. It **Bohemia** would become necessary to send reinforcements **evacuated.** to this exhausted army which, in a year's time, without serious battles, had lost sixty thousand men, mostly from disease or hardships. It was decided to evacuate. Marshal de Broglie tried to bring his troops back from the Bavarian frontiers in time to join the army of the Rhine, the movements of which were directed from France by Marshal de Noailles. But the junction was not effected.

The struggle was concentrated in the Rhenish and Flemish provinces, where Noailles, at the head of forty thousand men was **Battle of** prepared to meet the so-called "Pragmatic" **Dettingen.** army of George II, who purposed to aid Maria Theresa and was assembling his troops in the Electorate of Hanover. This was in the spring of 1743. The battle took place on June 27 at Dettingen, a village of Lower Franconia, while Broglie was still at Donauwerth on the confines of Würtemberg. The French lost the day, though Noailles attained his object of preventing the English from entering Bavaria. The battle was lost through the fault, not of the Marshal but of his nephew the Duc de Gramont. The latter, instead of waiting for the attack, foolishly charged the enemy with his French guards, and thus upset all Noailles' plan of defence, and rendered the artillery unable to fire for fear of shooting Frenchmen. The soldiers in their flight crossed the river by swimming, and long retained the sobriquet of "Ducks of the Main." In the general encounter the English King was almost made a prisoner. Since the morning he had been riding at the head of his troops armed with an enormous pistol and a sword of prodigious length, which he drew from time to time saying : "On at the King of France ! he is my enemy ; you shall see how I will fight him." While he was uttering these vaunts, his horse shied at the cannonade and threw him; he found himself surrounded by French horsemen who would have carried him off had not help arrived just in time. This incident was maliciously revealed by the King of Prussia, who took a wicked pleasure in making his uncle ridiculous.

It must be admitted that the English army, and especially the infantry, were capable of resisting " like a wall of brass "— to quote Noailles. George dined on the battlefield, but he retired immediately afterwards, even leaving behind the wounded, whom Lord Stair commended to the generosity of Marshal de Noailles. "The two generals," Voltaire records, "wrote letters which allow us to see how far politeness and humanity can be carried amid the horrors of war." The losses had been equal; more than two thousand men were killed or wounded on either side. The result of the day of Dettingen was absolutely negative. Lord Stair asserts that the French committed one great fault and the English two : "Yours," he said, " was in your not knowing how to wait ; our two were, first, that we put ourselves in obvious danger of being destroyed, and then, that we were not able to profit by our victory."

In short, as Pitt remarked, it was less a victory than a " fortunate escape."

A few days later Noailles, in a spirit of courtesy and kindness, went to meet Charles VII, who had left Augsburg and taken **Noailles visits** refuge at Frankfort. He knew how precarious **the Emperor.** was the situation of the errant Emperor. He made him a generous allowance of forty thousand crowns, that being the most that France could do at this unfortunate time. Charles obtained a suspension of hostilities, promising Austria the absolute neutrality of the Imperial troops. This was the signal for the French armies to quit Germany. They were only auxiliaries, and as their ally disarmed, they retired.

The blow was painful to the prince : " I am fully sensible," he wrote to Noailles, " that the King is touched by the situation I am in. My reply must be akin to that the Duchesse who was loved and esteemed by Louis XIV (Marie de Mancini) made to that Monarch when she found herself deserted : ' You are the King ; you love me, and I have to go.' I in my turn will say : ' You are the King, you are touched by my fate, you are the most powerful king among my allies, and you desert me and I lose by your desertion all that I can lose. . . . My situation is the most terrible ever known in history.' "

Louis replied in person and excused himself to the best of his ability. He expressed " the deepest grief " at the thought of the Emperor's " consenting to an agreement with the Viennese Court," but he promised never to desert him in so sad an extremity, to assist him with fresh subsidies, and to continue the war until his Imperial Majesty was " re-established in full possession of his States." The King was really sincere. He used the same language to Noailles, though he added : " It is perfectly true to say that we are no longer at war, since the Emperor has declared his neutrality, and we only went to war because of him. However, we are at war. I can hardly believe that such a thing has happened, or could ever happen ; but we are in a century of extraordinary things."

At this time Louis resolved to show himself to his army, and he received the praises he merited from his immediate **Treaty of** circle. They were pleased to see in him the **Worms.** blood of Louis XIV and Henri IV. Under cover of an armistice the Chancelleries were now very active. The Treaty of Worms, on September 23, 1743, brightened the prospects of the Austro-English Coalition. Charles Emmanuel joined George II and Maria Theresa. He deceived the French, who, up to the last moment, had hoped to see the King of Sardinia united with them ; but they forgot that that prince was guided by the Italian proverb, and that he always wished " to have his foot shod with two slippers at once." The Spanish troops in Italy, supported by some French detachments, were thus compelled to fight not only the Austrians but the Sardinians, and to dispute with them the territories belonging to the Queen of Hungary, the coveted Milanese province among them.

Louis replied with the secret treaty of Fontainebleau on October 25. This treaty between France and Spain guaranteed **Treaty of** Naples to Don Carlos, Lombardy to Don Philip, **Fontainebleau.** Bavaria to the Emperor, and further indemnities. As Argenson says " we engaged ourselves to make the greatest and the most impossible conquests in Italy." Philip and Elizabeth profited by Louis' favourable disposition ; to please them he was to be engaged in two different quarters, to declare war on George II and Maria Theresa, and even to expose his own person. These grandiose schemes were complicated by a conspiracy.

England was always threatened by the possibility of a Stuart restoration. Among those who favoured the re-establish-

134

ment of the Catholic line on the throne of William of Normandy, the French were at this time in the front rank. The *entente cordiale* was merely an historic memory. Charles Edward, eldest son of the Pretender, lived with his father at Rome, but he hoped to distinguish himself by a great deed : "My head must fall," said he, "or be crowned." He succeeded in evading the vigilance of the spies in the pay of Austria, who watched his least movements. He reached Livorno in disguise and landed at the port of Antibes. He offered Louis' ministers to **Invasion of** attempt a diversion in England against the **England** House of Hanover, which was then fully occupied **planned.** with continental affairs. But the attempt failed, though a plan was drawn up, and Maurice de Saxe was deputed to command in England in the name of James III, should occasion arise. At the beginning of 1744 the Comte de Saxe went to Dunkirk to superintend the preparations for the expedition. On his return to Versailles he was greeted with his nomination as Marshal of France, a distinction afterwards most brilliantly justified at Fontenoy.

Meanwhile, after the battle of Toulon in February 1744, in which the English Captain Mathews was driven off the French coasts by the combined fleets of France and Spain, war was declared with Great Britain on March 15. The nominal object was to stop the "piracy" and pillage which continued to be committed in defiance of international law and the most solemn treaties.

A similar message was sent to the Queen of Hungary on April 26, when the Austrians tried to enter Alsace and preceded their attempt "*by declarations as bold as they were indecent.*" Menzel, the daring chief of this army, insolently pledged himself to reconquer Alsace and give Lorraine back to its former masters. The King resolved to attack the Dutch possessions of Maria Theresa, and proceeded to do so in spite of the protests of Holland.

Thus, in the spring of 1744, there was a considerable display of arms. The Prince de Conti went to the aid of Don Philip, **Louis sets out** crossed the Var, and performed great feats on the **for Lille.** other side of the Alps. Louis XV set out for Lille. Altogether four French armies were in action. Besides the army of Italy commanded by the Prince de Conti, there was the defensive army in Alsace under the command of old Marshal de Coigny, and the Royal Army, which was divided into two distinct portions, one of which was preparing to enter Flanders with Louis, while the other, as a reserve under Maurice de Saxe, was on its way to protect French territory on the left bank of the Rhine.

The nation watched these movements with pride. Not a single complaint was made when heavy taxes were raised to meet the expenses of this war, in which three hundred thousand men were engaged. The Court would have liked to form an escort for the young monarch in accordance with the tradition of Louis XIV. By the Court we mean the Queen, the Dauphin, and above all the favourite of the day, Madame de la Tournelle, who was now at her zenith and had lately been created Duchesse de Châteauroux (October 28, 1843); she received the actual possession of that Duchy and all the prerogatives and revenues attached thereto, amounting to eighty-five thousand livres per annum.

The Queen attempted to get leave to go, though it caused her no little embarrassment. The Duc de Luynes says as much, and shows us the stage at which the relations between the King and Queen had arrived at this time. Not daring to speak, the Queen wrote a letter. As the King was at Choisy and she feared that a letter from her might seem strange, she awaited his return and herself handed it to him as she left the *petit lever*. The duke adds, "I have not seen the letter, but I have heard it said that she offered to follow him to the frontier, in any manner he pleased, and that she did not ask for a reply. Probably this last suggestion will be all that will be accorded her." However, the King did reply by a refusal on the grounds of the expense of her journey.

The Dauphin, who was close on fifteen, said : "You must not be annoyed, mother, that I am so sorry to stay behind with you. I cannot understand why the King has left me. The young de Montauban, who is small and weak, has gone, and I, who am tall and strong, might well have gone too."

When the Dauphin pleaded for his first experience of war the King made the proper reply : "I honour your desire, but your person is too valuable to the State until the succession to the Crown is assured by your marriage."

The Duchesse de Châteauroux applied to Marshal de Noailles. He also made the expense a pretext to bar the way.

Thus Louis left, without the Court, with a certain amount of secrecy, during the night of May 4, 1744, after a banquet at which a large number of people were present. He did not bid farewell either to the Queen or to his daughters, but he wrote to them. He told his daughters that he feared a mutual emotion. The Dauphin alone had an interview with his father, who spoke to him " in the presence of Monsieur de Châtillon [his tutor] with considerable affection."

In company with Noailles, the King visited the fortresses of Condé, Valenciennes, Maubeuge, and Douai, giving commands **Louis XV** and holding reviews. He was very popular : **at the** " he speaks kindly, and in a way to turn all men's **frontier towns.** heads in his favour." He was cheered everywhere and greeted with cries of, " Vive le Roi ! We have a King at last ! " Besenval says : " he attracted the gaze of all ; his face so fair and noble, his eyes so proud and yet so mild—all these natural advantages, whatever the impression they created at Versailles, were further heightened by the occasion." At Lille, especially, the reception organized by Maurice de Saxe was extraordinarily enthusiastic. On May 17 the army advanced on the Lys near Menin. The King joined it on the 23rd ; he reconnoitred the place " within pistol shot," and himself indicated the principal points of attack. He supervised the investment, and the town capitulated on June 4 after seven days in the trenches. This first conquest was followed by the capture of Ypres on June 24, and of Furnes on July 11, for which the Comte de Clermont was responsible.

A former ally was greatly interested in this victorious march, and decided to offer his support to Louis. This was the King of Prussia, yielding to necessity and self-interest. The moment was well chosen for an intervention on his part. He wished to profit by the presence of the Austrian troops on the Rhine and in Italy to attack Maria Theresa from the side of Bohemia. The negotiations lasted several months, and out of the mass of correspondence which passed it may be interesting to quote a letter written by Frederick to Madame de Châteauroux, which clearly indicates the influence of the new duchess, and the part she played in the most delicate matters. " I am flattered, Madame," wrote the King of Prussia, " that it is partly to you that I am indebted for the favourable disposition in which I find the King of France, and his willingness to form the lasting bonds of an eternal alliance between us. The esteem in which I have always held you is now mingled with a sense of indebtedness. It is unfortunate that Prussia is compelled to ignore the obligations she is under to you. However, the sentiment will remain deeply engraved on my heart, as I would have you believe ; ever your affectionate friend, Frederick."

Although matters were far advanced there was still some delay. It was only when he saw the martial attitude of Louis **Treaty with** that Frederick finally decided to instruct his **Frederick** plenipotentiary, Rottenburg, to sign a treaty in **the Great.** Paris on June 5. Without having the least suspicion of what was happening, Prince Charles of Lorraine crossed the Rhine. He was driven back by Coigny, but he returned in force, and threw his troops upon Alsace. France was invaded. Thereupon Louis left Maurice de Saxe to continue a defensive campaign in Flanders, and advanced to Metz with twenty-six battalions and thirty squadrons, commanded by Marshal de Noailles. The King intended to be in the front rank in the defence of his kingdom.

Following the King, though a day behind him on the march, were seen coaches of a very unmilitary appearance. They **The King at** contained the Duchesse de Châteauroux and her **Metz.** sister, Madame de Lauraguais. These ladies were dull at Plaisance on an estate of Pâris-Duverney and they made every effort to obtain permission to follow the operations. The Princesse de Conti, mother of the general who was acquitting himself so well in Italy, was able by skilful intrigues to satisfy the favourite. The Duchesse de Chartres, the Princesse de Conti's daughter, who had but lately married, wished to go and join her husband, since he was reported to have had a fall from his horse and to be slightly injured " because of his weight." The two princesses left with the King's consent. "Such," says Barbier, "was the beginning of the ' Court of women

138

with the army.' " Presently others arrived at Lille—Mesdames de Châteauroux and de Lauraguais, the Dowager Comtesse d'Egmont, Mesdames de Roure and de Bellefond and the Duchess of Modena, who was then in France owing to the invasion of her own states. One after another these ladies were obliged to ask the Queen's permission to leave Versailles, as etiquette demanded. Marie was patient at first, but when the Duchess of Modena presented herself, the Queen momentarily lost patience, and said with some asperity : " She may make her stupid journey if she likes ; it does not matter to me."

The favourite had gained her point. But she had to pay dearly for this " stupid journey," and the pleasure of playing **The favourite** the part of *vivandière*. The disapproval was **with the Army.** universal. Songs were written giving voice to the most violent sarcasm at her expense, and during the progress of herself and her sister, nothing but hoots and jeers were heard. However, the favourite soared far above terrestrial incidents and after the capture of Ypres she proudly wrote to her uncle, the Duc de Richelieu : " Assuredly, dear uncle, we have agreeable news, which gives me the keenest pleasure. I am overwhelmed with joy. Ypres captured in nine days ! Can you not see that nothing could be more glorious or flattering to myself, and that his great-grandfather in all his greatness, never did as much ? But subsequent events must be kept at the same pitch ; they must always maintain this appearance. We must hope ; and I flatter myself that it will be so, for you know that it is my nature to see everything in a rosy light, and that I believe my star, which I value (for it is not a bad one), influences everything." She posed as a martial Egeria with some dignity, it must be admitted. But the star of which she was so proud was soon to lose its lustre.

So Louis was at Metz preparing for great deeds and abandoning easy conquests. We come now to August 4, 1744. On the preceding day Schmettau, the envoy of Frederick II, had come, bearing the congratulations of his master who admired, possibly with sincerity, the haste with which Louis flew to the succour of his people. On the 7th a magnificent supper was given in honour of the Prussian officer, during which there were premature celebrations of the exploits which were to end the conflict in

Alsace and Bohemia. The excitement was the stronger since the dispatches from Italy announced a fresh victory, the capture of Castel Delphino by the Bailli de Givry.

On August 8 the King woke up with a fever, owing to the fatigue of the journey, the excessive heat, or the too generous **The King's** libations of the night before. The malady grew **illness.** worse and on the 11th he was given up for lost. At his bedside were the Duchesses de Châteauroux and de Lauraguais, who took it upon themselves to impose silence on every one, and jealously guarded the entrance to the royal chamber. However, they had to admit the Princes of the Blood —the Duc de Chartres and the Comte de Clermont—and dignitaries like the Duc de Bouillon, the Grand Chamberlain, and the Bishop of Soissons, the King's chaplain. The King himself understood the gravity of his condition, and Madame de Châteauroux was compelled to leave him. He made his confession to Père Pérusseau, and when it became a question of administering the last sacrament, Fitz-James, the Bishop of Soissons, insisted on the immediate departure of the favourite. Louis did not hesitate, but ordered the duchess to leave Metz. The rite of extreme unction was administered by the Grand Almoner in the presence of the Princes of the Blood and the great officers with extraordinary pomp. Fitz-James made himself the spokesman of the dying king, and declared that he asked pardon from all for the bad example he had given.

The road from Versailles to Metz was furrowed by the coaches that bore Marie Leszczynska, the Dauphin, and Mesdames. **The Queen and** At Saint-Menehould the *cortège* met the carriages **Court at Metz.** of Madame de Châteauroux travelling in the opposite direction, pursued by the invectives of the populace.

The Queen went to the King's bedside and was alone with him. He embraced her, saying : " I have caused you much sorrow which you do not deserve ; I beg you to forgive me for it."

" Do you not know, Monsieur," she replied, " that you never need pardon from me ? God alone has been offended. Concern yourself with God alone, I beseech you." The Queen burst into tears, but she wrote to Madame de Maurepas that she was " the happiest of mortals." The King was better, and everything was to be hoped from so fervent a conversion.

The fears which threw all France into consternation were

changed into joy as soon as it was known that Louis was out of danger, that he had repented, and was prepared to make amends. The people of Paris embraced the horse of the messenger who published the news of his convalescence. A poetaster named Vadé was able to say with truth : " he is Louis the Well-Beloved," an expression which echoed the sentiments of the nation. The enthusiasm was such that the King exclaimed : " What have I done to make them love me so much ? "

For all too short a time he was a king after the heart of his devout Christian subjects. The people rejoiced to see that Louis merited their affection, and they trusted him and were ready to follow him in his new path.

He began to talk of rejoining his troops. Meanwhile, according to Voltaire, he sent to remind Noailles that when Louis XIII was being carried to the tomb, the Prince of Condé was winning the battle of Rocroi. Unfortunately the Marshal had nothing of the great captain about him. Too much was expected of this timid time-server ; he could do nothing except when he had a pen in his hand.

Noailles was in Alsace in pursuit of Charles of Lorraine, who had received orders to retire and come to the support of Bohemia against the King of Prussia. The prince abandoned his positions, Saverne and Haguenau, taking care not to risk a battle and so diminish his army. It was most important to prevent him from crossing the Rhine. But owing to the slackness of the pursuit he succeeded in effecting his object ; he burnt the bridges behind him to obstruct his enemies, though they made no attempt to strike at him. Public opinion about the Marshal was unequivocal. It was rumoured that he had a wholesome fear of cannon balls, that he had given as many as thirty-five different orders in a day, that he never knew what course to take. One night a wooden sword was fastened to the door of his house in Paris, where insulting songs were current about him :

> Amis, débaptisons Noailles :
> Tout autre nom mieux lui convient.
> Comment, le sien rime à batailles !
> Eh ! morbleu ! c'est rimer trop bien ! *

---

* Friends, let us rechristen Noailles, any other name would better suit him. Why his name rhymes with *batailles!* Eh ! morbleu ! The rhyme is too good.

He returned to Metz to find a cold reception. His influence was at an end. Louis no longer asked him for his advice, and for the future used him only in purely ornamental services. He sent him, for instance, to Spain in the following year as ambassador extraordinary to Philip. Close relations ceased between the King and his Nestor.

At this time—on August 23—Frederick invaded Bohemia with eighty thousand men, and there he heard what had been **Frederick** done. He wrote Louis a letter in which his **invades** ill-humour was apparent, and he said quite **Bohemia.** plainly to Schmettau : " I do not know what to think of Marshal de Noailles' behaviour (he had almost accused him of treason). . . . I desire you to make strong complaints to the King of France."

He would have had the French troops join him in Bohemia. But only half measures were adopted. The Comte de Clermont, with a small detachment, endeavoured to join Charles VII's army for an advance into Germany. He took Constance in September and Munich in the following month. The main body of the French forces was directed to the further side of the Rhine, above Strasburg; thence they invaded the nearest territories of Austria and besieged Freiburg, the capital of Breisgau. The King was still weak and convalescent, but he arrived at the town, and it was captured in his presence on November 8. Frederick had taken Prague on September 15, but had been driven out again two months later by Charles of Lorraine. Then came winter to suspend operations.

Louis returned to Paris on November 13. In spite of a cold and rainy evening and of a wind which was strong enough **Louis' entry** to extinguish the illuminations, a large crowd **into Paris.** assembled to greet him. The enthusiasm was enhanced when they saw how thin he was and how much he had changed. Frederick, and with him all France, was anxious to know whether the convert of Metz would keep the promises he had made so solemnly, and whether he would continue faithful to the Queen. France feared and hoped, but Frederick prayed that the favourite would regain her influence and be useful to him. Hitherto, Louis had listened to the Duchesse de Châteauroux alone, and the King of Prussia relied on her to make his ally act, to urge him to strong measures, and in particular to persuade him to appoint a minister of foreign affairs, who would be ready to accept advice in furtherance of Prussian policy. This post had been vacant since the dismissal of Amelot, Chauvelin's successor, on March 27, 1744. Two important events took place at this time—the disgrace of the Dauphin's tutor, the Duc de Châtillon, who had openly expressed his approval of the dismissal of the favourite and had delivered a moral lecture thereon for the edification of his pupil ; and the disgrace of Monsieur de Balleroy, private secretary of the Duc de Chartres, and related to the family of Fitz-James. His fault was that he belonged to the religious party. These two had been singled out because the striker had not dared to aim higher. During the five days fête in Paris the prevailing topics of conversation were Madame de Châteauroux and her victims, and her probable reinstatement. But, as Barbier says, no one dared speak openly.

As soon as the King returned to Versailles these rumours were confirmed. It was reported that Madame de Châteauroux had been received privately by Louis, and that she had reason to be contented with the results of the interview. Everything was to be forgotten, the insults of Metz were retracted and the forfeited rank of lady-in-waiting was restored to her. Paris was stupefied, and public opinion was voiced by the women of the Halles when they cried : " As he has taken back his favourite we shall no longer say a *Pater* for him."

Two days after her visit to the King the duchess in her turn caught a fever and was almost immediately in a critical condition. During the fortnight that her illness lasted **Death of** the public followed its progress and phases with **Madame de** more curiosity than emotion, without attempting **Châteauroux.** to disguise the fact that they considered that this mysterious illness was opportune. In the Rue du Bac where the Duchess was staying with Madame de Lauraguais there was a constant stream of messengers from the King, the Queen, and the Court, inquiring for her. The dying favourite made her confession to the Jesuit Père Segaud and received the last sacraments. She died on December 8.

She was buried three days later, at seven o'clock in the

morning, in the chapel of Saint Michel in Saint-Sulpice. A time when the streets would be little frequented was purposely selected for fear of popular demonstrations like those that had occurred at the funeral of Madame de Vintimille.

The King's grief was very great, and the people had to restrain their joy for fear of injuring his health. But, in the peace which preceded new campaigns, preparations were made for the marriage of the Dauphin to the daughter of Philip V, and these occupied every one's attention. During the fêtes which celebrated this event Louis forgot his grief, as at Christmas he forgot his contrition of August ; he did not approach the Holy Table, as was the custom of the Court.

CHAPTER XI

" AS STUPID AS THE PEACE "
1745–1749 ·

The marriage of the Dauphin. Madame Lenormand d'Etiolles at
the masked ball at Versailles. Madame de Pompadour's *rôle*.
Death of the Emperor. The Marquis d'Argenson, Minister
for Foreign Affairs. The defection of the Elector of Bavaria.
The Battle of Fontenoy. Louis' advice to his son. A letter
from Voltaire to Argenson. New victories. Military events in
Italy (1745–1746). Conditions of peace. Louis XV and Maria
Theresa duped. Discontent of the people. The announcement
of the peace.

IN 1745 the Dauphin was slender and graceful, as he is
represented in the pastel by La Tour in the Louvre. He
was like his mother, and the good Queen's subtle and
resigned smile was to be seen again on the face of this boy
Marriage of of sixteen. The Dauphine, the Infanta Maria-
the Dauphin. Teresa-Raphaëlla was four years older than her
husband. She was ugly, red-haired, and austere, but she
inspired the Dauphin with a deep love. The Dauphin was
married for reasons of State to assure the succession, and for
family reasons to cement the reconciliation of the two crowns.
At the same time he was made happy, a rare event in diplomatic marriages. His happiness only lasted two years, for
Maria-Teresa-Raphaëlla died in July 1764, after giving birth
to a daughter who died in infancy.

The marriage celebrations at Versailles and Paris were
magnificent ; memoir-writers and draughtsmen have preserved
them for us, and help us to picture the rejoicings of the time.
There is an engraving by Cochin of the masked ball given at
Versailles on February 25, 1745, at which Louis noticed for the
first time Antoinette Poisson, an elegant, graceful, and very
pretty young lady of the Court, who had already appeared

frequently at the royal hunts, in the forest of Sénart. She was the wife of Lenormant d'Etiolles, nephew of Tournehem, the Director of Public Works. She became by the King's favour Marquise de Pompadour and even a duchess. She was then radiant in all the charm of her twenty-four years. Madame de Châteauroux was already forgotten by Louis, and the little *bourgeoise* was about to enter upon twenty years of absolute power.

Madame Lenormant d'Etiolles.

Madame de Pompadour appears to posterity surrounded by the writers and artists whom she patronized with so gracious an appreciation. She had the head and the heart of a true patriot, and yet history is obliged to admit that the influence she exercised for a quarter of a century over political matters was harmful. On the surface her reign was nothing but laughter and pleasure ; the atmosphere in which she lived seemed to be tinted with rose and blue ; we see her through the pictures of Boucher with which she loved to surround herself. Around the Marquise were to be heard the murmur of light conversation and the applause which hailed her as a sovereign when she trilled ariettas from an opera in the theatre of the " Petits Appartements," a worthy pupil of Jélyotte ; the air was filled with madrigals. Such are the futilities we connect with the Pompadour.

But this fairy Eldorado vanished before the eyes of those who understood, and the hour of disaster was at hand. There was no one capable of steering the tempest-tossed vessel to anchor-age—least of all Louis. No statesman, not even Choiseul, was strong or disinterested enough to dethrone the favourite and to give a lesson to this King, so eager to avoid the responsibilities of his throne.

However, before the final reckoning, there was one more bright incident to record in the annals of the eighteenth century. On May 11, 1745, the gallant descendants of the heroes of ancient France were gathered round the King and his son. All the chivalry of the French nobles was concentrated at Fontenoy, and if Louis earned a halo by his presence at this triumph of French arms, what should be the crown of the real victors ?

Some months previously it was almost decided to make peace. Important tidings received in their winter quarters took the belligerents by surprise. On January 20 the phantom Emperor, Charles VII, died of aggravated gout, leaving a son who was too **Death of the Emperor Charles VII.** young to undertake the government of the Electorate of Bavaria and still less able to claim the Imperial throne. The real cause of the war thus disappeared ; it was left to the Chancelleries to decide what should be done.

The new Minister for Foreign Affairs, the Marquis d'Argenson, found at the outset that his task was difficult. He was of a speculative turn of mind, and had long interested himself in international politics in the seclusion of his retreat. He thought himself ready for action. But he had little knowledge of men. He was an intimate friend of Voltaire and trusting in him, he believed in the good faith of Frederick. He had not sufficient foresight to arrange a peace with Maria Theresa at the price of consenting to the election of Francis, Grand Duke of Tuscany, to the Imperial crown ; nor had he the courage to secure a concentration of forces in the heart of Germany, and so bar the way to Austria and annihilate her claims. His policy was one of uncertainty and hesitation. Two years were wasted in attaining a result which might have been realized in 1745.

The King of Prussia might have assisted with his advice, but he was scheming. Appearing all along to consult France, **Defection of the Elector of Bavaria.** he made overtures for an alliance with England and Holland, and while he was engaged in these futile attempts an event occurred which ended the uncertainty of the French minister. The young Elector of Bavaria yielded, placing himself at the discretion of Austria, and acknowledging her supremacy over all Southern Germany. He subscribed to an ultimatum dictated by Maria Theresa and retained his Electorate by submitting to the following terms : renunciation of the Empire and of the slightest claim to any part of the Austrian succession ; complete adhesion to the Pragmatic Sanction ; promise of the electoral vote of Bavaria in favour of the Grand Duke, and immediate rupture of all alliances with Louis and Frederick. These terms were embodied in the Treaty of Füssen on April 22.

At this juncture when Frederick asked for French support

he received very little encouragement. The French and Prussians were allies in name only ; they acted separately and each defended their own interests without any concerted plan. Louis resolved to resume the Flanders campaign and to follow up the conquests of 1744. All preparations had been made during the winter by Marshal Saxe, and when the King and the Dauphin arrived at headquarters on May 8, Maurice had invested Tournai and was prepared to try conclusions with the enemy composed of English, Dutch, Hanoverians and Austrians to the number of sixty-five thousand, under the command of the young Duke of Cumberland, the second son of George II.

The engagement took place to the south-west of Tournai in the direction of Antoing, near the village of Fontenoy. A Battle of memorable day it was, and marked by many Fontenoy. deeds of valour showing the spirit of both armies. Some weeks before Fontenoy it was feared that Maurice de Saxe would be unable to accompany the army, for he was suffering from dropsy. Voltaire meeting him in one of the galleries at Versailles asked him if he would not endanger his life if he went with the army. Maurice answered indifferently : " It is not a question of living but of setting out." He was tapped for his complaint, and then directed and won the battle from a wicker carriage which drew groans from him at every jolt. The English were full of confidence and saw themselves already in Paris. Cumberland had declared : " I will get there or I will eat my boots." " Here is an Englishman who is a bit of a Gascon," remarked Maurice, " but if he likes to eat his boots we will make it our business to prepare them for him."

The English officers were equally sure. At the first en- counter with the French, they greeted them as they would have greeted acquaintances on a public promenade. Then there was a halt, while Lord Charles Hay, Captain of the Guards, came forward to say to the Comte d'Auteroche, Lieutenant of the Grenadiers : "Monsieur, let your men fire."

" No, Monsieur, this honour shall be yours ! "

There is another version of this dialogue, which has been popularly accepted, in which Auteroche is supposed to have said :

148

" Messieurs the English, fire first ! " Be that as it may, it is probable that under the veil of courtesy the French were obeying Maurice's orders. His tactics were not to make too much use of his muskets. He held that " troops should never be in a hurry to fire first, as if they fire in the presence of an enemy who reserves his reply, they are bound to be defeated." The English fought valiantly. Their impenetrable column of infantry made success doubtful for several hours. For a moment every one thought of Dettingen, but the last charge was terrible, and the " French vivacity " was irresistible. The Dauphin " with a natural impulse took his sword in hand with perfect grace," wishing to join the charge, and was only restrained with difficulty. The young Duke de Gramont, who had been responsible for the defeat of Dettingen, died at Fontenoy. A bullet struck his horse :

" Take care, sir, your horse is killed," some one cried to him.

" And so am I, sir," he answered.

His thigh was shattered and he died an hour later.

The slaughter was terrible. At the end of the day Louis left the hill of Notre-Dame-aux-Bois with his son, and passed before his victorious regiments who greeted him with wild cheers, and threw themselves on the ground to kiss his feet. Then he pointed to the heaps of corpses and said : " See, my son, what a victory costs. Learn to be chary of the blood of your subjects." Developing the King's idea the Marquis d'Argenson wrote to Voltaire : " Triumph is the most beautiful thing in the world : cheers for the King, hats in air and on bayonet ends, the master complimenting his warriors, joy, glory, affection ; but the groundwork all this is human blood, and shreds of human flesh. . . ."

" I think that this check will take down the English pride a little," wrote Maurice de Saxe. " The action lasted for nine hours, and although I am dying I stood the fatigue as well as if I were in full health. The King and his only son insisted on being present on the other side of the river, and practically without means of retreat. . . . I cannot say enough of the King's firmness of mind and calmness. He did not disturb our operations by giving orders counter to mine, which is often to be feared when a monarch is present with his Court, and cannot see things as they are."

Some amends were due from Voltaire to make the people forget his untimely affection for the King of Prussia. He **Voltaire's Letter to Argenson.** made them, not in his poem *Fontenoy*, which is lacking in spontaneity, but in the following short note addressed to his friend, Argenson : " What a splendid occupation for a historian ! " (He had just been made Royal Historian.) " The kings of France have not performed so glorious a deed for three hundred years. I am wild with joy. *Bon soir, Monseigneur.*"

A generous impulse of the Marquis d'Argenson made him wish to follow up this glorious battle with proposals of peace. He ordered the Abbé de La Ville, the plenipotentiary at The Hague, to make overtures to the States-General of Holland. " On the occasion of so complete a victory," he said, " when the Netherlands lie unprotected and our victory is practically assured, an offer of peace made in all sincerity would be the act of a hero and a statesman." He spoke in Louis' name.

But it was not to be, and peace had to be sought sword in hand. Frederick, to quote his own expression, met the bill which Louis had drawn on him at Fontenoy by his victories of Friedberg in Silesia and Kesseldorf in Saxony. He then signed with Austria, on December 25, 1745, the Treaty of Dresden, by which his rights in Silesia and the province of Glatz were acknowledged. In Italy the Infante Don Philip won the battle of Bassignano, but lost that of Placentia. On the death of Philip V, in July 1746, his successor, Ferdinand VI, terminated the active intervention of the Spanish troops and kept them on the defensive.

France was thus left to fight alone—in Flanders against the allies defeated at Fontenoy, in Italy and the South of France **New Victories.** against the Austrians, who were now free from the pressure of the Prussians. She bravely stood her ground. Raucoux, in 1746, and Lawfeld, in 1747, were brilliant sequels of Fontenoy ; once again the ability of Maurice de Saxe was manifested. Mention may be made also of the capture of Berg-op-Zoom by Löwendal, and the siege of

Maestricht. Flanders became French once more and Holland had to witness the invasion of her territories.

In Provence, Maillebois, with the assistance of Chevert, repulsed the Austrians and Sardinians who had occupied Cannes and Antibes, and were preparing, with the encouragement of the English, to besiege Toulon. In consequence of these achievements the Republic of Genoa revolted, and succeeded in throwing off the foreign yoke. Its success was due to the Duc de Boufflers and the Duc de Richelieu, and to Belle-Isle's unsuccessful diversion at Col d'Assietta which induced the King of Sardinia to withdraw all his troops from the coast.

After this the preliminaries of peace were mooted at Breda, **Peace of Aix-la-Chapelle.** and a treaty was drafted which was signed subsequently at Aix-la-Chapelle on October 30, 1748.

What had France gained? She had heroically defended the Emperor, but on the death of Charles VII she had lost interest in the Imperial election, and as a result the crown went to Francis of Lorraine, husband of Maria Theresa, and the aspirations of France's enemy were assured. Frederick at least acquired Silesia. But Louis kept none of his conquests in Flanders, because, as he said, he wished to " act like a king and not like a tradesman." He was content that the Duchies of Parma, Placentia, and Guastalla should go to his eldest daughter's husband, the Infante Don Philip, who had become the pretext for the war after the death of Charles VII. In America France recovered Louisburg and Cape Breton—a meagre return for her expenditure of lives and money.

The King of Sardinia, like Frederick, gained territory. The Republic of Genoa won its independence. The Duke of Modena, the Regent's son-in-law, recovered his duchy, which he had lost in supporting France.

In spite of her defeats, the real triumph was with England. From the commercial point of view, which with her was the most important, she obtained the right of importing negroes (*Asiento*) and of trading with the Spanish colonies for four years. Politically, she obtained a renewal of the stipulation made at Utrecht for the demolition of the fortifications of Dunkirk, and secured the banishment of the Stuarts from France.

Charles Edward, called also the Chevalier de St. Georges,

who had been under French protection, and was the nation's guest in Paris, was arrested at the Opera, conducted to **Charles Edward** Vincennes, and thence over the frontier. This **banished** outrage aroused severe comments ; the King did **from France.** not escape satires and libels, and he was told :

" He is a king in chains. What are you on the throne ? "

Maria Theresa also was deceived. Intelligent observers saw in the Treaty of Aix-la-Chapelle a Protestant victory over the two most ancient Catholic monarchies in Europe. After this appeared the first signs of a *rapprochement* between Hapsburg and Bourbon, and of that reversal of alliances which has been so warmly defended by many modern historians.

The people were greatly discontented with the results of the war, although on the cessation of hostilities the burden of **Popular** the taxes was lightened. The women of the **Discontent.** Halles expressed the general feeling when they abused one another for being " as stupid as the Peace "—which passed into a catch-phrase. Their ignorance of the undercurrents of diplomacy excused their downright judgment, and in truth the popular conception was not far wrong. The treatment of the Stuart Pretender displeased the people and drove them to express their resentment.

They also wanted to know why all the towns of Flanders, in which the *fleurs-de-lis* had waved, had been taken for nothing. Again, it was suggested that the King of France's eldest daughter deserved more than three insignificant Italian duchies ; it had been hoped that she would become a queen and wear a real crown.

Peace, none the less, was proclaimed on February 12, 1749, with all the customary pomp.

A procession was formed numbering more than eight hundred people. Among them was Bernage, the Provost of **Proclamation** the Merchants, clothed in his magnificent dress, **of Peace.** " a robe of crimson and tan velvet," enriched with golden embroidery. The first municipal magistrate was accompanied by the sheriffs, the Public Prosecutor and the Attorney-General, the Protonotaries and the Receiver-General, the King-at-Arms, six heralds, a Master of the Ceremonies, Gentlemen of the Châtelet, and the Lieutenant-General of the Police. A fanfare of trumpets, drums, hautboys, and cremonas lent its aid to the ceremony. All these imposing officials started from the Place de Grève where a large crowd had been waiting since the morning to see " this magnificent spectacle." The King-at-Arms especially attracted attention ; he was mounted on a white horse and rode by himself preceded by his heralds. In his left hand he held the King's ordinance which he was to proclaim, in his right a sceptre ; his heralds-at-arms carried wands.

After three flourishes of trumpets, accompanied by solemn ringing of bells, the procession started on its long itinerary. It stopped thirteen times at the principal open spaces of Paris, amongst others at the Place du Carrousel, the Grand Châtelet, the Halles, opposite the Pillory, the Place des Victoires, the equestrian statue of Henri IV on the Pont Neuf, the Place Saint Michel, and the Place Maubert. At each halt the King-at-Arms uncovered and said in a loud and clear voice : " *By the King's command!* " Then he put his Majesty's proclamation into the hands of one of the heralds, saying : " *You, Herald-at-Arms of France, do your duty.*" The Proclamation of Peace was read. It was preceded by three flourishes of trumpets and cries of " Vive le Roi ! " from the Archers, but the spectators did not take up the cry. The crowd was curious, but not in the least enthusiastic. Louis' unpopularity was just beginning.

PRINCIPAL SOURCES. The same as for the preceding chapter. The description of the Publication of Peace is taken from the unpublished official report in the *Registres du Bureau de la Ville* (Archives Nationales, H., 1863, fols. 59–85).

CHAPTER XII

LOUIS XV BECOMES UNPOPULAR
1749–1757

Pamphlets and libels. Madame de Pompadour's position. Her character. Licence of the great nobles. Discontent of the clergy. Parlementaires and courtiers. Seditious books. The risings of 1750. The École Militaire and the nobility of the sword. Death of Maurice de Saxe. Birth of the Duc de Bourgogne. High price of bread in Paris. Death of Madame Henriette. Illness of the Dauphin. The *tabouret* granted to Madame de Pompadour. Quarrels between the Clergy and the Parlement. The conversion of the Marquise. Damiens' attempt. The Court in 1757. The favourite's omnipotence. Dismissal of Machault and the Comte d'Argenson.

THE nation hoped that the Treaty of Aix-la-Chapelle would cause an appreciable reduction of taxation, but the actual reduction was insignificant. Consequently there were loud complaints when it was known that **Pamphlets and** the Royal expenditure had not diminished, and **Lampoons.** that the fêtes at Versailles and the building operations at Choisy, Bellevue, and Fontainebleau had depleted the Treasury. Songs, verses, and satires were published against the King. One of these pamphlets said : " Louis, if you were once the object of our love, it is because all your vices were not yet known to us. In this kingdom depopulated by you and given over to the mountebanks who are reigning with you, all Frenchmen have come to hate you." The King found on the floor of Versailles missives containing the following words : " You are going to Choisy : *why don't you go to Saint-Denis ?* " On the Louvre and the Pont Neuf the following warning was posted :

Crains notre desespoir ; la noblesse à des Guises,
Paris des Ravaillac, le clergé des Clément.*

---

* Beware of our despair ; the nobility has its Guises, Paris its Ravaillacs, and the clergy their Cléments.

There also appeared a brochure called "The Five Wounds of France"—an attack on the whole reign—the *Constitution*, the *Convulsions* (one of its disastrous effects), *Law's System*, *Cardinal Fleury's Ministry* and the *Peace of Aix-la-Chapelle*. There were murmurs also against the reduction of the army. Twelve regiments had been suppressed and there had been a general retrenchment of the military establishment.

But Louis' greatest unpopularity arose from the new favourite. It began to be known that all responsible positions **Madame** and places under government were at the disposal **de Pompadour.** of Madame de Pompadour. When the Naval Minister, the Comte de Maurepas, was dismissed, there were grounds for the belief that his disgrace was due to the favourite, who was said to be thus avenging herself on him for some satirical remarks. The Queen, however, had to be gracious to the favourite, for she knew that she had her rival to thank when her husband treated her kindly.

It must be confessed that Madame de Pompadour was extremely attractive. She was anxious to please or at least to *appear* amiable. Her skill was great ; never has actress played her part so well. She had more charm than real beauty ; her round face, regular features, magnificent complexion, superb hands and arms, and intelligent eyes would have been of little value but for her talent for putting people at their ease. Her conversation was gay and witty, and gave evidence of a taste and a fund of information much above the average. None knew better than she how to treat every one suitably. Her tact was remarkable and she gave evidence of it by holding receptions at her toilet, so as to avoid difficulties of etiquette. She understood Louis perfectly and possessed the valuable art of being able to amuse the most unamusable man in the kingdom. She realised that this Bourbon was meant for a private rather than a public life, so she transformed the Court to suit his caprice, arranging a large number of supper parties, journeys, and select gatherings to which only intimate friends were invited.

While life went on in this way at Versailles, the Clergy and Parlementaires were meditating revolt. The former wished to escape their burdens of State and the payment of the regular taxes ; the latter objected to the curtailment of their prerogatives and privileges. Even the courtiers who surrounded Madame de Pompadour complained bitterly as soon as they left her presence. Everywhere, in the salons, in the cafés, and on the promenades, men complained against the Government without caring if they were heard. The police contented themselves with espionage and arrested nobody, as they would have been obliged to arrest every one. A breath of revolution was passing over the nation and spreading " like gangrene." Montesquieu's *Esprit des Lois*, by its comparison of the monarchic with the republican system, furnished arguments to the enemies of the Government.

Hitherto religious quarrels had merely divided the Jesuits and Jansenists, but about 1749 the war between scepticism **Sceptical** and faith was initiated and daring publications **Books appear.** began to appear. Diderot was sent to Vincennes for his *Letter on blindness for the use of those who see*. Toussaint's book *Les Mœurs* was ordered to be burnt for its impiety. The Parlement accused the author " of establishing natural religion on the ruins of all outward faith," and of objecting to " the punishments with which human justice corrects theft and murder." Toussaint was the forerunner of Jean-Jacques Rousseau and Beccaria. The Abbé de Prades delivered a lecture in the Sorbonne in which he compared the miracles of Jesus Christ to the cures of Æsculapius, and under the influence of the Jesuits the Sorbonne denounced him in spite of having previously received him. He retired into exile at Berlin, but was recalled to retract his essay publicly.

In 1750 there were risings in Paris caused by the kidnapping of girls and boys. It was said that they were destined to be **Riots in 1750.** shipped to America where they were to be employed in the proposed new Canadian silkworm farms. Some too zealous constables, actuated by greed of gain, instead of taking foundlings for this purpose, seized workmen's children, " who were wandering in the vicinity of their homes, or who had been sent to church or to fetch something," and the tumult among the people was great in the Faubourg Saint-Marcel and the Faubourg Saint-Antoine. On May 22 the house of a commissary in the Rue de Clichy was wrecked with stones because a constable had taken refuge there. The same thing happened to a restaurant-keeper in the Croix-Rouge who had given shelter to an archer. The next day the rising became more serious; at Saint-Roch shots were fired, a spy called Parisien was murdered and his corpse was dragged to the house of Berryer, the Lieutenant-General of Police, against whom fierce threats were uttered. The culprits were placed on their trial, but it was realized that the whole populace was implicated. In June of the same year, when the King went from Versailles to Compiègne, he travelled to Saint-Denis without crossing Paris, dreading seditious cries, and afterwards a road was made which still bears the name of the *Route de la Révolte*.

Thus Clergy, Parlementaires, courtiers, writers, men of letters, and men of the people were all discontented and believed themselves to be victims of injustice, under the influence of the spirit of revolt which was driving France towards revolution. The Marquis d'Argenson wrote these prophetic words in September 1751 : " Every class is discontented. Everything is in a highly inflammable state, a rising may grow into a revolt and a revolt into a *national revolution* which would result in the election of tribunes of the people and electoral assemblies of the communes. Thereby the King and his ministers would be deprived of their excessive power to do harm." It is true that when d'Argenson himself was in power he did not find his authority excessive.

To create a diversion some popular schemes were set afloat. On January 1, 1751, under the auspices of Madame de Pompadour, the École Militaire was founded, in which five hundred sons of gentlemen were to be educated free, the preference being given to those whose fathers had been killed on active service. The building in which they were established still exists and is a fine specimen of eighteenth-century architecture; it is situated near the Invalides at the end of the Champ de Mars. The public took much interest in it. " We shall see," said Barbier, " two neighbouring houses, one the cradle and the other the tomb of soldiers."

Some months earlier an edict was passed establishing a new nobility, to which not only those who reached the rank of general, but those also who had become captains and whose

157

fathers and grandfathers had served in the same capacity—
patre et avo militibus—acquired a prescriptive right. The nobility
thus created did not owe its immunities to the power of money,
like the court officials, but to personal service, often of a
distinguished nature. These just favours were some consolation to the soldiers now in mourning for the victor of Fontenoy,
who had just died, to the deep regret of his companions in arms.
They felt that one century could not produce two such heroes.
He died at the Château of Chambord, which Louis had given him
for life as a reward for his services. He led a sumptuous life
there and had made it a second Versailles.

Maurice de Saxe died bravely. He said to Sénac, the court
physician, sent to him by the King : " My friend, you come too
Death of late. This is the end of a beautiful dream ! "
Maurice He was a Protestant. The Queen said of him :
de Saxe. " It is a pity we cannot say a *De Profundis* for a
man who was the cause of so many *Te Deums !* " His body was
taken to a Lutheran chapel at Strasburg, and later Pigalle
erected a monument to the great captain whose glory was not
surpassed even by that of Turenne. His face was bright and
intelligent. La Tour has immortalized him in a wonderful
pastel at the Louvre, of which there is a beautiful replica in the
Dresden Museum. Maurice honoured the House of Saxony as
the natural son of the Elector, Augustus II, King of Poland,
and he honoured France also by his brilliant services to her.

A gloom was cast over the Court in 1751 by this sad
event and by the censures passed upon the monarch from the
vantage-ground of the pulpit. Père Griffet, who preached
the Lent sermons at Versailles, alluded to the King's conduct,
and inveighed against worldliness even in the presence of
Louis himself—an attentive listener. The Jesuits, and with
them the Queen and the Dauphin, hoped that the universal
jubilee festival would bring Louis back to religion. But Louis
performed his Lenten devotions very carelessly. All the while,
ballets and comedies were being rehearsed behind the scenes at
the Marquise's theatre, in preparation for private performances.
At the sermons Louis was merely amused, treating them as
though the words of truth could not apply to him and were
addressed only to his Court.

158

On September 12 the Dauphin's first son, the Duc de Bourgogne was born, but there were no manifestations of public **Birth of the** rejoicing. The official celebrations aroused no **Duc** enthusiasm; bread stood at twopence a pound; **de Bourgogne.** the high prices and the poverty increased; taxation became heavier; the complaints of the clergy and the Parlement troubled the country; and honest folk had no heart for merrymaking. The prevailing listlessness was so great that when the Duc de Gesvres, Governor of Paris, caused money to be thrown to the people, there were not ten persons present to pick it up. Artisans and merchants had some cause to be discontented. The Dauphin and Dauphine on November 26 went to a *Te Deum* at Notre Dame and their reception was unfavourable. More than two thousand women assembled near the Pont de la Tournelle and cried to them : " Give us bread ! We are dying of hunger ! " The Dauphin ordered the distribution of some small coins, but the women only cried the louder : " Monseigneur, we do not want your money ! We want bread. We love you ; send away this Pompadour who is governing and ruining the kingdom. If we only had her here there would soon be nothing left of her to serve as relics." On their return Louis asked the Dauphine if she had not received many benedictions.

" Benedictions ! " she answered, sobbing, "they asked me for bread ! "

On the death of Madame Henriette on February 10, 1752, a terrible blow for Louis, the people cried out again : " See **Death of** what happens when you offend God and make **Madame** your subjects unhappy ! God takes away your **Henriette.** beloved daughter." Louis was tortured with grief and remorse ; the Queen's party hoped to be victorious this time. But, after two days, it was apparent that there was to be no change, and the Marquise was more powerful than ever.

Some months later the Court was again alarmed ; the Dauphin had small-pox and seemed to be in danger. Louis **Illness of** did not enter the sick-room. The Queen was less **the Dauphin.** timid and went to see her son. The Dauphine took her place at her husband's bedside and ordered those who assisted her to forgo all ceremony and not to consider her. " I

159

am no longer Dauphine," said Marie-Josèphe, " I am only a nurse." Pousse, a doctor who had been summoned from Paris, knew nothing of the Court or its etiquette. He saw the princess simply dressed, attending to the various requirements of the sick-room, and said one day : " Do exactly what this little woman tells you, for she understands wonderfully what is wanted." And turning to Marie-Josèphe he added, " What is your name, my child ? "

When the Dauphin began to mend the King was compelled by custom to show himself to the Parisians and to go with his family to Notre Dame for a thanksgiving service. The price of bread had been lowered so that his Majesty should be better received. Nevertheless, a poor wretch climbed on to the Queen's carriage, near the Point-du-Jour, to show her some black bread, crying : " There, Madame, that is what we have to pay three halfpence a pound for."

Louis changed horses at the Petit Cours, where he was cheered by some bystanders, but in Paris nobody cried *Vive le Roi !*

In spite of these sentiments Louis chose this very time to complete Madame de Pompadour's satisfaction by according

Madame de Pompadour's Honours.
her the *tabouret* and the privileges of a duchess. The favourite was presented, with great ceremony by the Dowager Princess de Conti, and thus fresh jealousy was aroused, since for the future she would be entitled to the privileges of the wives of dukes and peers. The *tabouret* was the right to sit down at the *Grand Couvert* and in all Court assemblies, and was the highest honour at Court. It was a dignity to which no *bourgeoise* had ever yet attained. The Dauphin greatly resented this inopportune favour and the event caused what was then called a " ruffling of feathers," at Court. Sharp words passed between father and son. The Dauphin asked permission to dine with the Archbishop of Paris, and received the following answer from the King : " My son, you ought to wish me to live long, for you are not yet able to govern yourself." The Dauphin, who was deeply sensible of his duty, could not completely ignore the Marquise, but towards his father he behaved for the future with only an outward show of respect.

The antagonism between the Clergy and the Parliament increased. Bouettin, Curé of Saint-Etienne-du-Mont, refused the last sacraments to a Jansenist priest named Le Mère, because he had not a confessional certificate signed by an ecclesiastic who had submitted to the Bull *Unigenitus*. There was a general disturbance in Paris ; ten thousand people followed Le Mère to the grave. The Parliament did not dare to attack the Archbishop of Paris, Christophe de Beaumont, who was responsible for the scandal, " but they issued a warrant of arrest against the Curé of Saint-Etienne." The King interfered and quashed the warrant as derogating from his authority.

Friction between Clergy and Parlement.

The trouble spread to the provinces and almost brought about a revival of the League. The Parliament addressed a remonstrance to the King like " the harangues which the Romans made from the tribune." The magistrates pointed out the disorders which the Constitution had caused in Church and State, and they reminded the King that Louis XIV had only allowed the Bull to be registered with the addition of certain amendments safeguarding Gallican liberties. " The impious," they said, " have made use of the dissensions which have arisen between ministers of religion to attack religion itself. The proud philosopher, madly jealous of the Divinity Himself, and seeing with regret the homage which is rendered to Him, thinks this a favourable moment to introduce a monstrous system of unbelief." This was an allusion to the first volumes of the *Encyclopædia*. " It has been reserved for our generation," they continued, " to hear without comment in the first University of Christendom a public lecture (that of the Abbé de Prades), in which all the false principles of unbelief were systematically expounded."

The Chief President, in a private interview, said to Louis, " Sire, you are being deceived ; it is time you realized it. Schism needs small forces to dethrone kings, whereas it takes great armies to defend them." A commission of prelates and Parlementaires was appointed to discuss the question, but it never sat. The troubles increased, the Ultramontanes continued to refuse the sacraments, and the Jansenists to protest. They disputed over opinions and doctrines. Contradictory decrees

were issued at the same moment by the Parliament on one side
and the King's Council on the other, and thus "two practically
equal powers crossed one another in their operations." The
anarchy was complete. "Everything is falling in turn," wrote
d'Argenson. "Meanwhile opinion gains ground, rises and
spreads until it may cause a national revolution."

The Parliament sent in remonstrances in quick succession,
but the King persisted in his refusal to listen. Matters were at
Struggle between King and Parliament. their worst in May 1753, and in the night of May 8
musketeers went from door to door to present
the presidents and councillors with *lettres de
cachet* ordering them to go to the residences which
had been assigned to them. The *Grand Chambre* was excepted
from this punishment, but it desired to share the fate of the
rest, and so was sent to Pontoise as in 1720. The *Grandes
Remontrances,* which had fired the powder, were published on
May 23, although they had not been officially read. These
Grandes Remontrances were a political and religious manifesto
of the utmost significance, for they revealed the temper of the
Parlementaires and already foreshadowed the revolution to
come. They censured the clergy, showing how the Church
had encroached on the temporal authorities. The following
was among the phrases used : " The authority of the successors
of the Apostles is a ministry, not an empire." The Throne was
censured : " If subjects," said the Parliament, "owe obedience
to kings, kings on their side owe obedience to law." The
conclusion was particularly stirring : " No, Sire, we will not
allow the triumph of a schism fatal to religion and capable of
striking a deadly blow at your Sovereignty and the State. In
vain do they try to compel us to become powerless spectators
of the misfortunes of our country and thus incur responsibility for its woes. If those who wrongfully use your name
are trying to reduce us to the cruel alternatives of either suffering
disgrace from your Majesty, or betraying those duties that an
inviolable zeal for your service imposes upon us, let them
know that that zeal is boundless, and that we are resolved to
remain faithful to you, even though we become the victims of
our own fidelity."

All the provincial parliaments joined with the Parliament

of Paris; there were even suggestions of a Convocation of the States-General.

There were numerous attempts at repression, but they only inflamed the resistance. The one dominant idea was that the nation is above the monarch, *as the Church is above the Pope.** The Ultramontane Party seized upon this as a weapon. The Bishop of Montauban published a charge in which he recalled the fate of Charles I, and insinuated that the Parliament of Paris, like that of London, *was capable of condemning the Sovereign to the scaffold.*

We have here an example of courageous championship of the liberties of ancient France, when the highest institution of
Unrest in Paris. the kingdom, an institution which was independent of the State both in its origin and in its functions, addressed such reprimands to the Government. But it must be admitted that the effect was small. Under the name of the *Chambre Royale* a sham Parliament was created, a weak anticipation of the Maupeou Parliament. But the Châtelet, the last remnant of the judicature, a court of first instance, refused to recognize it. Whereupon the Government wished to suppress the Châtelet. " I learn," writes d'Argenson on this subject in December 1753, " from one of the chief magistrates of Paris, that the Parisians are in a state of subdued excitement. Military precautions are being taken, the watch is doubled each day, and patrols of Swiss and French guards are to be seen in the streets. The same magistrate tells me that he believes, if the Châtelet is suppressed, the shops will be shut, barricades will be constructed, and thus the revolution will begin."

The Ultramontane reaction became very violent in 1754. Christophe de Beaumont, Archbishop of Paris, deprived of their authority all confessors who did not show sufficient zeal for the Constitution. Père Laugier, a Jesuit, preached before the King against the Parliament, and concluded " in the style of an Attorney-General," urging the abolition of this institution as impious and destructive of religion. The Protestants of the Cévennes were threatened with new dragonnades. In March 1754, five thousand Huguenots of Nîmes left the Kingdom. This quarrel between the Jansenists and Ultramontanes

* d'Argenson.

was the preface of the *Cahiers* of the States-General of 1789.
The fever of opposition in 1754 is a forecast of the Revolution.
And if the storm cloud did not burst, it was not, as Rousseau
says, because of the publication of his *Lettre sur* (or rather
against) *la musique française.* . . . " When you read," he says,
" that this pamphlet perhaps prevented a revolution in the
State, you will think you are dreaming ! " It was still less,
as the Duc de Luynes would have us believe, because of the
arrival in Paris of a troop of *Opera Buffa*, and of the actor
Manelli, which set the partisans of French and Italian music at
loggerheads. The real reason was that the Court realized the
danger and changed its policy. In June it caused a report to be
spread of the recall of the exiled Parlementaires and the expulsion of the Jesuits. Only the first was true. On August 30
the *Chambre Royale* was suppressed by letters patent, and on
September 4 the Parliament returned to favour almost at the
Birth of very time that the Duc de Berry, the future
Louis XVI. Louis XVI, was born on August 23. It was said
that these measures were the work of the Marquise ; they were
designed to calm the hatred which pursued her and the insults
with which she was loaded.

Magistrates were muzzled by the *law of silence*. Louis XV
ordered them not to revive religious quarrels and to maintain
public peace. This law hardly pleased the clergy, and especially
the bishops, who asserted that they had received their mission
from Our Lord " to preach His Name on the housetops," and to
be in subjection to God and not to men. There were fresh
refusals of the sacraments at Boulogne and at Paris. The
magistrates asked for explanations from the Archbishop, but
he did not listen to them, so they complained to the King. Louis,
Archbishop of intent upon keeping the peace, exiled Monseigneur
Paris exiled. de Beaumont to Conflans on December 3. The
reconciliation between the King and Parliament was complete,
but the Archbishop of Paris resisted and continued the war.
He was next ordered to go to Lagny, a little further from his
faithful followers. Then the Parliament declared, in March
1755, that the Bull was not a rule of faith and forbade all clergy
to attribute this character to it. The *law of silence* was scarcely
observed at all, and the Constitution was " nationally annihi-
164

lated." * At this pass the King, foreseeing war, annulled the decree so as to persuade the Assembly of the Clergy to vote him several millions. There was a tacit agreement between the magistrates and the Monarch, and as soon as he had secured the *freewill offering* (*don gratuit*), as the ecclesiastical tax was called, Louis met all the requests of the bishops with a refusal. This was followed by a general relaxation of stringency. The *Encyclopædia* was allowed to reappear; tolerance was shown to the Protestants and they were allowed to build places of worship. But the Archbishop of Paris, supported by the Jesuits, would not own defeat and, finally, at the *lit de justice* held on December 13, 1756, they persuaded the King to order the Constitution to be respected as a decision of the Church. The Archbishop's exile was made less strict and he returned in October 1757. Once more the omnipotent favourite was the cause of this abrupt change of policy; she had special reasons for supposing that her reign would one day end, for Louis was now interested in her merely from force of habit, and because no superior attraction had yet arisen. Her enemies lost no chance of intriguing against her and of putting temptation in the King's way, and she, playing a dangerous game, was prepared to use any means to serve her ends.

The memory of Madame de Maintenon haunted her, so she made preparations to secure her retreat with feminine adroitness, **Madame de Pompadour's Conversion.** combining the trickery of a Tartuffe with the craft of a Dorimène. She thought of becoming converted, and did not hesitate to apply to a Jesuit, Père de Sacy, an innocent accomplice and a very saintly man, to unravel the tangled skein of her position. This took place at the end of 1755. The Marquise at that time gave evidence of the most fervent piety; she went every day to Mass, fasted on Friday, and held receptions no longer at her toilet, but at her embroidery frame. It was even thought that she would cease to use rouge. Suddenly, on February 8, 1756, to the surprise of everyone, she was appointed Lady of the Palace to the Queen. A letter from the King informed Marie Leszczynska of the appointment and she answered: " Sire, I have a King in Heaven Who gives me the strength to endure my troubles, and

* d'Argenson.

a King on earth whom I shall always obey." The next day Madame de Pompadour performed her new duties " with an easy air, as though she had never done anything else."

Such was the reward of her return to the faith—her " quarter conversion." " Extremists said already," writes the Duc de Croÿ, " that after the death of the Duchesse de Luynes, the post of Superintendent of the Queen would be revived in favour of Madame de Pompadour; that her great influence would continue and even increase, if it were possible, and that she would equal or surpass Madame de Maintenon, whom for some time she had been carefully imitating."

The Marquise certainly owed some return to the Jesuits. She had made Père de Sacy believe that her example would bring back the King to his religious practices; she conjured up a vision of a devout Court firmly supporting the Church, and she persuaded Louis to insist upon the acceptance of the Constitution. Later, when she returned to her old life, she helped to complete the ruin of the clergy who had procured her the position of Lady of the Palace :

La maison est à moi ; c'est à vous d'en sortir.*

Once more the course of justice was suspended ; many parlementaires sent in their resignations, and there were general **Damiens'** signs of discontent. On January 5, 1757, a **attempt.** fanatic named Damiens tried to assassinate the King as he was leaving Versailles for the Trianon. Immediately all was forgotten in anxiety for the King's health. The suspense, however, was not long, as the wound was not serious, and in spite of fears of a fresh attempt, it was soon ascertained that Damiens had no accomplice.

The citizens of Paris had been as much distressed as everyone else when the King was ill at Metz in 1744, but now they remained indifferent, and nursed their resentment at the exile of the Parliament.

The attitude of the Court at this critical moment is interesting. The King behaved well, and when the surgeons told him of his safety, he showed no more pleasure at being out of danger than he had showed fear when he thought he was lost. He said to one

* The house is mine ; it is for you to go.

of his courtiers: "The wound was not very deep, yet it went to the heart." His conduct to the Dauphin was moving; he spoke long and affectionately to him, expressed his regret at the scandal he had caused, and recommended his son to study the happiness of his people. He wanted to confess. His titular confessor, Père Desmarest, who certainly had not a very heavy duty to perform, was at Paris; but the Abbé Soldini was brought to him and remained "three-quarters of an hour with the King, behind his curtains."

All eyes were turned on the Dauphin as the rising sun; on the 5th he was treated as King, and that evening he presided at the Council of Ministers. Argenson says he showed intelligence, dignity, and eloquence beyond all expectation. Men must be put to the test before they can show their true value.

The Queen and Mesdames thought only of the King's conversion "which would have given them more authority"* and would have dismissed the Marquise for ever. The Comtesse de Toulouse, on behalf of the King's children, approached Bernis. She asked him to advise the Marquise to retire, adding that this retreat would not diminish the confidence and friendship of the King, and would assure her of Monsieur le Dauphin's protection for the rest of her life, besides covering her with glory in the eyes of all Europe.

Madame de Pompadour's future was the topic of all conversation and, if Bernis is to be trusted, people were more **Position of** interested in what was likely to become of the **Madame de** favourite than in the accident to the King. All **Pompadour.** means of access were closed to her; the royal family were sufficient to fill the Chamber. The friends of the Marquise were no longer numerous. "At Court, disgrace causes courtiers to fly away, like pigeons from a cot at the entry of a sparrow-hawk."* Most of the people who went to see her went "to see what appearance she was presenting, under pretence of interest."† However, some were faithful to her. Bernis and the Prince de Soubise managed to overcome the intrigues of the Comte d'Argenson, Minister of War, and the indecision of Machault, Minister of Marine, and saw that Madame de Pompadour was allowed to wait at Versailles in safety.

* Cheverny.   † Du Hausset.

For eleven days she was left in uncertainty as to her position, as she had no message from the King " who was under the eyes of all his Court and all his family." At last, on January 16, the courtiers noticed a change in Louis. Instead of looking sad and severe he now appeared calm and bright. A smile passed over his lips and happiness brightened his handsome face. Thus his intimates knew that he had visited Madame de Pompadour. " They had tried indirectly," says Cheverny, " to prove to him that people were ill disposed towards him and that this was probably a conspiracy. . . . Madame de Pompadour took a different view ; she told him that Damiens was only a dangerous madman, and that it was not a conspiracy. She spoke of the general alarm which had spread through the kingdom, how all the Parliaments had been horrified at the deed. She said that this accident would protect him from anything of the kind happening again. . . . Thus she poured so much balm on his wounds that that evening he dressed, and the next day he reappeared at the hunt and at the suppers in the *Petits Appartements*. The pious cabal was defeated and the Marquise became more powerful than ever.

She took advantage of this omnipotence to secure the disgrace of Machault and the Comte d'Argenson, against whom she had a personal grievance ; she also resented their attitude in the Damiens affair. These two ministers, and especially Machault, were men of considerable experience, and their disgrace took place at a time when war was imminent and their services would have been inestimable. They were sacrificed in spite of the King and in spite of public opinion. Cheverny, in his *Mémoires*, says of them : " Monsieur le Comte d'Argenson was Minister for War. Naturally gifted, with a handsome appearance, a prodigious memory, and the refined eloquence of a courtier, and believing his position secure, he originated vast intrigues in the hope of persuading Louis to make him Prime Minister. Monsieur de Machault's plans were deeper and better carried out."

The favourite restored to power.

Louis, on this occasion, showed his habitual dissimulation. He treated the two victims " equally well both publicly and privately." Bernis remembers that two days before his disgrace
168

d'Argenson said to him : " You are reticent, but you know quite well that Machault is packing up ; the Marquise wishes to see no more of him. It is a question of a week at most."

Machault and d'Argenson were exiled together on February 1, 1757. Neither of them had suspected his own disgrace. The **Dismissal of** wording of the letters that the King had sent to **Machault and** them was very different. It is evident that **d'Argenson.** Louis was distressed at having to obey the Marquise when he wrote to Machault : " Although I am persuaded of the probity and uprightness of your intentions, present circumstances force me to ask you to return my Seals and to resign the office of Secretary of State for the Navy. *Be always assured of my protection and my friendship.*" A pension of 20,000 livres was granted to Machault. The note which d'Argenson received was cold and imperative : " Monsieur d'Argenson, as your service is no longer necessary to me, I order you to send in your resignation of the office of Secretary of State for War, and your other duties, and to withdraw to your estate of Ormes."

Bernis, who was devoted to Madame de Pompadour, owns that this was a fatal error. The Marquis de Paulmy, who succeeded his uncle d'Argenson, and Moras, who replaced Machault, brought " confusion and disorder into their respective departments." The Marquise, " with her childlike confidence," thought that with her help all would be well. . . . Neither Bernis nor the new allies had any illusions on that subject. Disasters were hanging over France which would increase the already considerable unpopularity of Louis and his favourite. **Execution of** As for Damiens, he was condemned to be drawn **Damiens.** and quartered. We will not here give the details of this terrible execution. It will suffice to say that, according to Barbier, the criminal remained " more than half an hour seated in front of the scaffold looking on calmly whilst everything was prepared for his punishment." They took an hour and a quarter to kill him. " Many people," says Madame du Hausset, " and even women, had the barbarous curiosity to watch this execution, among other Madame P——, a very beautiful woman, wife of a farmer-general of taxes. Some one told the King of this and he put his two hands over his eyes, saying : " *Oh ! the horrible woman !* " They say that she and others had intended to flatter the King by their action.

PRINCIPAL SOURCES. *Mémoires* or *Journaux* of the Marquis d'Argenson, Barbier, the Duc de Luynes, Dufort de Cheverny, Président Hénault, Madame du Hausset, Bernis ; *Correspondance* of Madame de Pompadour (Malassis) ; *Journal historique ou Fastes du règne de Louis XV*, 1766 ; *Vie privée de Louis XV* (Moufle d'Angerville) ; Glasson, *Histoire du Parlement de Paris*, 2 vols., 1901 ; Rocquain, *L'ésprit révolutionnaire avant la Révolution*, 1878 ; Aubertin, *L'ésprit public au XVIIIe siècle*, 3rd edition, 1889 ; E. & J. de Goncourt, *Madame de Pompadour*, new edition, 1899 ; P. de Nolhac, *Louis XV and Madame de Pompadour*, 1904 ; C. Stryienski, *La Mère des trois derniers Bourbons*, 1902.

CHAPTER XIII

THE SEVEN YEARS WAR
1756–1763

Rivalry between France and England. Dupleix in India. Events in America. Capture of Port Mahon. War breaks out. The proposals of Maria Theresa. Frederick's attitude. Invasion of Saxony. Marshal d'Estrées. Richelieu. Madame de Pompadour obtains the command of the French forces for the Prince de Soubise. The Comte de Clermont. The English plunder the coasts of France. Bernis. Choiseul. Elizabeth of Russia. Contades. Broglie. Saint-Germain. The Chevalier d'Assas. Death of Elizabeth. The defection of Russia. The Family Compact. Preliminaries of peace. The treaties of Paris and Hubertsburg. Bouchardon's Statue of Louis XV.

CARDINAL FLEURY had continued the Regent's English policy and had allowed himself to be duped by his pretended friend, Walpole. The British Government had been continually waiting for a propitious moment **French and** to dispute with France the possession of her **English in** colonies in India and America and to destroy **India.** her fleet. In Asia, the settlements which were originated by Colbert, founded by Lenoir and Dumas, and developed by Dupleix, were compromised by the rivalry between the latter and de La Bourdonnais. At the Peace of Aix-la-Chapelle, France had to give up Madras to England and only kept Pondicherry, Mahe, Chandernagore, and Karikal. Nevertheless, Dupleix continued to conquer the Mogul Empire with the intention of establishing European supremacy, and being both an able statesman and a man of action, he understood that in order to exercise a victorious authority in India he would have to gain influence over one or other of the puppets dignified by the title of *Nizam* or *Nabob*, whose motions he would govern and who would be the mouthpiece for his orders.

171

THE EIGHTEENTH CENTURY

The English historian, Macaulay, says : " The arts both of war and policy, which a few years later were employed with such signal success by the English, were first understood and practised by this ingenious and aspiring Frenchman." It was Louis' government which stopped the progress of this great pioneer of French colonization. Dupleix was master of a territory which stretched from the River Narbada to Cape

Dupleix. Comorin, comprising a tract of land as large as France. But he had to contend with Clive, a young English adventurer, endowed with the military talents in which his adversary was lacking. Clive was supported by a regular army, whilst the Frenchman had nothing but the sweepings of the galleys. The King would not make the sacrifices which might, in spite of all, have assured success. Like a faithful disciple of Fleury, he gave in to the demands of the English Cabinet and recalled Dupleix in 1754. Dupleix has been much misunderstood. Some days before his death in 1763, he published his *Mémoires*, which are pitiful reading : " I have sacrificed," he says, " my youth, my fortune, and my life in loading my nation with honour and riches in Asia. . . . I am in the most abject poverty. The little that remained to me has been seized. I have been obliged to obtain suspension decrees to prevent myself from being dragged to prison. . . ."

Colonel Malleson has said of Dupleix : " The rivals who profited by his disgrace place him on a pedestal (his bust is at Calcutta amongst those of other great Europeans) hardly less elevated than those which bear Clive, Warren Hastings, and Wellesley." *

In America matters were going no better for France. The Peace of Aix-la-Chapelle had not determined the boundaries

Events in America. of the English and French colonies there. The Canadians were defending their territory by fortifying the Valley of the Ohio and protecting the St. Lawrence and the Mississippi, so as to keep the English between the Alleghanies and the sea. Some of the islands of the Antilles were still in dispute. Nevertheless, French commerce was

---

* Colonel Malleson's actual words are : " Not the less will even the descendants of his rivals place him on the pedestal of Clive, Warren Hastings, and Wellesley."—*History of the French in India.*

expanding ; a new impulse had been given to shipping by two great ministers, Rouillé and Machault. England, jealous of the French maritime power, had determined on her destruction. In June 1755, without any declaration of war, Admiral Boscawen, then in Newfoundland, seized two French frigates, the *Alcide* and the *Lys*. The English thus commenced hostilities with a scandalous surprise attack. The chase continued, and more than three hundred vessels fell into the English nets. The Duc de Mirepoix, French Ambassador in London, and Bussy, the Minister at Hanover, were ordered to return immediately without taking leave of the Courts to which they were accredited.

A reprisal was necessary and it was complete. A French fleet, commanded by the Marquis de la Galissonnière, trans-
Capture of ported troops to Minorca under the command of
Port Mahon. Marshal de Richelieu. After a brilliant assault the fortress of Port Mahon was taken on May 20, 1756. The French were thus masters of the Mediterranean. It was an eloquent reply to Boscawen. The rejoicing was great in Paris. England made Admiral Byng responsible for his defeat, and he was shot on board his own vessel.

During these operations war was declared by England on May 17, and by France on June 16. Unhappily, Louis could not fight England without securing peace on the Continent.

He had to take into account that his ally Frederick had deserted him, and by the Treaty of Whitehall on January 16, 1756, had agreed to support British interests, and to defend the Electorate of Hanover which still belonged to George II, and was later menaced by the French Army. At this point Maria Theresa interfered. The obvious desire of the Empress-Queen was to get back Silesia from Prussia. Ever since 1750, through her ministers, Kaunitz and Starhemberg, she had been making
Maria Theresa's overtures for an alliance with Louis, and now, in
overtures. 1755, the moment seemed favourable. Kaunitz had a complete insight into the ways of the Court of France, having spent two years there with the object of obtaining this knowledge, and he knew to whom he should apply at this serious juncture. From Vienna, where he was continuing his brilliant career under Maria Theresa, he wrote to Madame de

Pompadour : " Monsieur le Comte de Starhemberg has matters of great importance to propose to the King, which are of such a nature that they can only be communicated through some one whom his most Christian Majesty honours with his complete confidence, and whom he will indicate to the Comte de Starhemberg." The man honoured with complete confidence was Bernis, who had just returned from Venice, where he had been ambassador, and was expecting to be made minister. Louis discussed the matter with him and with the Marquise. It was decided at the meeting of Babiole, in September 1755, that the Austrian proposals should be considered. Starhemberg then revealed to Louis the King of Prussia's negotiations with England through his representative, the Duke of Brunswick. Nothing was known of these negotiations at Versailles, because the French Ambassador had been withdrawn from London. The news was an important trump in the Austrian Minister's game. Frederick, who was allied to France by a treaty which held good until July 5, 1756, signed in January of the same year a treaty with George II against France. Faced with this outrageous action Louis did not hesitate. He decided to reverse his alliance. On May 1 France signed with Austria the first **First Treaty** Treaty of Versailles ; the two Powers promised **of Versailles.** mutual guarantees and the help of twenty-four thousand men against any aggressor. At the end of the year the Czarina Elizabeth subscribed to this Treaty, rejecting an alliance with England which her advisers had urged her to conclude.

The outlook was gloomy ; France had to contend with the rivalry of England on the seas and in the colonies and also fight on the Continent. Louis was, perhaps, supported by the idea that his adversaries belonged to a different religion, but he had embarked on a double enterprise, which was the most disastrous of the eighteenth century. Frederick followed England's example, and without declaring war invaded Saxony, in August 1756, with the evident intention of marching to the borders of Bohemia and so threatening Maria Theresa. This caused consternation at Versailles, especially to the Dauphine and her friends. The first victims of the hostilities were Augustus III, her father, who fled to Warsaw, and her mother, who remained at Dresden to receive the insults of the King of Prussia's representatives.

Thus both family interests, and the engagements she had made, prompted France to support Austria. In face of the Prussian aggression she could not be content with the stipulations of the Treaty of May 1. Since war had been declared it was best to do all that was possible to terminate it quickly and successfully. Louis was ready to make any sacrifice ; he said of his intimate connection with Vienna : " It is my work, I consider it good, and I mean to maintain it." He sent the Comte d'Estrées to Maria Theresa to arrange the plans of the military operations. Over a hundred thousand Frenchmen were placed at the disposal of the Empress to form the armies of the Rhine **Second Treaty** and of the Main ; one was to invade Hanover and **of Versailles.** the other to support the armies of Maria Theresa. This new Convention was signed at Vienna on February 28, 1757, and ratified by the second treaty of Versailles on May 1, 1757.

The Comte d'Estrées was made a Marshal on his return, and, in spite of the competition for the post, obtained the command of the great army of the Lower Rhine. Madame de Pompadour had wanted this post for her friend, the Prince de Soubise.

Meanwhile Frederick advanced on Prague, which he captured on May 6. But he sustained a sanguinary defeat at Kollin, on June 18, inflicted by Marshal Daun. " Fortune," wrote the King of Prussia, " is turning her back on me. She is a woman and I am not gallant. I ought to have expected it ; she has joined the ladies who are making war against me." These ladies were Maria Theresa, the Czarina Elizabeth (whose armies were watching the Pomeranian frontiers) and Madame de Pompadour. Frederick evacuated Bohemia.

D'Estrées entered the lists and chased the Anglo-Hanoverian forces across Westphalia to the Weser, which he crossed at Hameln. **Victory of** On July 26, aided by Chevert and three Princes of **d'Estrées at** the Blood Royal, the Duc d'Orléans, grandson of **Hastembeck.** the Regent, the Prince de Condé, and the Comte de la Marche, he defeated the Duke of Cumberland at Hastembeck. The news of the victory of Hastembeck did not reach Paris before the departure of a courier sent with a letter from the King to d'Estrées telling him : " You are replaced by the

Maréchal de Richelieu." A friend of d'Estrées, who knew what was going to happen, had warned him, and urged him to offer battle, hoping thus to save him, as he thought none would dare to recall a general who had just won a victory. . . . The public was furious. An engraving was published in which Marshal d'Estrées was shown thrashing the Duke of Cumberland with a branch of laurel, and as the leaves fell the Marshal de Richelieu was picking them up. D'Estrées had supporters even at the Court. The Comte de Maillebois, a son of the old Marshal, who had taken part in intrigues, and whose conduct at Hastembeck had been open to question, was imprisoned at Doullens.

The intrigues at Versailles compromised the success with which the campaign had begun. Richelieu committed fault **Marechal de** after fault. On his own responsibility he signed **Richelieu.** the fruitless Convention of Closter-Zeven on September 8, 1757, an action which met with strong disapproval at Versailles. The other army was commanded by the Prince de Soubise. In face of the enemy there was personal animosity between the two generals. Richelieu made a pretence of going to the assistance of Madame de Pompadour's *protégé*, but his only real object was to secure the defeat of his rival. He wore his troops out with forced marches, disheartened his soldiers, and encouraged pillage while reserving the greater part of the booty for himself. The Pavillon de Hanovre, which still exists on the Boulevards of Paris, was built on his return from the campaign with the proceeds of his robberies, and testifies to their extent. "The disorder," wrote Marshal de Belle-Isle, "the insubordination, and the brigandage of Monsieur de Richelieu's army, have passed all bounds. I have never seen anything which comes anywhere near it in all my fifty-six years' experience of war. It is certainly the General's fault, for he ought to be master, or he is not worthy to command. It is true that to this end he must begin by being himself irreproachable, and by giving an example of perfect disinterestedness." Each day new officers were sent from Versailles and thrust into the conflict by means of influence. They arrived with numerous retainers who were so many useless mouths to feed, to the detriment of the weary half-starved soldiers. At Gotha, when the Franco-Imperial camp commanded by Soubise and Hildburghausen fell into the hands of the enemy, they found a crowd of secretaries, cooks, and valets, valuable plate, toilet articles, scents, parasols, and even monkeys and parrots !

These carpet knights soon got tired of the camps, and then there were new appeals made at Court. "If an army is being formed," wrote General de Fontenay, Ambassador to Saxony, "the women clamour until those in whom they are interested receive appointments. After three months of the campaign, they go through the same performance to obtain permission for their friends to return."

There was current at his time a verse in which Marie-Josèphe of Saxony speaks to the Marquise—the Dauphine both as a Frenchwoman and a Saxon was suffering doubly from the misfortunes which were accumulating :

> Delphine à Pompadour a tenu ce propos :
> Madame, désormais, si vous voulez m'en croire,
> Vous vous contenterez pour votre propre gloire
> De faire des fermiers et non des généraux.*

The King of Prussia was in the heart of the Electorate of Saxony ; he had only twenty thousand men left. Soubise was **Frederick in** opposing him, in command of part of the Imperial **Saxony.** army. Richelieu at Halberstadt could have attacked Frederick's flank, having sixty thousand men at his disposal. The Austrian General, Marschall, was holding Lusatia with fourteen thousand men. But each hesitated. Marschall considered himself too weak and had no orders to advance ; Soubise was awaiting reinforcements and lacked supplies. Richelieu said that the season was too severe to undertake anything with such an exhausted army as his. The King of Prussia retreated, but very slowly, having no need to hurry from so indolent an enemy ; but he was not very confident. Besenval tells a characteristic anecdote of him. One evening in October 1757, the King had gone to bed and was sleeping on straw ; one of his grenadiers awoke him, saying : "Frederick, here is one of your men who had deserted and whom they are bringing back to you."

---

* The Dauphine said this to Pompadour : Madame, for the future, take my advice and content yourself, for the sake of your fame, with making farmers, and not generals.

" Bring him forward."

The King asked him why he had deserted.

" Your affairs," answered the deserter, " are in such a state that I left you to seek my fortune elsewhere."

" You are right," said the King, " but I pray you to remain with me during this campaign, and if things go no better, *I promise to desert with you.*"

Rossbach was fought on November 5. Frederick's twenty thousand men took the sixty thousand Franco-Germans by **Battle of Rossbach.** surprise. The Prince of Hildburghausen retired at the first cannonade and Soubise lost his head. The King of Prussia wrote : " The army of France seemed about to attack me on the 5th of this month. But it did not do me this honour and fled at the first discharge of our guns, without my being able to come up with it." The army of France ! Frederick forgot that France had allies ; so did the pamphleteers. They preferred to make songs against the French general and to revenge themselves on Madame de Pompadour. Soubise wrote to the King : " I write to your Majesty in my great despair. The rout of your army is complete." Was the Prince of Hildburghausen equally frank ?

In Silesia the Austrian armies took Liegnitz and Schweidnitz from Marshal Bevern and shut him up in Breslau. Frederick **Battle of Leuthen.** hastened to the spot, retook Breslau, and won the battle of Leuthen (Lissa). Daun, the Austrian General, brought back in December only thirty thousand men out of the eighty thousand he had once had. The King of Prussia had reconquered the lost ground, and his iron grip held Silesia, never again to be loosened. The victory of Leuthen, Napoleon said, " was one of the most complete which have ever been gained. By itself it would be sufficient to immortalize Frederick II." These compliments are permitted from general to general ; but what must be said of Voltaire, who crowned the brow of his Potsdam friend with laurels ?

The songs which were levelled at the generals and Madame de Pompadour amused the public and did no more. The **The Comte de Clermont.** Marquise retained all her prestige. The ministers submitted the most important questions to her before they were discussed in council. She interfered with the military operations, traced plans of campaign, marked maps with patches on the places she thought advisable to attack or defend. The appointments of generals were at her disposal and always caused the same complaints. Louis de Bourbon, Comte de Clermont, took Richelieu's place. He was the great-grandson of the great Condé; and was then fifty years old. Although Abbé of Saint-Germain-des-Prés, he had served in 1737 and had distinguished himself in many campaigns, particularly at Lawfeld under Maurice de Saxe. He did not wish to marry, although he was only a tonsured clerk, because he would have had to abandon his numerous benefices, and he preferred to lead an independent life. He was an Academician, but he had not delivered the customary discourse. The command, which he had solicited with much persistency from the beginning of the war, was not really suited to him, for there is a great difference between the officer who obeys orders and can execute them, and the general-in-chief who must show initiative. They laughed at him and called him *moitié plumet, moitié rabat* (which may be rendered *half-sword, half-gown*), and wrote this celebrated verse against him :

> Est-ce un Abbé ? L'Eglise le renie.
> Un général ? On l'a bien maltraité ;
> Mais il lui reste au moins l'Académie ;
> N'y fut-il pas muet par dignité ?
> Qu'est-il enfin ? Que son mérite est mince ?
> Hélas ! j'ai beau lui chercher un talent ;
> Un titre auguste éclaire son néant,
> Pour son malheur, le pauvre homme est un prince.*

The Comte de Gisors wrote a letter about Clermont to his father, the Maréchal de Belle-Isle. It was a serious criticism from a young soldier whose superior qualities were appreciated even by his adversaries. The tone of the letter proves that Gisors had no particular intention of disparaging his general ; it suggests that it pained him to have to make such damaging

* Is he an Abbé ? The Church repudiates him. A general ? He has been very badly treated. But at least the Academy remains to him ; even there did he not preserve a dignified silence ? What is he then ? How small is his merit ? Alas ! I search him in vain for a talent ; an august title advertises his nullity ; unfortunately the poor man is a prince.

admissions : " Until now I have not been able to speak openly to you. . . . M. le Comte de Clermont has no knowledge of the country and is incapable of forming any plan by himself, yet he will not allow himself to be governed consistently by any one person, but always follows the last advice. He has no foresight and is little troubled by the dangers at hand, is amused at trifles and wastes, his time in useless exercise. Such is our general."

In 1758 Frederick's enemies each took independent action. The French, Austrians and Russians tried to resist the King of **Battle of** Prussia on the Rhine, in Moravia, and in East **Crefeld.** Prussia. Clermont was beaten at Crefeld by Ferdinand of Brunswick on June 23. It was a repetition of Rossbach. Clermont wrote like Soubise : " We have only the shadow of an army left." At Crefeld the Comte de Gisors was mortally wounded and died at the age of twenty-six, a true Marcellus of the eighteenth century. The day after the death of this young hero one of his friends (M. de Vignoles) wrote : " We have just lost the best subject and the best man in the kingdom ; he was endowed with too many virtues to live in so corrupt an age. . . . My poor friend kept his consciousness till the last and prepared his own soul for death. He was mourned by the enemy as well as by ourselves."

Great hopes were placed in Marshal Daun and in the Muscovites who were advancing to threaten Frederick both in the south and the north. But the battle of Zorndorf on August 25 was indecisive. The Muscovites and the Prussians lay down to rest where they were, after terrible carnage lasting eleven hours, and the next day, Fermov, the Russian general, withdrew to the Vistula. On the Rhine, Chevert won the battle of Lütternberg on October 7 in the name of Soubise. Chevert had the glory and Soubise was given the Marshal's bâton. Frederick, freed on the Russian side, attacked the Austrians. Daun defeated him at Hochkirchen on October 14, but he failed to follow up his advantage, and was driven back into Bohemia. Frederick was once more triumphant in the most critical situation, although he had the mortification of seeing part of his states in the hands of Elizabeth's armies. England profited by the French disasters, and attacked the gallant garrisons and squadrons on the French coasts and in the colonies, all doomed to perish for want of aid. The Continental war exhausted France. Commodore Howe made a descent on Cherbourg on August 16, levied contributions, burnt twenty-seven ships, blew up with a mine the embankments which defended the port, and then retired, taking with him cannon and flags. The English tried to do the same at Saint-Cast, near Saint-Malo, on October 11, but were repulsed this time by some Breton volunteers commanded by the Duc d'Aiguillon. In Canada Montcalm did marvels with a handful of men. He wrote to the minister who had abandoned him : " We shall fight and we shall bury ourselves, if it be necessary, under the ruins of the colony." When Louisburg was taken on July 20 Montcalm tried to bar the way. But he was left alone, at the head of his little troop, augmented, it is true, by some valiant Canadians, and he died, a hero, at Quebec on September 13, 1759. He left the command to the Marquis de Vaudreuil, who could do nothing against the numbers of his enemies and was obliged to surrender Montreal. . . . It was a fatal blow to France's colonial enterprise and her maritime commerce.

The English raid the French coasts.

They take Montreal.

At Versailles, Bernis, who was appointed Minister for Foreign Affairs in June 1757, sued for peace or at least an armistice. He had " a beautiful dream," he wished to interrupt the war and only begin it again when they had " better actors and better concerted military plans." He found himself confronted with Madame de Pompadour who wanted war and intended to have it ; everything gave way before her. He had against him also Maria Theresa, who was more anxious than ever to avenge her defeats. Thereupon Bernis resigned ; the Comte de Stainville, recently created Duc de Choiseul, replaced him. This diplomatist had just served his apprenticeship as Ambassador at Rome and Vienna. He justified both the confidence and favour of the King.

Bernis.

Choiseul was an ugly man, but the defects of his face were forgotten in the brilliancy of his wit. He came of an eminent family of Lorraine, and had married a daughter of Crozat the financier. With her he received an immense fortune which enabled him to live as a great noble.

Duc de Choiseul.

His wife, a charming, gentle, and charitable woman, assisted his rise not only by her wealth, but by her grace and her qualities of heart and head. Choiseul's retinue had never been surpassed by any minister. All courtiers and all foreigners who had been presented were admitted to his house. He held his receptions at one o'clock and dined at two ; no matter how many visitors were present, all were invited to dinner. There was always one great table with thirty-five covers, and a second was prepared in case of need. A servant counted the guests as they arrived, and as soon as the number exceeded thirty-five the second table was made ready.

President Hénault has left a portrait of this splendid and intelligent minister, who " among the pygmies of the reign was something of a great man." After enumerating his virtues —frankness, vivacity, tact, and courage—he asks : " But had he then no faults ? Oh, yes ! Love of pleasure—he does not deny himself. He gives much time to it, as well as to making his court to the King, whether at supper or the gaming table. Obviously, this is so much time lost to business. But his friends reply that M. de Choiseul is able to use for these distractions the time which other ministers are compelled to devote to understanding a subject or to making up their minds. His wit and talents enable him to economize the hours which less active and less penetrating minds find all too short."

Choiseul's first diplomatic achievement was the third Treaty of Vienna, signed on December 30, 1758. It gave complete satisfaction to Maria Theresa, who was assured of the assistance of a hundred thousand Frenchmen. Besides this, her subsidy was doubled and she was promised that peace should not be signed until Frederick had restored Silesia. Choiseul forgot to demand a return for these assurances, or assistance of any kind in the struggle with England. In this he was at one with Louis, whose attitude was absurdly disinterested. The Czarina Elizabeth subscribed to this treaty and pledged herself, at Choiseul's instigation, to bring the enemies of France and Austria " to the terms of a just and reasonable arrangement."

In course of time Choiseul secured an unique position : he was in charge of three departments, Foreign Affairs, War and the Navy. He presided over each in turn, but on resigning he chose as his successors nonentities who would allow him to retain complete control, though it must be admitted he did not wait until he occupied any particular ministry before interfering with it. He was responsible for the new project of an invasion of England in 1759. The scheme was rather bold than **French Navy destroyed.** practical, considering the condition of the French fleet and the vigilance of the English. The Havre squadron was bombarded and burnt. The Toulon fleet succeeded in passing the Straits of Gibraltar, but was checked on reaching Lagos. Part of the Brest fleet, commanded by the Marquis de Conflans, was wrecked on the sand-banks of Belle-Isle-en-Mer, and what was left was annihilated by Admiral Hawke. Thus the last French ships were gone, and Berryer, the Minister of Marine, put up all the munitions of war remaining in the arsenals to auction. Thereupon Choiseul thought of opening negotiations with England through the mediation of Russia. He met with a certain amount of opposition from Louis, and his efforts were checked by an event of considerable importance, by which all calculations were upset. Frederick was defeated by the Russian army under Soltykoff at Künersdorff, some leagues from Frankfort on the Oder, on August 13, 1759. The King of Prussia fled from the field of battle and wrote some days later : " What a calamity ! I will not survive it. The consequences of the battle will be worse than the battle itself. I can see no way out, and in truth I believe that all is lost." Of an army of forty-eight thousand he had scarcely three thousand left, and he thought of committing suicide. It was the right moment to dictate peace ; the Russians wished it, but the Austrians were set on the re-conquest of Silesia. Soltykoff waited for Daun for five weeks and finally retired on East Prussia. Frederick recovered his spirits : " I thought they would march on the Rhine," he wrote, " but they take the opposite course. . . . I am announcing to you the miracle of the House of Brandenburg." This miracle was due to the procrastination of Daun, who revenged himself by capturing Dresden and driving the Prussians out of Saxon territory ; it was the greatest success of the campaign.

The French armies of the Rhine and Main did nothing of

note in this year.   The former was commanded by the Marquis de Contades, nominated by the Pompadour in place of the Comte

Contades. de Clermont, the latter by the Duc de Broglie, who managed to check Ferdinand of Brunswick at Bergen on April 13, and took Cassel and Minden.   Contades joined Broglie and disputed the command with him.   As a result there were bickerings and rivalry between the generals, and the early success was neutralised.   Brunswick took advantage of this and recaptured Minden on August 1.   The only benefit derived was the recall of Contades, whose disgrace was accentuated when Broglie was raised to the rank of Marshal : " the latter passed over the heads of more than a hundred of his seniors."   The *Amsterdam Gazette* announced the news in the following words : " This dignity has in his case preceded years of service and seniority.   If it had been the immediate reward of the brilliant victory of Bergen, the enemy would certainly have not been able to inflict the fatal day of Minden on us."   Maria Theresa gave Broglie the title of Prince of the Holy Roman Empire.

Misfortune followed misfortune.   In 1760 another rivalry arose between the Maréchal de Broglie and the Comte de Saint-

Broglie and Saint-Germain. Germain, causing them to separate.   Saint-Germain returned to Paris after his victory at Korbach on July 10, leaving sincere regrets behind him.   He was replaced by the Chevalier du Muy.   The latter was defeated at Warburg. He lost many men in conducting his retreat, and people said "the retreat of Monsieur de Saint-Germain caused many tears, and that of Monsieur de Muy much blood to flow."   The Marquis de Castries was charged by Broglie with the defence of Wesel ; he checked Ferdinand of Brunswick's son at the Abbey of Klosterkampen on October 15 and 16.   The battle is cele-

D'Assas. brated for the heroic death of the Chevalier d'Assas and Sergeant Dubois.   These two officers were on the extreme left of their regiment, which was gradually being driven back though maintaining its fire.   A comrade said that they were making a mistake and were firing on Frenchmen. D'Assas and Dubois went forward to find out if this were true.   Immediately the English surrounded them and threatened them with their bayonets, promising them their lives if they

184

would be silent. They cried out, " Shoot, it is the enemy," and fell, victims to their lofty courage.

The Russians and Austrians had important successes at Landshut and Glatz. The troops of Tottleben, Tchernychef and Lacy entered Berlin and remained there as masters of the capital for three days. But Frederick had his revenge at Torgau on November 3, and held his own in Saxony.

The next year similar vicissitudes continued until the defection of France's allies hastened the end. Soubise managed to overcome the intrigues against him and was made General-in-Chief, an appointment which caused widespread discontent. The Comte de Broglie distinguished himself at Cassel, but his father, the Marshal, was defeated at Villinghausen on July 16, owing to his haste to fight before the arrival of Soubise, of whom he was jealous. Then followed skirmishes round Cassel, where Ferdinand of Brunswick was trying to separate the two French armies, and so to prevent them doing anything. In Silesia the Austrian General, Laudon, took Schweidnitz and the Russians seized Kolberg and all Pomerania as far as Stettin. Frederick **Death of** was, as he said, " at his wits' ends " when suddenly **the Czarina** the Czarina Elizabeth died on January 5, 1762. **Elizabeth.** This catastrophe caused the immediate cessation of hostilities on the part of the Muscovites. The new Czar, Peter III, Elizabeth's nephew, was a Prince of Holstein and therefore more German than Russian. His first act was to offer to ally himself with Frederick, and he signed first a truce and then a peace. Tchernychef's army, which was occupying Silesia, now fired on its former allies the Austrians : " Russia's defection was in fact a desertion." These new friends, so quickly gained, saved Frederick and his kingdom ; " it was restored to him by the death of a woman and supported by the power which had been most anxious for its destruction. . . . On what do human things depend ? " adds the King of Prussia ; " the smallest events affect and change the destiny of empires."

As early as 1759 Choiseul undertook secret negotiations to bring about peace with England, but he had to deal with Pitt, **The Family** who was determined on war to the knife. The **Compact.** English minister, however, lost the support of his own compatriots and was overthrown. With the help of

Charles III of Spain, Choiseul's negotiations were successful
and resulted in the celebrated alliance known as the Family
Compact, signed by all the reigning princes of the Bourbon
dynasty in France, Spain, the Two Sicilies and Parma,
on August 15, 1761. For some time, in spite of temporary
quarrels, the interests of the two crowns, according to a time-
honoured expression, had been *effective*. The Treaties of Madrid
and Fontainebleau had sealed friendly understandings; but
since 1748 and the accession of Charles, King of the Two Sicilies,
to the throne of Spain (1759), the Bourbon power had extended.
Choiseul had the credit of giving definite form to the alliance
for which preceding generations had laboured, and more especially Louis' eldest daughter, Louise-Elisabeth, Duchess of Parma,
who had died at her father's court in December 1759. The
Family Compact affected Austria, for the policy of Maria Theresa
was bound up with the policy of Louis XV. France, Spain, and
Italy on the one side and Austria on the other now formed the
great Catholic league conceived by Louis XIV. But the
Jesuits, who would have been all-powerful in the seventeenth
century, had nothing to do with this; they were, on the contrary, almost simultaneously driven out of the different allied
monarchies and their order was even dissolved by Clement XIV
in 1773.

The time had come for negotiations, and Choiseul considered
that the Family Compact would serve to strengthen his hand
Peace in treating for peace. He was about to take up
Negotiations. the Ministry of the Navy, intending to bring new
life into it, to repair the losses of the squadrons, and to show
England that France was not abandoning her maritime power.
Unfortunately, the effect was only moral.

The campaign of 1762, carried on during the progress of
diplomatic negotiations, need not detain us, since the belligerents
Treaty of were awaiting events. The preliminaries of peace
Paris. were signed at Fontainebleau on November 3,
1762, and were followed by the Treaty of Paris on February 10,
1763, which put an end to the colonial war between France and
England. France retained nothing in North America except
the town of New Orleans. In the Antilles she ceded three of
the contested islands and only recovered St. Lucia. In Senegal

she only kept the Island of Gorea, and in Hindustan the five factories she still possesses. She gave up Minorca.

Amongst the most important losses was the entire empire of Canada and its dependencies. The only trace of French supremacy left in that beautiful country is the soft speech of the early settlers of the seventeenth century.

The Treaty of Hubertsburg on February 13, 1763, settled continental affairs and conceded Silesia to Frederick; there **Treaty of** was no other change in the map of Europe; the **Hubertsburg.** King of Prussia alone had what he desired. In return he promised his vote at the Diet of the Empire to the Archduke Joseph, Maria Theresa's eldest son, thus giving up the idea of obtaining the Imperial throne for a Protestant dynasty.

Austria found consolation in arranging the affairs of the East with Prussia and Russia; she was to have a share in the partition of Poland, and no longer needed to consult her ally of the Seven Years War.

France remained alone and impoverished, to contemplate the loss of her army, her navy and her colonial empire; she had fought not for herself but first for the King of Prussia, and then for the Queen of Hungary and Empress of Germany.

Shortly after the conclusion of peace Louis' statue was placed on a pedestal in front of the swing bridge of the Tuileries. The **Statue of** fête was dull, spoilt by the bad weather and by **Louis XV.** the gibes which were levelled at the monarch himself, who, indeed, was little worthy of apotheosis at such a time.

PRINCIPAL SOURCES. *Mémoires* of Duclos, Bernis, Rochambeau; Frederick II., *Mémoires de non temps* and *Correspondance*; *Correspondance du Général-Major de Martange*, published by Charles Bréard, Paris, 1878; Camille Rousset, *Le Comte de Gisors*, from the papers of Clermont and the Military Archives, Paris, 1888; *Correspondance secrète de Louis XV*, published by M. E. Boutaric, 2 vols., Paris, 1866; Macaulay, *Essay on Clive*; Rambaud, *Histoire de Russie*, Paris, 1879; Albert Vandal, *Elisabeth de Russie et Louis XV*, Paris, 1882; Soulange-Bodin, *Le Pacte de famille*, 1894.

CHAPTER XIV

CHOISEUL
1764-1770

Death of Madame de Pompadour. The parties. Expulsion of
the Jesuits. The affair of Père La Vallette. The Dauphin and
Choiseul. Death of the Dauphin. His character. The influence
of Marie-Josèphe of Saxony. Death of the Dauphine. Sadness
of the Queen's last years. Madame du Barry. The affairs of
Brittany. Trial of the Duc d'Aiguillon. Resistance and exile of
the Parliament. The Maupeou Parliament. Choiseul and Madame
du Barry. The cabal. Spain and the Falkland Isles (*Iles
Malouines*). The *lettre de cachet*. Choiseul exiled to Chanteloup.

A HEAVY task was awaiting the successor to this careless
and indolent monarch, who, though not lacking in intelligence, interested himself only in what was foolish
and futile. A diplomat, the Baron Le Chambrier, for many
years Frederick's *chargé-d'affaires* at the Court of Versailles,
has left a remarkable description of Louis XV. He shows us
the King not daring to trust himself in the affairs of government,
" persuaded that he knows nothing about them, and that his
ministers, if they are to do their duty properly, must not be
hampered by his opinions, nor contradicted in any of their resolutions." This was written in 1751 and what was true then was
much more so twenty years later, when a woman with complete
confidence in herself, governed France and had the satisfaction
of seeing foreign courts apply to her for support and protection.

It was supposed that if Madame de Pompadour disappeared
the ever-dependent Louis would submit to some nobler yoke.

In March 1764, business was suspended, ministers and
courtiers were agitated, and nothing was thought of but the
Death of
Madame de
Pompadour.
illness of the Marquise. Which was to win—the
Queen's party or the King's ? Would the
Dauphin, aided by his mother, gain some in-
fluence ? Would the King return to his family ?

188

CHOISEUL

On April 15 Madame de Pompadour died, fully conscious, and with admirable courage. General de Fontenay, the King of Poland's ambassador, has given a very graphic account of her last day : " This lady never made the slightest movement of anger or impatience during her illness. Two hours before her death her waiting-women wished to change her clothes. She said to them : ' I know that you are very skilful, but I am so weak that you could not help making me suffer, and it is not worth while for the short time I have to live.' The same day she dictated to Collin, her steward, a document four pages long, which is said to be very well composed. Seeing that he was much affected as he wrote she begged him not to grieve. . . . Many people whose fortune she made naturally mourned her death, but she was above all respected by all the poor of Paris, Versailles, and her own domains, and generally in every place where she has dwelt."

The King was greatly distressed. It was believed that he was quite unmoved, while all the time he restrained himself before the world and hid his grief under a mask. He pretended to be callous, said the Duc de Croÿ. Did Louis say the often-quoted words : " The Marquise will have very bad weather," when he was watching from his windows the coach that bore the remains of Madame de Pompadour from Versailles to Paris ? If the story be true, it does not prove the King's indifference ; it shows him still concealing his grief under this frivolous remark, while following with his eyes to the last her who had for nearly twenty years monopolized his existence.

The religious party hoped that the Marquise's death would help them to gain ground. But a blow, long **Expulsion of** foreseen, was struck at them when the Jesuits were **the Jesuits.** definitely expelled in November 1764.

For some time past the Order had been attacked by the Jansenists. Under Louis XIV they had detractors in Pascal, Saint-Simon and Noailles. They were accused of ruling the majority of the Catholic countries behind the scenes ; the education of the young was almost entirely in their hands, since the numerous colleges they had founded were superior to all others ; they had made their way into the Courts as confessors to the Royal families, and they had had a great influence in important diplo-

189

matic negotiations. Their power extended even to America and the Far East, where they made their religious, political and commercial conquests with as much zeal as ability.

They laid themselves open to legal attacks. Père La Vallette, the Superior of the Martinique Jesuits, had been a victim of **Père La Vallette.** English piracy, in 1755, before the declaration of war. His ships were captured and the industrial settlement that he directed was ruined. He failed for three million francs. Some merchants of Marseilles were among his creditors. The missionary was tried and condemned ; he appealed to his colleagues, but they refused to assist him, and reproved his proceedings on the grounds that they were forbidden by the statutes of the Order. The Parliament of Paris interfered, and ordered the General of the Jesuits, Père de Sacy, to pay what was owing to the Marseilles creditors, amounting to over a million livres. Not satisfied with this victory, the magistrates, who had Jansenist leanings, took action against the Society itself, and after an examination of its rules, decided that these contained principles which were inconsistent with monarchical laws and even with Christian morality. By a preliminary decree of 1761, Loyola's doctrines were condemned and the Colleges of the Fathers were ordered to be closed. The next year, in spite of the efforts of powerful champions, all the personal property of the Jesuits was sequestrated, and by 1764 the suppression was complete. Louis was for a long time undecided, but at last he gave way to Choiseul. According to the Bachaumont report the joy of the *bourgeoisie* and people at this suppression was " excessive and almost indecent." The Jesuits themselves confessed that the people were stoning them with the stones of Port-Royal, the destruction of which had been their work.

The Queen, the Dauphine, the Dauphin and the Royal princesses were dismayed ; they now had to choose the directors of their consciences from among the secular clergy. As for the King, he tried to make a joke of it and speaking of his confessor he said, laughing : " I shall not be sorry to see Père Desmarets an Abbé." This frivolity was one of the most remarkable features of Louis' character, apparent even on the gravest occasions.

The Dauphin took an active part in the defence of the Jesuits, but he could do nothing against a minister whom he irritated by his importunity. Choiseul once said to him in the heat of argument : " Perhaps, Monseigneur, I shall one day **The Dauphin** be unfortunate enough to be your subject. But **and Choiseul.** certainly I shall never serve you." This was reported to Louis, who said to the Dauphin : " My son, you have so offended Monsieur de Choiseul that you must forgive him everything." From this conversation it is easy to gather what an abyss separated the King from the son he was to lose so prematurely. The last years of the reign were to be saddened by a succession of deaths.

First, the Dauphin died at Fontainebleau on December 20, 1765, in the thirty-seventh year of his age. He lingered six **Death of the** months with pulmonary tuberculosis, and during **Dauphin.** that time his faithful companion, Marie-Josèphe of Saxony, mother of the three last Bourbons, nursed him continually. The Dauphin was little known, but after a life of retirement he was obliged " to be ill in public." * Every evening he received the first gentlemen of the chamber, the great officers and the young noblemen attached to his person. He conversed with them and seemed quite cheerful. In the morning, after mass, he allowed every one to see him, even the ambassadors ; he asked their pardon for the inconvenience he was causing them by obliging them to remain at Fontainebleau. His words, actions, and sentiments all proved how solid were the qualities of his heart and mind. He was extremely considerate of all who tended him. To the Queen's first physician, who sat up with him one night, he said : " Ah ! my poor Lassone, I am distressed at the bad night I have given you. Go and lie down ; you must be very tired."

He excused himself in amusing ways. To the Duc d'Orléans he declared : " I must be tiresome, as from time to time I enter- **His character.** tain you with a little agony." It was necessary for the Dauphin to die to be appreciated, and the public without exception expressed sincere regret. Philosophers enlarged on his liberal ideas and summed up his policy in his favourite phrase : " *We must not persecute.*" They loved to repeat this maxim, forgetting that they never acted up to it, but only replied on it for themselves. Diderot delighted in recalling

* Proyart.

the fact that the Dauphin had disapproved of the expulsion of Rousseau, saying that the author of *Émile* was a man to be pitied, not to be persecuted. Voltaire liked to think that the Dauphin read Locke during his last illness, and knew the tragedy of *Mahomet* by heart. " If this age," he concluded, " is not that of great talents, at least it is that of cultivated minds."

It is well known that the prince used to say in speaking of what he intended to do later : " *If I ever have the misfortune to ascend the throne.*" He would say also that the people would be his family and himself their head.

Nine days after the death of her husband, the Dauphine wrote to her brother Xavier : " September 29, 1765. God has willed that I should survive him for whom I would have given a thousand lives. I hope that He will grant me the grace to spend the rest of my pilgrimage in preparing myself, by sincere penitence, to rejoin his soul in Heaven, where I do not doubt he is asking that same grace for me."

The Dauphine Marie-Josèphe.

The poor wife only lived a year after her husband ; she was the victim of her devotion and succumbed to the same malady. She left three sons who were all destined to reign, and two daughters, Clotilde, who became Queen of Sardinia, and Elisabeth, the unfortunate sister of Louis XVI. During her widowhood, she took charge of the education of these children and wrote instructions for the Dauphin. Her chief preoccupation was to prepare him for his future, and she told him to meditate on this phrase from the *Mémoires* of Louis XIV : " Nothing is so dangerous as weakness, of whatever kind it be." Did Marie-Josèphe foresee how much need her son would have of such advice ?

The Dauphine's constancy gained the affection of her father-in-law ; Louis admired in others the virtues he did not possess himself. In the year 1766 he was under the beneficent influence of the Dauphine. The Princess could have had the power of the Marquise, and have brought back the King to his family, had she consented to a reconciliation with Choiseul. But on this point she was inflexible ; she would sacrifice everything rather than insult the memory of her husband. She was able, however, to obtain some favours ; amongst other things

CHOISEUL

her confessor Nicolay, Bishop of Verdun, was promised the
succession to Cardinal de Luynes, Archbishop of Sens, though
his attitude to Choiseul's policy was definitely hostile. Little
by little the Dauphine would have gained more power ; she
would have won the heart of the King ; he would have
allowed himself to be ruled by this new Egeria. But Marie-
Josèphe died on May 13, 1767, and Choiseul immediately
regained all the favour he had lost. Louis no longer had
anyone in his family capable of guiding him. His daughters
were not clever enough to take up Marie-Josèphe's part, and
the Queen, who had never counted for much, was now relegated to her oratory, preparing to die as virtuously as she had
lived.

To the great grief of Marie Leszczynska her father died in
February 1766. Stanislas was really the only being in the world
Death of King who truly loved the Queen ; his letters to his
Stanislas. dear daughter are almost masterpieces of paternal
affection. To quote one of these short notes would be to quote
them all, for the subject is always the same, though the expressions differ a little. They come straight from the heart and
sing the praises of the imcomparable *Maryneczka*. The same
refrain recurs all through in phrases such as the following :
" You are my *alter ego* and my thoughts are as near yours as
my heart, since I live only for you. In the name of God, keep
your dear health, it is all I care for in the world. I am not
young, yet I would fain be three months older to make myself
younger by the pleasure of seeing you. I kiss the tears that
you are shedding, those little pearls which are jewels of infinite
value to me." It is thus that poetry is unconsciously created.
Stanislas would have been very much astonished if he had been
told that these pages, yellowed with age, were the most sincere
and harmonious things in his life.

The death of her father on February 23, 1766, following on
that of her son, was a cruel grief to the Queen. "As for me,"
Death of the wrote Marie, "I am sad, and shall be so all my
Queen. life. My only consolation is the thought that
those I mourn would not wish to return to this vale of tears,
as the *Salve* calls it."

Soon after this the Queen began to languish ; she was ill

for months, and fell into a pitiable decline. Like a forsaken flower, she died on June 24, 1768. " This estimable princess," said the Duc de Croÿ, " had harmed no creature and deserved the regrets of the nation. The goodness of her character could be seen in her most gracious countenance." Here we recognize the model of La Tour, whose delightful portrait in the Louvre perpetuates her calm smile and reveals the resignation she showed both as woman and as wife.

At this time the King encouraged his daughters to believe that he would for the future submit to no new yoke. For two years he gave proofs of a certain consideration for the queen and showed some signs of remorse. When Lassone came to tell him that Marie was no more, he went to the death-chamber, approached the bed, and kissed the forehead of his hapless and forsaken wife. But he soon forgot the lesson he had learnt in the advent of Madame du Barry.

Blind to the seriousness of the revolts which were threatening the royal power, he entrenched himself in his divine right, and never realized how that right was discredited.

As an example of his folly, he allowed the Duc d'Aiguillon, the Governor of Brittany, to receive incoherent orders and to **The La Cha-** get himself into the most difficult position. He **lotais affair.** annoyed the magistrates of Rennes by the unjustifiable arrest of La Chalotais, the Attorney-General, who was famous for his struggle against the Jesuits, and for his opposition to the vacillating policy adopted with reference to Breton affairs. From province to province, the various States claimed their prerogatives and clamoured for the liberty of the people. The Parliament of Paris unanimously declared itself in favour of the Breton cause. With a sudden assumption of authority Louis commanded the Parliament to be silent, saying that he could not tolerate the formation " of an imaginary body " which believed itself the mouthpiece of the country and the guardian of principles. But the Duc d'Aiguillon was obliged to retire when the Parlementaires of Brittany refused to deliberate and the judges refused to try La Chalotais. He came to Court in April 1770 to vindicate himself and to solicit the judgment of his peers. Louis ordered his trial. There was considerable curiosity to see whether the evidence given would justify the accused and show the contradictory nature of the instructions he had received. The Parliament sat in the King's presence, at Versailles itself. But there were only two sittings, after which Louis stopped the proceedings, removed and destroyed the documents, and declared the Duc d'Aiguillon immune from all further charges. The Parliament returned to Paris and declared the Duc " deprived of his rights and privileges as a peer until he should be purged of the suspicions which stained his honour." The King quashed this decree, and at the instigation of Chancellor Maupeou he issued an edict fulminating against the Parliaments, their insolence and their illegal claims. He asserted that he held his crown " from God alone " ; that the legislative power belonged only to him, supreme and undivided ; that there were limits to the right of remonstrance, and that the magistrates could " set no limits to his authority." This edict **The Parliament** was issued on September 7, 1770. It was duly **in exile.** registered, but the Parliament refused to reassume its functions. Consequently, it was sent into exile. The provinces made common cause with Paris and everywhere the agitation was extreme. " All heads were turned," wrote Besenval, " and even in the streets one heard cries about injustice and tyranny." The Counsellors of State and the Masters of Requests replaced the former magistrates and represented the former Parliament.

Maupeou, the author of the edict, was little concerned at the public excitement, the animosity aroused by this *coup d'état* and the opposition of the princes of the blood—Orléans, Chartres, and Conti. Elated by his victory, he took no heed of the fact that he was the object of public contumely and that the King, his accomplice, had become extremely unpopular. In themselves his ideas are defensible. But they owed their existence rather to a hatred of the Parlementaires than to a true love of justice, and this is a sufficient justification for the strictures of history.

Such was the origin of the new Parliament, which was supported by the celebrated triumvirate: Maupeou, Abbé Terray, Controller-General, and the Duc d'Aiguillon, who soon replaced Choiseul. All three were staunch supporters of Madame du Barry.

Choiseul had succeeded Bernis owing to his support of Madame de Pompadour. He was overthrown because he did **Choiseul** not seriously take into account the favourite who **and Madame** replaced her. He could not believe that a woman **du Barry.** of such humble origin would succeed in having herself presented at the Court, and would establish herself both in the Court and in the Council. Madame du Barry, aware of the contempt with which Choiseul and his friends treated her, resolved to overthrow him with the assistance of Aiguillon. The cabal easily found grievances against the Minister. The ground of the accusations was an unsuccessful attempt he had made to found a settlement in Guiana. He had spent thirty million *livres* in sending out twelve thousand people from Alsace and Lorraine ; but practically all of them had died of fever. He had taken the loss of the French colonies to heart and had hoped to retrieve it ; for the result he was only partially to blame.

Choiseul was responsible for the successful conquest of Corsica, which became French in 1769, though it must be admitted that the undertaking was costly and was naturally resented at a time when there were loud cries of poverty. His enemies did not lose the opportunity of making this a grievance against him, hiding the fact that but for Choiseul's prompt action, England would have deprived France of that valuable Mediterranean island. They also disregarded the twelve years in which the minister had successfully maintained the new Austro-French policy, his attempts to strengthen the army and navy, his defence of Poland against the menace of a Russian invasion, and his schemes to avenge the Seven Years War. At least he had commanded the respect of the neighbours across the Channel.

With this object—always an important one to him—he had decided in June 1770, on his own initiative, to encourage **Spain and the** Spain to provoke England in a dispute which had **Falkland** arisen between the English Governor of the Falk- **Islands.** land Isles and the commander of two Spanish frigates, who had come to protest against the illegal occupation of the Archipelago. A war of such importance would have created a diversion. Choiseul would have been indispensable and would have escaped his enemies. But Spain hesitated to support him, and he was obliged to reveal part of his secret and come to the Council with a request for credits. Terray granted what he required, wishing to drive him into a corner and force him to throw off all concealment. Choiseul declared that while he hoped that peace would be maintained, he was prepared for all eventualities. Terray had no intention of paying the promised eight millions; and in consequence the embarrassment of Choiseul was assured. The cabal was triumphant and accused the minister of being responsible not only for the war which was then imminent, but for the inexcusable resistance of the Parliament. He defended himself against these accusations; less easily in the case of the first than in that of the second, and this made Louis waver. The King did not know whether to support Choiseul, who asserted that the exile of Maupeou and Terray would make the Parlementaires quite amenable, or Maupeou, who assured him that he would deliver the kingdom for ever from their remonstrances. But the complaints of the favourite, supported by her partisans, became louder at the critical moment. Louis yielded to the solicitations of the " dame," as she was called in diplomatic dispatches, but he hesitated for a considerable time. He kept the *lettre de cachet* intended for Choiseul on his person for three days, fearing it should be prematurely delivered. He knew of what his circle was capable.

On Christmas Eve, December 24, 1770, in the morning, the Duc de la Vrillière, who under the title of the Comte de Saint-Florentin had frequently discharged similar missions during the past forty years, entered the Duc de Choiseul's apartments and handed him the King's note : " I order my cousin the Duc de Choiseul to place his resignation of his office of Secretary of State and Superintendent of Posts in the hands of the Duc de la Vrillière and to retire to Chanteloup * until the receipt of further orders from me." The instructions given to La Vrillière included the following : " But for Madame de Choiseul, I would have sent her husband to some other place, because his estate is in his own Governorship. But he will behave as though he were not there, and will only see his family

Choiseul dismissed.

* Chanteloup is close to Paris.

and any others I permit to visit him." This was a delicate concession.

The event caused a sensation in Paris and abroad. The Duke accepted his disgrace with courage and without affectation. His numerous friends hastened to his side, and there was soon a large number of coaches at the door of his house in the Rue de Richelieu. Many people came to write their names as a last proof of their esteem and affection " for the great minister whom France was losing." Never did disgrace do more honour to the victim.

His fall decided Charles III of Spain to make the sacrifices demanded by England to secure the maintenance of peace ; but the Parliament was sacrificed. Maupeou was master of the situation.

PRINCIPAL SOURCES. *Correspondances des agents diplomatiques en France avant la Révolution*, published by Jules Flammermont, Paris, 1896 ; *Mémoires* of Madame du Hausset , *Journal inédit* of the Duc de Croÿ (1718–1784), published by the Vicomte de Grouchy and Paul Cottin, 4 vols., Paris, 1906–1907 ; *Mémoires* of Bachaumont ; *Lettres inédites du roi Stanislas à Marie Leszczynska* (1734–1766), published by Pierre Boyé, Paris, 1901 ; *Correspondance secrète entre Marie-Thérèse et le Comte de Mercy-Argenteau avec les lettres de Marie-Thérèse et de Marie-Antoinette*, published by the Chevalier d'Arneth and M. A. Geoffroy, 3 vols., Paris, 1875 ; *Correspondance secrète inédite de Louis XV sur la politique étrangère*, published by M. E. Boutaric, 2 vols., 1866 ; *Mémoires* of Besenval, Georgel, Dumouriez, and Hardy ; *Mémoires sur la mort de Louis XV* by the Duc de Liancourt (in Sainte-Beuve, *Portraits Littéraires, III*) ; Sorel, *La Question d'Orient au XVIIIᵉ siècle*, Paris, 1878 ; A. Geoffroy, *Gustave III et la Cour de France*, 2 vols., Paris, 1867 ; Duc de Broglie, *Secret de Roi*, 2 vols., Paris, 1888 ; Flammermont, *Le Chancelier Maupeou et les Parlements*, Paris, 1883 ; P. de Nolhac, *Marie-Antoinette Dauphine*, Paris, 1878 ; Maurice Boutry, *Antour de Marie Antoinette*, Paris, 1906 ; Claude Saint-André, *Madame du Barry*, Paris, 1908.

CHAPTER XV

THE DEATH OF THE KING
1770–1774

Marie-Antoinette Dauphine. The Dauphin. Marie-Antoinette's strength of mind. Madame du Barry. The Princess de Lamballe. The "King's Secret." The Partition of Poland. Choiseul's intervention. How Maria Theresa yielded to political necessity. Louis' indifference. Maupeou's reforms. Goëzmann and Beaumarchais. Louis' conversation with Maupeou. The King falls sick. The intrigues of Madame du Barry's faction. The fourteen representatives of the Faculty. Louis criticized by the Duc de Liancourt. The Archbishop of Paris' intervention. Dismissal of the favourite. The last sacraments. The two processions.

IN the last year of his ministry Choiseul had witnessed the consummation of a marriage, for which he was chiefly responsible. On May 16, 1770, the Dauphin married Marie-Antoinette, Archduchess of Austria, the former being sixteen, the latter fourteen and a half years old.

An English prose writer, Edmund Burke, in his *Reflections on the Revolution in France*, perhaps best conveys to us the

Marie-Antoinette. poetic impression produced on the Court by this charming princess : " It is now sixteen or seventeen years since I saw the Queen of France, then the Dauphiness, at Versailles ; and surely never lighted on this orb, which she hardly seemed to touch, a more delightful vision. I saw her just above the horizon, decorating and cheering the elevated sphere she had just begun to move in."

Burke only saw the surface. A courtier, the Duc de Croÿ, who was extremely well informed as to all that happened at Versailles, describes the clouds which came to disturb the brightness of the heavens. " Madame la Dauphine," he wrote in his *Journal*, " is more and more of a success. Her face was the fairer for her graciousness ; she had charming words for every one, and her curtsies were so delightful that in a short time all were pleased. All said that she must be counselled to remain as she was and listen to nothing which would change her. But it was feared that it might be said that she over-did it, and that if she changed it would be the fault of those around her." These fears, so awkwardly expressed by de Croÿ, who was not so good a stylist as he was a psychologist, were only too well-founded.

It would have been natural that the Dauphin, in spite of his youth, should act as Mentor. But he received Marie-Antoinette coldly, he was heavy and ungainly, **The Dauphin.** morally and physically awkward. Caraccioli, the Neapolitan ambassador, wrote to his Court where Marie-Caroline, the Dauphine's sister, was reigning, that the prince was not handsome, nor had he any of the fine deportment of his grandfather, and that he showed himself " boorish and rustic to such a degree, that he seemed to have been born and educated in a wood, *selvaggio e rozzo a segno che sembra nato ed educato en un bosco.*" His judgment is echoed by well-informed contemporaries. However, Caraccioli did not fail to do justice to the Dauphin's moral qualities. He described him as simple and natural in his conversation, hating lying and flattery, without vanity or pride, austere from principle both as regards himself and as regards others, the friend of justice, and with an excellent heart in spite of his rough and harsh exterior. In this also the diplomat was not deceived. All that remained was to know if there were in Louis the makings of a king and of a statesman. Marie-Antoinette did not find the support she required, and she complained that her husband had only one ruling taste—hunting—and to this he sacrificed both his private and his public life. He was not a lovable husband, and he did not prepare himself to reign.

Louis received his granddaughter graciously. Marie-Antoinette replied to his affectionate sentiments with a formal **Court Parties.** respect. She did not love her grandfather. She was hurt to see a Du Barry occupying the first place at the Court and exacting its prerogatives. Mesdames her aunts naturally persuaded the young Dauphine to humiliate the King's friend by not condescending to speak to her. Maria

Theresa, according to Mercy-Argenteau, the Austrian ambassador at Paris, entreated the Dauphine to be less uncompromising, and to make some concessions ; this was politically expedient at this time, when the fate of Poland was about to be decided with the utmost secrecy, and Maria Theresa was about to betray her friend and ally, the King of France. But this queen of unassailable virtue could not have grasped the extent of the scandal at Versailles. It might also be questioned whether she really understood her daughter.

Marie-Antoinette did not hesitate between the two counsels, but she followed neither to the letter. Both from pride and **The Dauphine** modesty she adopted a line of conduct which **and Madame** could satisfy no one but herself. On one or two **du Barry.** occasions she made some trivial remark in the favourite's presence, but she did not directly address her, and she did not encourage a reply. The Dauphine had plenty of character, and she showed it in these delicate circumstances. Her attitude towards Madame du Barry proves her virtue and candour ; she did what was demanded of her by her mother and Louis, but no mud stained her ermine robe, no defilement polluted it.

Marie-Antoinette became more or less isolated, sorely though her warm heart needed affection. Unhappily she could find **The Princesse** no consolation in her mother's letters. The stern **de Lamballe.** and imperious Maria Theresa estranged her daughter with her unreasonable demands and ceaseless scoldings, admonishing her to read and engage in intellectual studies little suited to the life at a Court where balls, plays, excursions, the chase, and riding, were indispensable distractions to the young princess in her isolation. Marie-Antoinette soon conceived a warm attachment for Madame de Lamballe, widow of the son of the Duc de Penthièvre. In the society of this charming woman she forgot the tyranny of etiquette and the already growing cares of politics for which she had little taste. There were many complaints that she would not abandon herself with more complaisance to the parties who fought over her. At this time her aunts gave her the name of " the Austrian." That campaign of calumny which pursued her to the foot of the scaffold soon began. The first attacks came from her family circle.

Maria Theresa was obliged to resign herself to her daughter's wilfulness in refusing to allow herself to be led. The Empress found consolation in congratulating herself that the incompetence of the new minister, the Duc d'Aiguillon, who was incapable of grasping or deciding matters of business, would allow the Court of Vienna to pursue secret negotiations with Russia and Prussia without fear of interruption. Louis had always been interested in Poland, and it was thought that now her fate was to be decided he would defend her. But he remained indifferent.

For a long time the King had had his *Secret*; he had been carrying on a private correspondence with the object of check-**The King's** ing the encroachments of the Czars. These pro-**"Secret."** ceedings, which were unknown to all, even the favourites, had captivated and amused him, but he eventually gave up the pastime, like a wearied gambler. He had pursued this policy for nearly twenty years, taking pleasure in countermanding the official instructions of his ministers. He sent money to his Polish dependents, often considerable amounts, with the object of influencing the royal elections, originally in favour of the Prince de Conti, and then, when the latter quarrelled with Madame de Pompadour, in favour of the Saxon succession. Ultimately he came to wish simply for the freedom of the Poles and a return to national kings. But he did not allow himself to be disturbed by the schemes which were nullifying all his monetary sacrifices, and his often skilful manœuvres. As one of those who were in his confidence wrote : "We cannot but admit that the partition of Poland could not have taken place but for our negligence in preventing its inception, and the insufficiency of the means we adopted to arrest its course."

The original idea of this spoliation came from Frederick. At the instigation of France the Turks had declared war on **The Partition** Russia in 1769. Hereupon, Frederick, who was **of Poland.** disturbed by the progress of Russia, made proposals for an alliance with Joseph II to maintain the neutrality of Germany. Austria, on her side, was alarmed when the Russian armies invaded Moldavia and Wallachia, and she prepared at once to assist the Turks. This would have meant a general war in the north, for the Prussian King, who was tacitly

bound to the Czarina, asserted that he could not abandon his ally.
A conference was held between Frederick and Joseph at Neustadt
on September 3, 1770, where it was decided that it was time for
mediation, and that the intermediaries between Russia and the
Porte should be themselves. France was entirely disregarded.
Maria Theresa at first disapproved of her son's policy, but in
the end she gave way in spite of the treaties which bound her
to Louis XV.

In the meantime France was sending Poland money, and
even some adventurous officers like Dumouriez and Vioménil.
The latter were handicapped by the undisciplined troops placed
under their command. With such support it was difficult
to resist the Russians, for under pretext of protecting the
members of the Orthodox Church, Catherine had invaded
Polish territory, and was already treating it as a conquered
country. At this juncture Choiseul, who was favourable to
the Polish cause, was dismissed, and his successor, the Duc
d'Aiguillon, made a point of not following his predecessor's line
of policy. Aiguillon essayed a reconciliation with Prussia,
and Prussia made pretence of listening in order to put him
off the scent. He became the laughing-stock of European
diplomatists, and was considered to be "blundering along in
the dark."

The negotiations between the three Powers progressed,
though Maria Theresa still hesitated. Seeing this, Frederick
Maria Theresa sent one of his confidants to Vienna to win over
and Poland. the Empress' confessor. She allowed herself to
be persuaded that she ought to yield "for the good of her soul."
"Thereupon," wrote the King of Prussia, "she began to weep
terribly. Meanwhile the troops of the three Powers entered
Poland and took possession of their shares, the Empress weep-
ing all the while. But of a sudden we discovered, to our great
surprise, that she had taken far more than the portion allotted to
her, for she wept and took the while, and we had much difficulty
in persuading her to be contented with her share of the cake.
That is what she is." The French ambassador at Vienna,
Prince Louis de Rohan, who was later to play a part so fatal to
Marie-Antoinette in the affair of the necklace, confirms this
description of the Empress' attitude. "I have seen," he said,

" Maria Theresa weep over the misfortunes of oppressed Poland. But this princess, who is an adept at the art of not allowing her real feelings to be known, seems to have her tears under control ; with one hand she holds her kerchief to wipe them away ; with the other she seizes the sword with which to carve her third share." This letter was confided by Aiguillon to Madame du Barry, who had it read to her during a supper, as though it were addressed to herself. Marie-Antoinette could never forgive Rohan for having ridiculed her mother and for having chosen the favourite, as she thought, for such a confidence.

The actual Partition Treaty was signed on August 5, 1772, when each of the spoilers had already taken possession of the Polish provinces allotted to them. The event was received at the Court at Versailles with indifference. Its significance was not understood, in spite of the remonstrances of the Comte de Broglie, head of the secret diplomatic service, who said : " The position of Poland as regards France and all the other Powers of Europe is that of a member cut off from society, a citizen deprived of his natural rights, reduced to slavery, civilly dead, and in consequence no longer possessing either property or personality in the social order. Such in the political order is the fate of a nation once called illustrious, which has had the son of its king proclaimed Czar at Moscow, received the homage of Prussia at Warsaw, and delivered a proud and humbled Austria under the walls of Vienna."

Louis replied : " From the distance of five hundred leagues it is difficult to aid Poland. I could have preferred that it should remain intact, but I can give it little more than my good wishes." Through all he adhered to the Austrian alliance, and did not want war.

" I must not speak of Polish affairs before you," he said to the Dauphine, " for your relatives are not of the same opinion as ourselves." With this astonishing levity the King allowed French influence to be destroyed by this unjust dismemberment where the strong triumphed in defiance of the law of nations. The decadence of Turkey and the anarchy of Poland had excited the covetousness of the Powers ; but they preferred to agree rather than fight with one another. " Their rivalry," says Sorel, " was the cause of their alliance, but the alliance did not make the causes of their rivalry disappear. On the contrary, it gave them a new stimulus, and the only effect of the treaties of St. Petersburg and Warsaw was to add to the Eastern question another which was more urgent, more serious and more menacing still—the question of Poland. If it had been possible to stop at the treaties of 1772, the Partition would have ranked not only as a lucrative, but as a skilful and politic stroke. But history does not stop. Facts once established bring their inevitable consequences, and as a lasting revenge of right against might, wrongful deeds and immoral treaties find their echo in the inextricable embarrassment which results from them."

The dismemberment of Poland mattered little to Louis. The internal affairs which troubled the end of his reign left **Louis'** him equally unmoved. The Maupeou Parliament **indifference.** excited contempt and ridicule and alienated many who were faithful to the ancient liberties of the Parliaments. "The King in the midst of his own Court," said a diplomat (the Chevalier d'Eon) with some justice, "had less power than an advocate at the Châtelet." The great evil was that the ministers of the time, such as the Abbé Terray, the Duc d'Aiguillon and the Duc de la Vrillière, found the heavy task laid on them beyond their powers.

Maupeou established superior councils, or purely judicial tribunals, in Paris and certain provincial towns. Litigants were **Maupeou's** able in this way to find judges in other places **Reforms.** besides the capital and to save a great deal of expense. The Chancellor also decreed the abolition of the sale of offices, and the gifts to the judges, but these reforms produced fresh abuses. If offices could no longer be bought, they were too often obtained by arrangement. Meanwhile Maupeou was overwhelmed with satires. But nothing did so much damage to his authority as the attacks of Beaumarchais in his famous quarrels with Goëzmann, a counsellor of the new Parliament. The latter was accused of having yielded to offers of bribes in a suit brought by the future author of the *Barbier de Séville* against the Comte de la Blache, heir of Pâris-Duverney. Madame Goëzmann had accepted a sum of money, and when the action was lost, had refused to return it in full. In four brilliant documents full of wit and spirit but also, unfortunately, of bad taste, Beaumarchais brought his cause before the bar of public opinion. He secured the condemnation of Goëzmann and his wife, but he himself was censured by the court, and on the day on which judgment was delivered, February 26, 1774, princes, gentlemen, and ladies of quality came to write their names at the house of the brilliant controversialist. The affair caused general indignation. A play upon words found popularity and was passed round Paris: " Louis Fifteen has established the new Parliament, fifteen louis (the sum in question in the suit) will destroy it." The King himself in the end was amused by the incident; according to his custom he spoke of this scandal as though some one else were governing, and he were an enlightened dilettante. The conversation he had with the Chancellor was reported everywhere.

" Well, well, your Parliament is getting itself talked about; it seems that this Goëzmann is a bad character who must be got rid of."

" Sire, that must not be attributed to me, he came from M. le Duc d'Aiguillon."

" Yes, but they say there are others."

" That may be so, Sire; it must be so even : the new Parliament is a youth sowing his wild oats. It will behave wonderfully later."

" They said that this Parliament would not take. It is taking well; it is taking with both hands."

Louis was trying to remedy the harm by making jokes; he retained Maupeou who showed himself so skilful in frustrating attacks. But a very serious thing occurred to decide the Chancellor's fate.

Towards the end of April the King who was taking a holiday at Trianon "felt himself troubled with pains in the **Illness of the** head, shivering, and lumbago. Either his fear of **King.** declaring himself ill, or the hope that exercise might do him good led him to refrain from altering the arrangements that he had made the evening before." He went to the hunt, returned in the evening to the Trianon, and placed himself in the hands of Madame du Barry and Laborde, his body-servant. He had a bad night. Lemoine, the first physician in

ordinary, thought that Louis, who was always inclined to fear
death, was exaggerating his sufferings. The first surgeon, La
Martinière, abruptly ordered the King to return to Versailles,
and had the royal family warned. They were at last permitted to
see the invalid for a short time. Suddenly he became worse.
He was bled twice ; a third bleeding was proposed, and it was
certain that Madame du Barry would be sent away. The young
woman tried to postpone the evil moment and was supported
by her ministers. The palace was full of intrigues ; those
in power tried to keep their places by hiding the truth. Louis
now thought only of himself and the fourteen representatives
of the Faculty. "He would have liked," said the Duc de
Liancourt, "to augment their number. He made all fourteen
feel his pulse six times every hour. And when any of this
numerous Faculty were not in the room he called for them so
as always to be surrounded by them, as though he hoped that
with such satellites, illness would not dare attack His Majesty."

On April 29 the doctors noticed red marks on the King's
face and diagnosed small-pox. The Dauphin and his brothers
Small-pox were forbidden to come near the King. The
diagnosed. King's daughters refused to leave their father,
thus defeating the intriguers by their filial piety, though their
devotion was foolishly ridiculed. The Duc de Liancourt as
Grand Master of the Wardrobe witnessed the King's last days,
and has left an uncompromising account of them. He gives a
grim reason for the little effect " the conduct of Mesdames, which
was so worthy of respect," had on the Court and Paris. He
said in very plain words, " that the object of their sacrifice did
not deserve such abnegation," forgetting that he was speaking
of a father. " The King was so debased and so despised, especially the latter, that nothing that could be done for him could
possibly interest the public. What a lesson for Kings ! They
must know that though we are obliged to give them marks of outward respect and submission, if we are forced to judge their
actions we avenge ourselves for their power over us by despising
them profoundly when the object of their conduct is not our
welfare, and does not deserve our admiration. Indeed, we
did but judge the King as he was judged by all his kingdom."

The next day there was a crowd at Versailles. On May 1,

the Archbishop of Paris, himself very ill, went to the King and found there Madame du Barry, who immediately retired. Louis, who did not know from what he was suffering, told the Prelate to withdraw. For the next few days there was considerable difficulty in preventing the Archbishop, who had taken up his abode in Versailles, from entering the Palace. The King seemed better. He was in full possession of his senses, and spoke "in his ordinary tone of voice." He was so well "that it seemed very much as though he would have a wonderful recovery, and that there would be no change, to the great dismay of Paris." Madame du Barry's circle was triumphant. But they were soon to lose all hope. Besenval tells us that " the crowd of rogues, intriguers, and spies," with which the King's courtiers had peopled Versailles, began to be filled "with great alarm." It was impossible to hide from Louis any longer that he had small-pox. He had to realize that this was serious for a man of sixty-four. At last he spoke to his favourite : " Now that I know my condition, I must not have a repetition of the Metz scandal. If I had known what I know now, you would never have entered. I owe my-**Madame du** self to God and my people. Therefore you must **Barry dismissed.** go away to-morrow. Tell d'Aiguillon to come and speak to me to-morrow at ten." The King arranged with the minister for her departure, and in the afternoon of May 4, Madame du Barry went to Rueil, accompanied by the Duchesse d'Aiguillon, who had offered her hospitality in her country house. About six o'clock the following conversation took place between Louis and Laborde.

" Go and find Madame du Barry."

" She has gone."

" Where has she gone ? "

" To Rueil, Sire."

" Ah, already ! "

In lucid moments he thought only of this woman. He had meant, said the Duc de Croÿ, " to put her in safety somewhere where he could find her again if he wanted her, to spare her the insults which had been offered to Madame de Châteauroux at Metz, and if it should come to the last sacrament, to have no obstacle." He forgot to summon his confessor, who was waiting in an adjoining room and waited there for two days more. The Archbishop of Paris and the Cardinal de la Roche-Aymon, the Grand Almoner, were also watching. On May 6, they were able to say a few words to the King who answered : "I cannot at present ; I am unable to put two ideas together." Mesdames were in a cruel position ; they were afraid of alarming their father, and did not dare to interfere.

At last, in the night between the 7th and 8th, Louis asked for his confessor, the Abbé Maudoux, and had several conversations with him. Then he summoned his grandchildren and made all arrangements for the eucharistic ceremony. Mesdames were to remain at the door of the room, the Dauphine and her sisters-in-law in the Council Chamber, the Dauphin and his brothers at the bottom of the staircase; the servants alone were to approach the dying man with the clergy. The Cardinal delivered an exhortation, and the King communicated. Then, going to the door of the room, the Grand Almoner addressed the Court which was assembled in the various apartments : "Messieurs, His Majesty charges me to tell you that he asks God to pardon him his offences and the scandal he has caused his people. If God gives him back his health, he will spend his time in penitence, in supporting religion, and in relieving his people." On which Louis said : "I should have liked to have had the strength to speak myself."

Last Sacraments administered.

There was a slight rally, and immediately Madame du Barry's *protégés* hastened to Rueil to give her the news and to assure themselves of her favour.

But suddenly the King's sufferings came on again with renewed force, and he had difficulty in breathing. Abbé Maudoux now never left his side and exhorted him to be patient : "Offer your sufferings to God as expiation," he said, and Louis answered : "Ah, if that were enough it would be very little ! I would suffer more than that."

How totally he had forgotten such sentiments ! They returned to his dying lips like an echo of the words he had spoken at the beginning of his reign. Between these two periods Louis had stifled conscience in pleasure, trying to escape the boredom which enveloped him like the shirt of Nessus, and

o

neglecting all his duties, especially those expected of the most Christian King.

Extreme Unction was administered on Monday, May 9, with great pomp. The room and the little camp-bed, with its curtains drawn back, were lighted by candles held by surpliced priests. The King was heard to say *Amen* in a firm voice. In the midst of these bright lights Louis, exhausted with pain, looked as though he had an enormous copper mask on his face. It was like a " death's head."

Some of those present affected " more self-possession than was necessary," practically no one wept, and in general there

The two Processions. was " more etiquette than sentiment." In the marble court which led to the royal chamber people passed the night waiting for " the proclamation." The weather was fine. On the next day the park was filled with people walking about " as usual " and the cabarets were busy. In Paris there was, if possible, even greater indifference. Louis was still able to speak on the 10th. Then at three in the afternoon the death-agony began. Sixteen large state coaches harnessed with eight horses immediately took the royal family to Choisy in accordance with the protocol. In the Avenue de Paris there was a large crowd acclaiming the new King. This formed a contrast which made those who had watched the sad spectacle " understand the vanity of greatness." It was impossible to expose the body at Versailles or in the Louvre as was the custom. In the night between the 12th and 13th another procession, composed of three hunting coaches accompanied by guards and pages with torches, set out for Saint Denis. One of these funeral carriages bore the mortal remains of Louis XV, surrounded with quicklime and encased in three coffins, so great was the fear of infection. This funeral procession, said Besenval, was more like " the transport of a burden of which men were anxious to be rid, than the last duties rendered to a monarch." On the way drunkards sang and made indecent remarks.

Louis was his own judge ; he said in his will : " I have governed and administered badly, because I have little talent and I have been badly advised."

What could be added to so frank an admission ?

[The same sources as for the preceding chapter.]

FOURTH PART
LOUIS XVI

CHAPTER XVI

THE CORONATION
1774–*June* 11, 1775

Louis XVI's reception. The King and Queen's bounty. Maurepas returns to power. Dismissal of the Duc d'Aiguillon. Activity of the Choiseul party. Vergennes. Dismissal of Maupeou and his Parliament. Complaints of the Viennese Court. Beaumarchais' opinions. Turgot, Controller-General of Finance. His first interview with the King. The Corn War. The rising at Versailles. The Coronation. Enthronement ceremony.

LOUIS XVI was received as a saviour. Everything seemed to smile on this twenty-year-old monarch, whose honesty was well known. He was simple and charitable, ready to reform abuses, to look into the finances, **Accession of** and reduce the sinecures. Up to this time he **Louis XVI.** had had no part in the government, and his tastes had not lain that way. The announcement of his grandfather's death caused him to utter a cry of despair ; for he feared for his youth and inexperience : " It seems that the universe is falling on me," he said, " I am the most unfortunate of men ! God ! what a burden is mine, at my age, and they have taught me nothing ! " However, though he was unknown, much was said in his favour, even outside his own kingdom. " You have a very good King, my dear D'Alembert," wrote Frederick II, " and I congratulate you with all my heart. A king who is wise and virtuous is more to be feared by his rivals than a prince who has only courage." The philosopher replied : " He loves goodness, justice, economy, and peace. . . . He is just what we ought to desire as our king, if a propitious fate had not given him to us."

It became known that on May 20 he had received one of the most important dignitaries of the old Court unfavourably.

"Who are you ? " he said to this individual.

"Sire, I am called La Ferté."

"What do you want ? "

"Sire, I came to receive your orders."

"Why ? "

"It is because . . . because I am Steward of the *Menus*."

"What are the *Menus* ? "

"Sire, they are your Majesty's *Menus Plaisirs* (amusements)."

"My *Menus Plaisirs* are a walk in the park. I have no need of you." Whereupon Louis turned his back.

The new king sent two hundred thousand livres to the poor of Paris, and renounced the *Joyeux avènement** which had **Royal Bounties.** cost twenty million francs under Louis XV. He thought only of the public welfare, and nothing of his private interest. In the preamble to the first ordinance of his reign, he said : " There are necessary expenses which may be consistent with the safety of our States : There are others connected with the Royal Bounty, which may be susceptible of moderation, but which from long usage have become the subjects of prescriptive right, and therefore can only be subjected to a gradual retrenchment. Finally, there are expenses which concern our person and the ostentation of our Court ; in this case we can more promptly follow the dictates of our heart."

The Queen also renounced the *Droit de Ceinture* (The Right of the Girdle, *i.e.* purse) † though this, it is true, was much less important than the *Joyeux avènement*. This due was levied in Paris every third year, and originally consisted of three *deniers* on each hogshead of wine. It was afterwards increased and extended to other commodities, such as coal.

Louis and Marie-Antoinette were cheered as soon as they were seen. They took up their residence at the Meute (La Muette) and walked daily in the Bois de Boulogne, whither all Paris came in crowds to see them. One day the Queen, "fair as the day and full of grace," went there on horseback. She met the King on foot, in the midst of his people, without escort.

---

* Joyful Accession, a grant given the king at his accession.

† At this period women wore the purse at the girdle.

She dismounted, and Louis ran up to her and kissed her on the forehead. The crowd clapped their hands, and the King thus encouraged gave her " two sound kisses." The applause was re-doubled. " They assure me," said the Duc de Croÿ, " that it was one of the most touching episodes that has ever been seen, the more so since it is long since the nation has been able to give vent to its tender feelings."

The enthusiasm was loyal and sincere. Louis XVI tried to deserve it in all good faith. He " barricaded himself with honest folk," and surrounded himself with men who would have the courage to remind him of his duties. The same idea guided him when he came to choose his ministers. He thought of Machault, whom Louis XV had always regretted, after sacri-ficing him to Madame de Pompadour. But he was not free, and others thought for him. Irreproachable as his intentions were, they had little stability. At this first serious trial he was caught in a trap ; the Comte de Maurepas returned to power.

Maurepas had been disgraced in 1749 for having written some insolent verses about the Marquise. He was born in 1701,

Recall of Maurepas. and had occupied the position of Secretary of the King's Household since 1718, so was said to have been a minister " since childhood ! " He did not lack wit—in fact he had too much of it—nor did he lack intelligence. But he used these gifts to settle even the most serious questions with *bons mots* and epigrams. His chief pleasure was to ridicule others. He had considerable experience of Court life, but that was not enough to fit him to direct the affairs of the monarchy. He was deceptive. Louis thought he had found the honest man he sought, when in reality he had laid his hand on one destined to be disastrous to the State.

There was, perhaps, no reason why this old man should have been appointed save, indeed, the persistence of the Duc de Richelieu and the Duc d'Aiguillon, to whom he was related. These latter, with the assistance of the Abbé de Radonvilliers, a former Jesuit and under-tutor to the Dauphin, secured Madame de Narbonne, lady-in-waiting to Madame Adelaïde for their cause. Madame Adelaïde, as " favourite daughter of the late King and aunt of the new monarch, was in a position of influence in the early stages." She joyfully undertook the intrigue and probably dictated the following letter which her nephew wrote to Maurepas : "In the just grief which overwhelms me, with all the nation, I have great duties to fulfil. I am the King. The name imposes many obligations, but I am only twenty years old, and I have not the experience I need. The certainty I have of your probity and of your profound experience of affairs induces me to beg you to assist me with your counsel. Come then as soon as possible."

The existing Ministers, who had assisted at the last moments of Louis XV, were as a matter of precaution in quarantine, and the intrigues were thus made all the easier. Maurepas returned from exile at Pontchartrain, and was received at Choisy on May 13. He was content to have the title of Minister of State without a portfolio, and to play the part of Mentor.

The Duc d'Orléans, and with him Monsieur (the Comte de Provence) the Comte d'Artois, and all the princes of the blood thought they would be admitted to the Council, but they were disappointed. This ostracism annoyed the King's brothers, and for a while it was feared that the Duc d'Aiguillon would remain in power. But the Queen desired the fall of the Minister, and, in spite of Maurepas, he was compelled to send in his resignation on June 2. Marie-Antoinette was begged by Mercy to overcome her antipathy, but she refused. The Austrian ambassador would have liked to see d'Aiguillon in charge of Foreign Affairs until the definite conclusion of the Turkish hostilities. Fears were also expressed at Vienna as to the possibility of Choiseul's recall, for his supporters were active about the Queen. He would, it was thought, have interfered with the new Austrian policy : his "restless and turbulent head," said Joseph II, "might have thrown the kingdom into the utmost difficulties." Marie Antoinette failed to secure his reinstatement, but consoled herself by receiving Choiseul at Court with all the grace and charm of which contemporaries speak.

Dismissal of D'Aiguillon.

"Monsieur de Choiseul," she said, "I am charmed to see you here. You made my happiness, and it is right that you should witness it."

The King who was somewhat embarrassed, found nothing to say but: " You have got fatter; you have lost your hair; you have become bald."

Choiseul received.

He could not pardon the Minister for having intrigued against his father, the Dauphin.

Choiseul understood that he was not likely to regain favour. He soon returned to Chanteloup, after having experienced indications of his continued popularity; he received thousands of visits during the three days he spent at Versailles and Paris.

With reference to these two events in which the Queen had played a part, Maria Theresa said: " I have noticed that in spite of the deference that she * seems to show to your counsels, she goes her own way in matters on which she is prejudiced. I was struck by her attitude in the D'Aiguillon and Choiseul affairs, and especially by the revengeful spirit she displayed to the former."

The Duc d'Aiguillon was replaced in the control of Foreign Affairs by the Comte de Vergennes, who had distinguished himself as ambassador at Constantinople and was then at Stockholm. It seemed a good appointment, since Vergennes was prudent and safe, and had a respect for sound traditions. He was known to be slow in making up his mind, but full of zeal and devotion. " The Comte de Vergennes," said Choiseul some years previously, " always finds arguments against anything which anyone proposes to him, but never has any difficulty in carrying it out. If we asked him for the Grand Vizier's head to-morrow, he would write that it would be a dangerous business, but he would send it to us."

Vergennes.

Maurepas congratulated himself on this choice which was inspired by Maupeou; every change in the Ministry was anxiously watched by the latter in his own interest. The appointment of the Comte de Muy to take D'Aiguillon's place at the head of the War Department was also satisfactory to the Chancellor. The Comte de Muy had been a friend of Louis' father and was one of the heads of the religious party who supported the new Parliament. Maupeou also had the satisfaction of knowing that Turgot, the new Naval Minister, had always been opposed to the old Parlementaires. It now only

* Marie-Antoinette.

remained to replace La Vrillière and Bertin, who had no influence, and Terray, although the latter was ready enough to support any party. But Maupeou had to fight the Palais Royal party, the Duc d'Orléans, and his son, the Duc de Chartres (later Philippe Egalité) who offered him a strenuous opposition. These princes had refused to be present at the ceremony of the "Catafalque" at Saint Denis, and to listen to the funeral oration of Louis XV, giving as their reason that they did not wish to meet the new Parliament. Consequently they were exiled from Court. The news of their disgrace excited much feeling among Parisians, with whom the old magistrates had always been popular.

On the evening of July 26, the King and Queen, accompanied by Monsieur, Madame, and the Comtesse d'Artois, passed through Paris on their way back from Saint Denis, where they had been to visit their aunt, Madame Louise. They were very coldly received, a fact which they felt deeply.

Maurepas was vigilant; and on this occasion, he gave evidence of his powers of intrigue. Although Louis believed in **Maupeou dismissed.** Maupeou, Maurepas succeeded in persuading the King that to retain the Chancellor and his tribunals would cost him the love of his subjects. The Queen, at Maurepas' instigation, put in her word. He told her that Maupeou was the principal author of the calumnies which had been spread about her with the object of causing a quarrel between her and the King. She used all her power, which was already considerable, and Maupeou was exiled on August 24, 1744. The Chancellor said when he left : " The King wishes to lose his crown. Well, it is his to lose." Terray was dismissed on the same day. Everywhere it was said : " It is the Saint Bartholomew of Ministers," and the Spanish ambassador is reported to have answered : " Yes, but it is not the Massacre of the Innocents."

The next day was the Festival of Saint Louis, and there was great rejoicing in Paris. Maurepas was able to tell his master that the people had never celebrated August 25 so loyally. The manifestations were continued on the 26th. The new Parlementaires were hooted when they left the Royal audience, and in the evening effigies of Maupeou and Terray were hung at the gallows of Sainte-Geneviève.

Hue de Miromesnil, Chief President of the Rouen Parliament, was made Keeper of the Seals ; Turgot was transferred to the Controller-Generalship, resigning his former office to Sartine ; Lenoir accepted the post of Lieutenant of Police. In spite of the opposition of the clergy and nearly all the ministry except Maurepas and Miromesnil, the recall of the old magistrates was decided. On October 21 the King signed the letters of **The Parliament** recall, and the old Parliament was summoned for **recalled.** November 9. Three days after, Louis held a *lit de justice* in Paris : " Gentlemen," he said, " the King, my most honoured lord and grandfather, forced by your resistance to his repeated orders, did what his wisdom dictated in order to maintain his authority, and to fulfil his duty of giving justice to his subjects. To-day I am recalling you to those functions that you ought never to have abandoned. Realize the value of my kindness and never forget it. . . . I wish to bury all that has passed in oblivion, and I shall be much displeased if I see internal dissensions trouble the order and tranquillity of my Parliament. . . ." At this sitting the Advocate-General pronounced the words States-General. The King gave him an angry look. The Parliament treated the grace they were supposed to have received with arrogance and disdain. They retained the right of remonstrance, but lost some of their other privileges. As the King and Queen left the Assembly, however, they were frantically applauded by the crowd, which was bitter against Maupeou. The young sovereigns had need of popular applause, and they took it as a proof of gratitude, not foreseeing that gratitude would be short-lived, and that by making concession after concession they would lose their kingdom. The recall of the Parliament was an act of weakness, but the King was persuaded to it by interested advisers, and by the supplications of the Queen, who wished to regain the goodwill of Paris. The whole policy of Louis' reign was to " please " either one party or another. Louis had some of the ideas of a statesman, but could never carry them out. He always gave way to Marie-Antoinette, and by degrees regular coteries formed around her, eager to take advantage of the inexperience of the young princess and the weak character of her husband.

Contemporaries, and amongst them even Royalists, deplored

the situation. "The worst," said Croÿ, "is that it was seen that with a thousand things in his favour, with much good sense and a just mind, the King would allow himself to be led, and would not learn to govern or act on his own responsibility, and that in many respects things would be exactly as they were in the times of the late King."

From Vienna, where these events were followed with much anxiety and interest, Maria Theresa wrote that "it is in-comprehensible that the King and his ministers should destroy Maupeou's work," and an Austrian diplomat added : " Certainly nothing is more desirable than to re-establish order in the administration of Justice. But the Empress seems persuaded that the King of France could have arrived at this salutary end without re-establishing the old authority of the Parliaments, which has so often shaken that of the most Christian Kings."

Remonstrances from Vienna.

From the monarchic point of view Louis' error was great : "if the King had taken the firm resolution of maintaining the work of his grandfather," says the Duc de Lévis, " that resolution alone would have been sufficient to consolidate it." The tribunals would have been purified, and would have shone with their old lustre. The nation would in time have given them its complete confidence, and the Government would have freed itself finally from a recurring cause of trouble that, in fact, increased instead of diminishing, and ended by dragging down the Government in its own overthrow.

When Louis recalled the old magistrates he created the new force which made the Revolution and by degrees gained control of France. Beaumarchais foresaw it ; he wrote to Sartine on November 14, 1774 : " *It is scarcely credible that a king, twenty years of age, who might be supposed to have a great love for his new authority, should have loved his people to such an extent that he should give them satisfaction on so essential a point.*" The brilliant controversialist realized the double consequence of this recall of the Parlemen-taires—the loss of Royal power, and the birth of a new supreme authority. Turgot, " honest Turgot," disapproved of the back-ward step, fearing the opposition of the Parliament to the useful and healthy reforms he intended to propose.

Beaumarchais' Comment.

" Fear nothing," said Louis to him, " I shall always support you."

The King was sincere, and he thought he was master. He had the greatest confidence in Turgot. In vain people tried to warn him against the ex-Intendant of Limoges, and his dealings with the philosophers and economists. Louis took his inspiration from his father, the Dauphin, who said : " Duties of State and religious duties should not be mixed." He also remembered his father's reflection on Madame de Maintenon's animosity towards Catinat : " If Monsieur de Catinat did not know God, he was to be pitied, but as he knew his own business, an army should have been entrusted to him."

Turgot Controller-General. " Turgot is an honest man," Louis had said in the same spirit ; " that is enough." And he made him Controller of the Finances in the place of Abbé Terray.

A letter from Mlle. de Lespinasse to Guibert, written on August 29, 1774, tells of the King's first meeting with Turgot :

" Then you do not wish to be Controller-General ? "

" Sire, I confess I would rather have remained Naval Minister . . . but it is not to the King that I give my services ; it is to the honest man."

" You shall not be deceived," replied the King taking him by both hands.

" Sire, I must impress upon your Majesty the necessity for economy, and that you must be the first to give the example. Monsieur l'Abbé Terray has no doubt already told your Majesty the same."

" Yes, he has told me, but he has not told me as you have done."

Turgot represented the moral energy that Louis lacked, but his energy was not supplemented by power of action or any sense of moderation. Like all his contemporaries, Turgot voluntarily withdrew himself into the desert of generous ideas without taking any human contingencies into account. He was thought to be contemptuous of public opinion ; he had no knowledge of men, and reckoned neither with their passions nor with their vanities. He wished to do good, but he seemed determined to see it in his own system alone. His friends who defended him, made certain statements which justify some of the criticisms : " He was thought to be susceptible to prejudice," said Condorcet, " because he formed all his judgments by himself, *and public opinion had no influence over him.*" Dupont de Nemours also shows the weak side of Turgot's character. He asserts that he was at his ease only with his intimate friends, and seemed cold and reserved to all other men. Between these and Turgot there was always a feeling of " mutual discomfort," which did him harm on more than one occasion. Turgot felt that the task he had undertaken was a heavy one. In the celebrated letter he wrote on leaving the King's cabinet at Compiègne, he declared that he wished to avoid bankruptcy, increase of taxation, and loans. This first official document of the Controller is the key-note of the new administration. The problem that the Minister set himself to solve was to find a remedy for the poverty of the people : " Sire," he said, " you must arm yourself against your own kindness with that kindness itself. Consider from whence comes this money that you are able to distribute to your courtiers, and compare the misery of those from whom this money must be extorted, sometimes by the harshest of means, with the position of those persons who have the greatest claims on your liberality." Turgot seems to have had more knowledge of men than he was given credit for, when he said : " I shall have to struggle against the generosity of your Majesty and those who are dearest to you. I shall be feared and even hated by the greater part of the Court, by all who look for favours. . . . The people, for whom I am going to sacrifice myself, are so easily deceived that perhaps I shall incur their hatred. . . . I shall be slandered, and perhaps with enough appearance of truth to deprive me of your Majesty's confidence."

It was the " league against abuses " which was to cause his downfall. Yet he was confident, for he was a staunch Royalist **Policy of** and trusted to Louis' intentions. He threw him-**Turgot.** self into his work with great energy. Among the events which give the best insight into the new Controller's methods are the Corn War, which reveals him as an economist, and the King's Coronation, which shows his political side.

On September 13 the Council signed a decree ordaining

the removal of internal restrictions on the sale of corn. A law
to this effect had existed since Machault's administration in
1749, but it had not been put into force. Up to this time a
peasant had had to sell his corn at a market ; he was not
allowed to deal directly with his neighbour or his landlord,
and was forced to go to the needless expense of transport,
market-dues, and warehousing. These exactions offended the
people's sense of justice ; it was only profitable to the middlemen
and monopolists, and made the Government the arbiters of
poverty or wealth. The grievance was not to be remedied
without difficulty ; abuses still persisted ; but gratitude is due
to the monarchy which showed the way to reform. The decree
was immensely popular ; the examples of Sully and Colbert
were recalled, and it was said of Turgot :

Ton nom vole avec eux vers l'immortalité.*

The words *property* and *liberty* lent particular eloquence to
this edict. However, there were critics. Turgot was made a
subject for ridicule to the ironic refrain of *chansons, chansons.*

Le Grand Ministre de notre France,
Doué d'esprit, d'intelligence
  Et de raison,
En réformant notre finance,
Repandra pourtant l'abondance.
Chansons, chansons.†

The Controller needed support ; but which amongst the
different Estates could come to his aid ? He could not ask
such a sacrifice from nobility, clergy, Parliament, or financiers.
He only had the people and the King on his side.

Soon, even the people were deceived by the Minister's
enemies, and they abandoned him. In April and May 1775,
The Corn War. the dearness of corn provoked riots which were
known as the Corn War. Turgot was the victim
of the monopolists, who reduced the agricultural interest to
poverty, and then excited it to revolt. The first disturbances

* Your name takes flight with them to immortality.
† The great Minister of our France, endowed with wit, intelligence and
reason, whilst reforming our finances will spread plenty around. Songs !
Songs !

took place at Dijon. Immediately the Controller removed other restrictions on the sale of corn, and increased the facilities for importation in spite of his economic principles. This to a certain extent relieved the public distress. However, riots continued to be organized, and spread from Pontoise to Versailles. It was obvious that some one was behind them, and the Keeper of the Seals had reason to say in the Parliament : " The march of the brigands seems to have been organized ; their approach is announced ; public rumours state the day, time, and place where their acts of violence will be committed. It would seem that a plan has been formed to devastate the country, to intercept navigation, and to prevent the transport of corn on the high roads, in order to reduce the great towns, and especially Paris, to a state of famine." The rioters sacked the granaries and threw the corn into the streets and rivers, but on their way from place to place they behaved quietly, as if they were under orders. Many of them had gold and silver in their pockets. According to a contemporary account, they were evidently creating a fictitious misery in the midst of plenty.

On May 2, the army of " John Barleycorn " * was at the gates and even in the court of the Château of Versailles. The King, **Riots in Versailles and Paris.** protected by his military Household, ordered that there was to be no firing and no violent measures. The Captain of the Guard suggested that he should retreat to Choisy or Fontainebleau, but Louis wished to remain. From his windows he watched a hostile crowd for the first time ; he appeared on the balcony and tried vainly to speak ; then he went indoors in extreme dejection, shedding tears. Yielding to the cries of the populace, he proclaimed that bread should be two sous the pound. Thus he disowned Turgot and his reforms. " Seeing the King's grief, the courtiers seemed also to be affected, but beneath the surface it was obvious that many of them were not displeased at the event." The next day Louis intimated to Turgot " that he was afraid he had made a political mistake and he wished to remedy it." A police order forbade the sale of bread above the market price.

On the following day the organizers came to Paris, and similar scenes were renewed there. Some of the squares might

* " Jean-Farine."

have been those of a town taken by assault. About eleven o'clock in the morning all was calm again. There was a revival of confidence in Turgot's efforts, and in his co-operation with the King. But it was said that both of them were "unskilled in the wiles of courts," and it was feared that Louis "had not the courage of his virtues."

It was necessary to make an example. The judges of the Châtelet examined the persons arrested on the morning of **Trial of the** May 3, and condemned a "gauze worker" and **Scapegoats.** a master-hairdresser to be hanged in the Place de Grève for having taken part in the sedition. The blow would have fallen with more justice in higher quarters, if the organizers of the Corn War had been handed over to the tribunal. But the King refused to disclose their names, and the affair was hushed up by order. Perhaps the most violent of these organizers was the Prince de Conti, a personal enemy of Turgot. According to Marmontel, he would have been well pleased "to ruin this troublesome Minister, from whom he expected nothing, in the King's opinion." The name of Terray was also mentioned, and with him the Jesuits, the clergy, the financiers, and the English, but the immediate cause of the revolt is still doubtful. One thing was well known, namely, that Turgot was accused by powerful adversaries of wishing to cut down their prerogatives. However, the King was victorious, understanding and supporting his Minister.

Strong in this support, Turgot tried to make some alterations in the costly coronation ceremony which was to take place **Attempted** at Reims on June 11, 1775. He was frightened at **Economies.** the expense, and made some suggestions, as, for instance, that the coronation should take place in Paris, since Henri IV had been crowned at Chartres; but it was decided that Reims should not be deprived of its traditional fêtes. Turgot wished to modify the following phrase in the Royal Oath: "I swear . . . to exterminate entirely in my States all heretics expressly condemned by the Church." Louis XIII and even Louis XIV had eluded this formula by declaring that they did not include Calvinists among the heretics. The Revocation of the Edict of Nantes, it is true, still existed in the national archives, but it was very much impaired by the difference of the Regent and Louis XV, in spite of having been enforced on rare occasions. For a time Louis XVI seemed attracted by this spirit of toleration, but eventually he gave way to Maurepas and the clergy. At Reims, nevertheless, he mumbled some inaudible words when he came to this part of the oath.

Some of the formulæ, however, were abolished, but from motives very different from those of Turgot. " The patriots **The Coronation.** were annoyed at the suppression of that part of the ceremony in which the Monarch seems to ask the *consent of the people.* However vain this ridiculous formula may appear, it was considered a mistake, a very great mistake on the part of the clergy, for whom this pious spectacle seems to be made, to cut the other part entirely out of the ceremony and retain only that which primarily concerned themselves." Here, again, the eternal struggle between the political and the clerical power came into play. In his *Essai sur la Tolérance*, Turgot insists that these two powers should not be confused, and should each remain in its own sphere. He deplored the fact that the same doctrine could have produced the Saint Bartholomew and the League, " alternately putting the dagger into the King's hands to kill the people, and into the people's hand to assassinate the king."

These details are necessary to a correct understanding of the philosophic movement and the forernnuers of the Revolution. **The Enthronement.** But it must not be supposed that the nation had forgotten its loyalty to the monarchy, for that loyalty was still strong and vigorous except in the case of certain reformers, such as Voltaire and D'Alembert. All the love which the people felt for their King was shown at the coronation. It had lately become the custom to greet the King whether in the theatre or in the street with cheers and applause ; and now at the time of the enthronement, near the end of the long ceremony, when the great door was thrown open, and even the people without were able to see the King ascend a throne placed in the centre of the screen, loud cheers were heard in the close outside, and even in the interior of the cathedral itself. The people thronged in ; birds were set free, singing as they soared, harmonies which were soon drowned by the trumpets, the firing of muskets, and the joyful peals of the bells in the town.

THE CORONATION

Louis had been wearied by the interminable ceremony, and had found his crown heavy and uncomfortable, but when he heard the shouts and the noise he began to share the general emotion. He was now robed in all his royal splendour ; he wore the great violet mantle, ornamented with fleurs-de-lys and lined with ermine, and he held the sceptre and hand of justice. The cathedral glittered with gold and jewels beneath the light of countless candles. Majesty was present both in symbol and in reality at the moment when its representative was thus acclaimed.

" I know," said the Duc de Croÿ, " that I have never felt such enthusiasm ; I was astonished to find tears in my eyes. . . . **Emotion of** The Queen was so overcome with pleasure that **the Queen.** her tears flowed in torrents. . . ." Marie-Antoinette tells of this day in a letter to her mother, in which she speaks of her emotion and of the enthusiasm of their subjects both " great and small " at the sublime moment when Louis XVI ascended the throne of his ancestors.

PRINCIPAL SOURCES. Besides most of the works cited in Chapter XIV, the *Mémoires* or *Correspondances* of Voltaire, Marmontel, Mlle. de Lespinasse, Jacob-Nicolas Moreau, Augeard, Weber, Dupont de Nemours and Madame Campan.—Correspondence attributed to Metra ; Abbé Baudeau, *Chronique secrète de Paris sous Louis XVI*, in *Revue rétrospective*, III ; *Souvenirs et Portraits* of the Duc de Lévis ; Abbé Proyart, *Louis XVI, jugé par ses vertus* ; Droz, *Histoire du règne de Louis XVI*, 1859 ; Condorcet, *Vie de Turgot* ; Foncin, *Essai sur le ministère de Turgot*, 1877 ; P. de Nolhac, *La Reine Marie-Antoinette*.

CHAPTER XVII

THE QUEEN'S SURROUNDINGS
1775–1776

Marie-Antoinette and Choiseul. The affair of the Comte de
Guines. The Princess de Lamballe, Superintendent of the
Queen's Household. Joseph II reprimands his sister. The
Sovereign's family life. The King's brothers. Their wives.
The royal aunts. The Queen's friends. Madame de Lamballe.
Madame de Polignac. Besenval, Adhémar, and Vaudreuil.
Favours granted to the Polignacs. Songs and satires. Portraits
of the Queen by Walpole and Tilly. Intrigues against Turgot.
The Edicts. Retirement of the Controller-General. Resigna-
tion of Malesherbes. The Comte de Saint-Germain and his
decrees. Maurepas' manœuvres. A monarchic crisis.

THE Queen tried to bring Choiseul back into power at
the time of the coronation. She congratulated herself on having obtained permission from the King to
interview the ex-minister, as she confided to the Comte de
The Queen and Rosenberg: "You will perhaps have heard of
Choiseul. the audience I granted Choiseul at Reims. It was
so much talked about that I do not doubt that old Maurepas
was afraid to go home and rest. You will, of course, guess that
I did not see him without speaking to the King about it, but
you cannot imagine what skill I employed so as not to appear
to be asking permission. I told him that I wished to see
Monsieur de Choiseul, and that I could not think which day would
be most convenient. I was so successful that the *poor man*
himself arranged the most convenient time for the interview.
I think I used a woman's power at that moment." This celebrated letter came into the hands of Maria Theresa, who sent
a copy of it to Mercy with this comment: "What a style!
What an attitude of mind! This only confirms my anxiety.
She [my daughter] is running straight to ruin, and she will be

lucky if in her downfall she is able to keep the virtues proper to her rank. If Choiseul becomes Minister, she is lost. He will take less heed of her than of the Pompadour, to whom he owed every-thing." Marie-Antoinette's brother, the Emperor Joseph II, sent her so violent a rebuke on this subject that Maria Theresa had it stopped, but the document has been preserved. His bitter reproaches refer to facts which must be noted.

It was decided that the Duc de la Vrillière was to retire. This Minister, an object of general contempt, was only supported by his sister, the Comtesse de Maurepas. He was the last repre-sentative of the Court of Louis XV, and had been in office for fifty-five years. The Queen had pressed Louis to send him away, since she wished to put Sartine in his place, but much to her displeasure Malesherbes, a friend of Turgot, was made Governor of the King's Household. The Queen, however, was satisfied on other points. At her instigation the Duc d'Aiguillon was definitely exiled to Gascony. "This departure was entirely my work," she wrote to Rosenberg; "the measure was full to overflowing; this dreadful man indulged in all sorts of espionage and evil talk." She extricated the Comte de Guines, **The De Guines** a *protégé* of Choiseul, who was French Ambassador **Affair.** in London, from a grave scandal. Guines was accused of using State secrets in order to gamble on the Stock Exchange, and of disowning his creditors to avoid paying his debts. To clear himself, he asked to be allowed to insert in his defence certain passages from his official correspondence. Vergennes and all the Ministers opposed this demand, saying that if they were to allow it no foreign Minister would ever dare make confidential communications to the Government. But the Queen supported Guines against D'Aiguillon who desired his ruin. In spite of the vote of the Council the King yielded to repeated requests and gave the ambassador the permission he desired. Here, as on more serious occasions, Louis allowed him-self to be led. He was sometimes obstinate, but never strong-willed. Guines won his case, which was tried by the Parlia-**The Princesse** ment in June 1775. The Queen gained another **de Lamballe.** victory by reviving the extravagant post of Super-intendent of her Household in favour of the Princesse de Lamballe, just when Turgot was finding extreme difficulty

229

in restoring order to the finances. The public grumbled; all these intrigues, exaggerated and wilfully misconstrued, greatly alarmed the Emperor. Consequently Joseph resorted to threats : " Why do you interfere, my dear sister," he wrote, " dismissing ministers, sending one back to his estates, giving office to this or that one, helping another to win his case, and creating a new expensive post at your Court ? Have you ever asked yourself by what right you thus intervene in the affairs of the French Government and Monarchy ? You, a charming young girl, thinking only of frivolity, your toilet, and your amusements all the day long, who do not read or listen to sense for one quarter of an hour in a month, who, I am sure, neither reflect nor meditate nor try to weigh the consequences of what you do or say ! The impulse of the moment is the only reason for your actions. The statements and arguments of your favourites win your credence and are your only guides." The Emperor, in this respect, touched the true source of the evil; people took advantage of the Queen, her inexperience, her kindness, and her desire to please.

The question of persons was the primary consideration in all the intrigues in which Marie-Antionette imprudently took part. She thus established a party at Court which used her as its tool, a secret ministry whose only principle was to secure places, sinecures, and reversions to the detriment of those who might have been of use to the State. Marie-Antoinette should never have allowed herself to play so dangerous a part.

Marie-Antoinette's position as Queen was, until 1778, as difficult as it had been as Dauphiness, and for the same reasons. **The Queen's youthful Frivolity.** The King, as always, was shy and undemonstrative ; Mercy complains that Marie-Antoinette " formed too poor an idea of the character and moral powers of her husband " ; but she was really an excellent judge. Tired of his coldness, she tried to spend her youth agreeably and to seek distractions. The husband and wife really only agreed on the subject of ceremony ; they both did their best to avoid it. Except for this single affinity, their tastes were opposite. The Queen loved dress, and social pleasures which she could enjoy with her intimates, cards, and amusements which were not spoilt by careful preparation ; she spent happy days far from the Court; at the Trianon, which had been a gift to her on the accession, she imagined herself a private individual whose mission it was to receive her friends, to do the honours to them, and to prepare charming and rustic surprises for their entertainment. She forgot that she had royal duties also, an error which her husband encouraged. She was pleasant and gracious with all the dignity of a queen. Louis was brusque and awkward; his natural clumsiness had caused his grandfather considerable disappointment. Marie-Antoinette sat up far into the night and got up late. The King worked with his ministers, but the pastimes which appealed to him were hunting and manual labour. Tired out by violent exercise, he became silent and taciturn and by no means an "evening man." They both tried to hide their little weaknesses; Louis was rather ashamed of his locksmith's work, and Marie-Antoinette of her passion for gambling. Sometimes she would put the clock forward so as to hasten the time when the sleepy King would go to bed, and the faro table could be brought out. She secretly bought diamonds, not satisfied with the jewels with which she was already loaded; her mother reproved her for it and told her her freshness was her chief ornament, but her taste for jewels was irresistible, and later it will be seen that her adversaries turned it into a deadly weapon against her. Such was their daily life. Nevertheless, Louis was captivated by his wife; he loved her as much as he was capable of loving anyone, but according to Mercy he feared as much as he loved her. Maria Theresa deeply regretted the situation at Versailles: " The King's kindness to her [the Queen] on every occasion, ought to make her respond with a perfect return, by giving up her dissipated life, which is so opposed to the King's character and tastes; I see with regret that although your remonstrances and those of Abbé Vermond [the Queen's reader] make some impression on my daughter, they are soon effaced by the suggestions of those around her and her own thoughtlessness." Louis, as King, had no more influence than he had had as Dauphin. Nor were his brothers in better case. The Comte de Provence was **The King's** gracious, learned, and clever, but he was also **Brothers.** conceited and crafty, and the Queen had been warned against this Court " Tartufe." In the depths of his heart he congratulated himself that there was no heir to the crown, and he built his hopes for the future on this circumstance. He was no more innocent than were his aunts of the scandal which was talked about the Queen. The Comte d'Artois was feather-brained and brilliant, and thus agreed better with his sister-in-law, whose tastes partook of the frivolity natural to her age. The future Charles X, at this time but lately married, was far from serious, and only thought of amusing himself in a princely fashion, throwing money away, and satisfying his most extravagant whims, while scarcely attempting to pay his creditors. He was the *enfant terrible* of the family. Sure of herself, Marie-Antoinette had an instinctive hatred for vice, as she had proved on her first arrival while Louis XV was still living, but she thoughtlessly allowed herself to be led by her brother-in-law into unfortunate amusements, the balls at the opera and the little theatres, and although all that could be said against this was that the King took no part in it, even that was too much.

The wives of the two princes were of the House of Savoy, and were very jealous of their sister-in-law's charm ; they held **Their Wives.** themselves aloof. Their Italian character was not trusted. The Queen who longed to assure the dynastic succession, was naturally envious of the Comtesse d'Artois, happy in the possession of sons, and she suffered a good deal in consequence. Mesdames, the royal aunts, had " little heads," and it was impossible " to put anything reasonable into them."* They did not love Marie-Antoinette, because her marriage was Choiseul's work. They had wanted a Princess of Saxony for the Dauphin. Their advice met with no attention, and tired of useless intrigue, Mesdames went into a retreat whence they only appeared on rare occasions to make disagreeable remarks which were of no effect. The real intimates of Marie-Antoinette were found elsewhere. The Queen had made certain ladies her friends and confidantes, sometimes with little consideration, as might be expected from a girl only twenty years old. Her chief desire was to escape the moral solitude which overcame her even in the midst of pleasures and fêtes. Her graciousness, which was even more marked than her beauty, made her seek and evoke the sympathy which she could not find in her family circle.

* Duc de Croy.

She chose her friends because they were charming, and attached them to her because they were unhappy. She wished to make them happy, but unfortunately in so doing she worked her own ruin.

The Princesse de Lamballe, her first friend, was a Carignan and cousin to Madame and the Comtesse d'Artois. She married, **Promotion of** in 1767, the Prince de Lamballe, son of the Duc **Madame** de Penthièvre and a princess of Modena, but she **de Lamballe.** was abandoned by her husband after five months and became a widow in May 1768. She had a position at Court when the Dauphine came to France. Marie-Antoinette made friends with this lovable creature with the melancholy, delicate face, and the childlike air. A poet represents her as embodying the three Graces, and adds :

> Il n'est qu'un point où vous et vos modèles,
> Douce beauté, ne vous ressemblez pas ;
> La volupté marche toujours près d'elles,
> C'est la vertu qui conduit vos pas.*

When she became Queen, Marie Antoinette wanted to create a post for Madame de Lamballe. She soon excited the jealousy of her ladies-in-waiting when they heard that the young widow was to be made Superintendent of her household. Her father-in-law, aided by Maurepas, who wished to gain the Queen's favour, carried this affair through and obtained for the lady a salary of 50,000 crowns, although originally it had only been intended to make it a third of that amount, 50,000 livres. The Duc de Penthièvres, who was a champion of etiquette, and had an eye to the main chance, insisted that the privileges of the post should be the same as they were for Mlle. de Clermont, Superintendent to Marie Leszczynska and last holder of the position, which had been suppressed in 1740. Louis and Turgot yielded, in October 1775, to the Queen's great joy. She had confided her hopes to Rosenberg : " The Maréchale de Mouchy is going to leave, so they say. I do not know whom I shall have in her place. But I shall ask the King to take advantage of the changes to make Madame de Lamballe

* There is only one point, in which you and your models, gentle beauty, are unlike ; voluptuousness walks alway near them ; it is virtue that guides your steps.

Superintendent. *Judge of my happiness! I shall make my great friend happy and I shall have even more pleasure from this than will she.*"

When we remember the sums expended by Marie de' Medici on the Maréchal d'Ancre, the astounding liberality of Louis XIV to Madame de Montespan and her descendants and to Madame de Fontanges, who had a stipend of 300,000 *livres* a month, Marie Antoinette seems moderate in the exercise of her power. The revenues of France amounted to 200,000,000 *livres*. It does not seem unpardonable to have revived the post of Superintendent, especially as the motive was goodness of heart and not vanity ; but the Court never made the slightest allowances for any of the Queen's actions. There were, however, other instances of the Queen's liberality which laid themselves more open to the bitter attacks made against them. It was surely unnecessary to expend 600 louis in paying the debts of the Comte d'Esterhazy, an Austrian by birth, who was domiciled in Paris. It was equally unnecessary to grant a widow's pension to the Comtesse de la Marche when that lady was only separated from her husband, and to give the Prince Eugène de Carignan, Madame de Lamballe's brother, a yearly salary of 30,000 *livres* and the command of an infantry regiment, especially since it caused complaints among the French officers.

Not content with the favour which had been conferred on her, the Princesse de Lamballe continued to make requests, and finally tired even the Queen. She aroused protests from all quarters, and was soon the centre of quarrels and dissensions. She complained to the Queen, who was irritated, and said she was badly served. " The Princesse de Lamballe, who is nearly always wrong," wrote Mercy, " is gradually losing ground with the Queen and I see the moment coming when Her Majesty will be filled with regret and find herself embarrassed at having re-established a useless post in her household."

Even before the appointment of the Princesse de Lamballe had been signed, Marie-Antoinette had found a new friend for **Madame de Polignac.** whom she conceived a great affection, an event which brought jealousy into the field. This friend was Gabrielle Yolande de Polastron, Comtesse Jules de Polignac. The family to which she had allied herself was much im-

234

poverished, but had counted among its representatives a celebrated Cardinal who had been a faithful servant of the House of France and the Catholic cause. The Comtesse, of whom there is a pleasing portrait by Madame Vigée-Lebrun, was a charming woman. " She had," said the Duc de Lévis, " the kind of head in which Raphael could combine intelligent expression with infinite gentleness. Others might excite more surprise or admiration, but one could never tire of looking at her." In our modern eyes Raphael's heads, though they are full of sweetness, perhaps lack intelligence of expression. The Comte de la Marck says practically the same as the Duc de Lévis and adds : " Never did anyone's demeanour express more modesty, reserve, and propriety than did hers."

The Queen had noticed Madame de Polignac at one of the summer balls about June 1775, and a close intimacy had sprung up between the two young women. " When I am with her," said Marie-Antoinette, " I am no longer a Queen ; I am myself." Henri IV had said practically the same thing. This intimacy, which lasted more than fifteen years, had greater influence than anything else on the Queen's future. Madame de Polignac had neither the wit, judgment, nor character to justify the speed with which she won the position of confidante, to the exclusion of all others at the Court. Yet she was the " depositary of all the thoughts " of Marie-Antoinette. The Austrian Ambassador was alarmed and foresaw the worst consequences from this " boundless confidence." Political aspirants did not neglect this open door ; the Queen was at the mercy of innumerable intriguers.

The Superintendent had the support of the Comte d'Artois, the Duc de Chartres (the future Philippe-Egalité) and all those Besenval, who composed the disaffected society of the Palais Adhémar, and Royal. Madame de Polignac's partisans were the Vaudreuil. Baron de Besenval, an indiscreet friend of the Queen, a man of wit, who loved " intrigue for intrigue's sake, even though it brought him nothing," and with him ambitious members of the *jeunesse dorée*, the Comte d'Adhémar, a pleasant singer, an excellent actor, a composer of elegant couplets, and Vaudreuil, the most important man of the group, behind whom Choiseul was concealed. This brilliant society met together at the house of the Princesse de Guéménée. The latter was a daughter of the Maréchal de Soubise, and was later to become the **Madame de** governess of the Children of France until her hus-**Guéménée.** band's failure caused her downfall. Outwardly, these evenings were easy social functions, but those present did not hesitate to interfere in affairs of State, to give the Queen interested advice, and in short to exploit her. They spoke with absolute freedom of all that was happening at Court ; they ridiculed those they wished to injure, laid traps for them, and practised every form of intrigue both small and great. It was at one of these evenings that Maurepas introduced himself to Madame de Polignac and told her of his desire to become Prime Minister, hoping that she would repeat his remarks to the Queen. Maurepas, who was always seeking his own advancement, was ready to sacrifice everything, even his most trustworthy colleagues, to his own ambition.

The three leaders of this party, Besenval, Adhémar and Vaudreuil, have been severely criticized by La Marck. None of them, he said, had any depth of judgment or exalted views, they were " people who were skilled in the artifices of the Court and nothing more." They did not possess " that power of observation which enables its possessor to grasp the events that are likely to have an important bearing on the future." This Polignac society was harmful not only to Marie-Antoinette but to the interests of the Monarchy itself. The wit, gaiety, distinction, and cleverness of the trio were deceptive, and cleverer people than the Queen might have been misled by them. Vaudreuil, in particular, gained a complete ascendency over Madame de Polignac, and found opportunity to satisfy his greed for favours.

The fair Comtesse was very susceptible to the handsome face and agreeable manners of Vaudreuil. To find an excuse for the scandal that began to be whispered, she declared that she was *above prejudices*. Her attitude towards religion was as doubtful as her moral standard. Lassone, the doctor, said one day to the Abbé de Vermond that he feared this intimacy might in the end affect the piety of the Queen. At first Madame de Polignac asked nothing for herself, though later she had her reward and became a duchess ; but her relatives, one after another, were benefited by reversions and offices, to the great disgust of those whose rank led them to count on reaping some of the harvest. The Rohans, Tessés, Noailles, Montmorencys and Civracs felt themselves aggrieved. In a few years the Polignacs had an income of nearly 500,000 livres. Two examples will suffice. Comte Jules de Polignac's father was well known for his stupidity, yet he was given the Swiss Embassy, because it was lucrative and got him away from Court, where his presence embarrassed his children. The Comtesse Diane de Polignac, sister of Comte Jules, was made lady-in-waiting to Madame Elisabeth, although the freedom of her conduct was likely to cause scandals.

The Queen's intimacy with her friend had the effect of increasing her aversion from ceremony, and this caused new subjects for complaint. It was said that the Court
Lampoons. only existed for a small and exclusive circle, that it was like a private house, where sympathy alone assured a favourable reception. A Queen of France owes herself to her subjects; she is bound to keep up the traditions, said the most indulgent of Marie-Antoinette's enemies. The most audacious songs, calumnies, and satires fell like rain on Paris, the provinces, and foreign countries. That the Queen did not spare her husband as a subject for her wit was well known. Some of the satires touch on this :

> La Reine dit imprudemment
> A Besenval son confident :
> " Mon mari est un pauvre sire."
> L'autre répond d'un ton léger :
> " Chacun le pense, sans le dire,
> Vous le dîtes sans y penser." *

La Marck, who knew the Court intimately and always spoke of the Queen with respect, deplored this tendency, though he tried to palliate it. "It was," he said, "a mistake for a person in her position, since those around her knew her weakness, and sought to amuse her at the expense of others."

There came a time when she knew how she had been deceived, and at last gave up Madame de Polignac. When people ex-

* The Queen said imprudently to her confidante Besenval, "My husband is a poor fellow." The other answered lightly, "Every one thinks so without saying it, you say it without thinking."

pressed astonishment at seeing her seek refuge amongst foreigners, she said :

"You are right, but at least they do not ask me for anything."

She lived as in a dream with absolute unconsciousness and refused to believe the warnings of her mother or her fears for the future. Yet in the midst of her life of diversions she must have found little amusement. In her fear of ennui she made continual efforts to avert it, but with small success. Her brother, Joseph II, in other respects too hard a critic, at least understood the psychology of Marie-Antoinette on this point ; he wrote to Mercy with reference to her mania for gambling, which caused Fontainebleau to be compared to Spa : "Her craving for pleasure and her anxiety to find those who can procure it for her, happy, contented people, is the only cause of these disorders, for at heart my sister does not like gambling." All Marie-Antoinette received from her circle was the basest ingratitude. The King, the only person who was really faithful to her, by his indulgence and loving weakness encouraged her tastes and extravagance. Louis by degrees awoke from his torpor and fell a victim to her charm. But he did not rightly understand his duties ; he admired the Queen in passive silence. The niceties of this situation formed the main problem of the Royal Household, as Marie-Antoinette shows in a confidential letter : "If I needed a vindication," she wrote to the Comte de Rosenberg, "I could safely rely on you. As a matter of fact, I am ready to admit more than you would allow. For instance, my pursuits are not the same as the King's, for his are only hunting and mechanical pursuits. You will agree that I should scarcely look my best at a forge ; I could not be Vulcan, and the part of Venus would displease him far more than my present tastes, of which he does not disapprove."

Marie-Antoinette needed firm guidance. All she found was a husband anxious to please her and abashed before the attractions of her triumphant youth. Another foreigner, Horace Walpole, gives us an idea of her irresistible charm. His words are well known and are the more valuable in that they are disinterested : "It was impossible to see anything but the Queen ! Hebes and Floras and Helens

Joseph II's estimate of the Queen.

Walpole's Portrait of the Queen.

and Graces are street-walkers to her. She is a statue of beauty, when standing or sitting; grace itself when she moves. . . . They say she does not dance in time, but if so it is certainly the time which is at fault." * This is how Marie-Antoinette appeared at a ball given on August 22, 1775, on the occasion of the marriage of her sister-in-law, Madame Clotilde, to the Prince of Piedmont.

A second portrait, by a Frenchman this time, the Comte de Tilly, is less enthusiastic, yet it gives an impression of the same

De Tilly's Portrait of the Queen. charm : " The Queen was then (about 1777) at her best. I have often heard her beauty spoken of, and I confess I have never absolutely shared that opinion. But she had that which is more valuable than perfect beauty on the throne, the look of a Queen of France, even at the moments when she tried most to seem nothing but a pretty woman. . . . She had two kinds of walk, the one firm, slightly hurried, but always noble, the other softer and more rhythmical, almost languorous, yet never encouraging people to forget their respect. Never have curtsies been made with such grace ; at a single inclination she greeted ten people, yet with head and glance she gave to each his due. In short, if I am not deceived, just as one offers a chair to other women, so one would almost always have wished to bring her a throne." It is a pleasure to quote so delightful an account, more especially since it bears the stamp of truth. In going on to speak of the Queen's character, Tilly brings us back to our subject and illustrates it in convincing terms. He laments the disgust Marie Antoinette showed : " for the forms surrounding royalty, which are more necessary in France than in any place I know," and " her incurable prejudice (though in general her nature was uncertain and hesitating) for or against those who were pointed out for her favours or her hatred, or whom she had herself classified, as she often did without any reflection."

The critic especially refers to the dismissal of Turgot, the gravest fault of the early days of the reign, and the work of the

Intrigues against Turgot. Queen's intimates. Turgot was marked out as a victim to be sacrificed to the extravagance and intrigues of the Court. A combination formed of the Polignacs,

* Letter to the Countess of Upper Ossory.

the Duchesse de Gramont, Choiseul's sister, and the Duc de Doigny, had no difficulty in persuading Marie-Antoinette and even the King, that the Minister had become the most unpopular of all Controllers-General.

Turgot was a man of the strictest integrity, but he was too abrupt and unbending. He imposed his principles without a trace of compromise, and it has been said of him in contrast to Terray : " He did the right thing in the wrong way, while the Abbé did the wrong thing in the right way." Sénac de Meilhan exaggerates, in his effort to make himself clear, but there is a certain amount of truth in the following judgment : " He did not know how to make allowances for the weaknesses of men, still less for their vices. Monsieur Turgot acted like a surgeon operating on a corpse, and forgot that he was operating on living beings."

Turgot was a convinced Royalist, and he was perhaps the only minister who could have saved the monarchy, as is proved by the consequences of his retirement. Some of those who followed him, men devoid both of talent and probity, showed the extent of the loss that France had suffered. A month before the Controller's disgrace, Louis had said : " Only Monsieur Turgot and I love the people." Turgot's schemes were soon abandoned, but among them were some of the reforms which the Revolution claimed as its own. For instance, he proposed the abolition of the *corvées*, to be replaced by a tax paid by all proprietors whether privileged or not, the suppression of Wardens, Freedoms, and Guilds which superficial observers at that time saw only as hindrances to commerce and industry, without understanding the profound reasons for which centuries of experience had imposed them on Western Europe.

These proposals increased the number of Turgot's enemies. Courtiers, financiers, Parliamentarians, and high dignitaries of the Church were all jealous of their prerogatives, and there was now also a *bourgeoise* aristocracy which swelled the ranks of those who were interested in preserving the traditional forms of society. A great lady summed up the whole question, saying : " Why make innovations ? Is not all well with us ? " Was this remark malice or naïveté ?

The opinion of the Parliament was similar and it wished to suppress Turgot's edicts. Louis disregarded it, and the edicts **Imprudent** were registered by order on March 13, 1776. But **Interference of** the Controller's isolation became more pro- **the Queen.** nounced. His enemies were uniting, and they even went so far as to forge letters purporting to come from Turgot, and containing sarcasms against the Queen and jests and offensive words about the King. " All this correspondence," said Dupont of Nemours, " was brought to Louis XVI. He communicated it to Maurepas, who, one may well suppose, failed to express any strong doubts as to its authenticity. Other letters were also intercepted, whether genuine or not, in which the most violent accusations were made against the Controller-General." His dismissal was decided. Tormented by her intimates, who used as their weapon Turgot's recall of the Comte de Guines from his embassy, the Queen yielded and obtained the desired order from the King. Louis, compromised by his contradictions, in the end listened to his wife. Mercy, who saw more clearly, declared that her influence would one day draw upon the Queen " the just reproaches of the King, her husband, and even of *all the nation*." These prophetic words alarmed Maria Theresa, but the Empress understated her terror in writing to her daughter, for fear of revealing the confidences of Mercy : " The public," she wrote, " no longer speaks of you with the same enthusiasm ; it thinks you occupied with small conspiracies unworthy of your position." Marie-Antoinette replied : " My conduct and my intentions are well known, and they are far removed from conspiracy and intrigue. There may be people who are disturbed about what is said between the King and myself ; but I will not renounce the confidence which rightly exists between my husband and myself to satisfy them. Moreover, I trust that the general opinion is not so opposed to me as some one has informed my dear mother." Marie-Antoinette denied having had any share in Turgot's dismissal. She dissimulated, blindly following the advice of her intimates. She was beginning " to use subterfuges in order to give a false colour to her actions," as Maria Theresa wrote to Mercy.

Turgot quitted his ministry with dignity. In a letter to the King he said, " My greatest hope is that you may come to know that I am wrong and that I have warned you of chimerical dangers. I trust that time may not justify me."

Fall of Turgot and Malesherbes. Malesherbes, who supported Turgot's principles and wished with him to reform the extravagance of the Court, was obliged to send in his resignation. The same combination overthrew both the reforming ministers, who had come before their time. As Walpole said : "Since their plans tend to serve the public you may be sure they do not please interested individuals. . . . Designing persons who have no weapon but ridicule to use against good men, already employ it to make a trifling nation laugh at its benefactors ; and if it is the fashion to laugh, the laws of fashion will be executed preferably to those of common sense." *

According to the President de Bachaumont, Louis said to Malesherbes on the day of his departure, May 12, 1776 : "How fortunate you are ! Would that *I* could retire ! "

The Comte de Muy died on October 10, 1775, and the Department of War was entrusted to the Comte de Saint-Germain, a **The Comte de Saint-Germain.** gifted officer, though of an advanced age, who had performed most of his service abroad, in Austria, Bavaria, and Denmark. His appointment astonished every one, since he was little known. Maurepas had brought him from retirement in Alsace. As minister he was allowed to issue decree after decree ; he suppressed a part of the King's Military Household, and increased the army by 40,000 men without extra cost to the Treasury ; he prohibited luxury and gaming, attacked the sale of offices, and made the famous strokes with the flat of the sword a substitute for imprisonment for light offences. This last innovation was considered an insult, and a soldier said : "Strike with the point ; it hurts less." Saint-Germain remained in power after Turgot's fall until September 1777 ; then he became very unpopular and yielded his post to his assistant, Monsieur de Montbarrey.

Amelot succeeded Malesherbes. Maurepas, who made light of everything, prepared the way for the new arrival by saying : "They must be tired of men of genius. Let us see if they will like a fool better." Amelot was faithful to his reputation.

* Letter to Sir Horace Mann.

Clugny, who became Controller-General, died a few months later, but he had time to re-establish the *corvées* and the Wardens and to institute a public lottery. His successor was one of the conspicuous personalities of the reign—Necker.

The country was in the throes of a crisis brought about by shallow intrigues. The Queen's youth, the King's lack of **The Decline of** energy, Maurepas' levity, were so many play-**the Monarchy.** things for the courtiers, who were anxious for change and eager to clear the way for their own advancement. The Duc de Croÿ said : " The young King, who did not shine in bearing or manner, was always good-natured, well intentioned, and clear-sighted, but he feared the embarrassment of making a choice or a decision, always a difficult thing, so that he avoided inquiry or discussion with anyone, except on rare occasions with Monsieur de Maurepas, whose good-nature did not incline him towards argument. The Queen was always pleasure-seeking ; she did nothing but run about to the shows in Paris, the balls at the Opéra and at Versailles, and was always in a flutter, hoping to escape boredom by perpetual motion." At this time the Comtesse de la Marck wrote to Gustavus III, King of Sweden : " Everything here is as God wills ; good sense, sound judgment, a regard whether for public or private interests are unknown. . . . A King who wishes to do good, but has neither the power nor the ability to compass it . . . a Minister [Maurepas], who was unstable and weak at forty, and is further enervated by age, who does the strangest things, and makes light of public opinion. . . . The Queen goes continually to Paris . . . incurs debts, invites lawsuits, decks herself in feathers and fripperies, and laughs at everything."

The monarchy was waning ; it sought assistance from Necker, a foreigner. The Queen needed advice and the Emperor came to give it her. But it was already too late.

PRINCIPAL SOURCES. *Mémoires sur la vie et le caractère de la Duchesse de Polignac*, by the Comtesse Diane de Polignac, 1 vol., 1796 ; *Mémoires* of the Comte de Paroy, of Marmontel, of the Baronne d'Ober-kich, of Tilly ; Reports said to be by Bachaumont ; *Letters* of Horace Walpole ; *Correspondance entre le Comte de Mirabeau et le Comte de la Marck*, 2 vols., 1851 ; Thévenot, *Correspondance du prince Xavier de Saxe* ; Sénac de Meilhan, *Du gouvernement et des mœurs*, 1795.

CHAPTER XVIII

THE EMPEROR'S VISIT
1777

Necker. Madame Necker and her Salon. *Éloge de Colbert. Sur la législation et le commerce des Blés.* Necker in power. The Emperor approves of Necker. Joseph II's visit. He repairs the blunders of the Archduke Maximilian. Proposals of marriage. A Mentor. The *Invalides.* Coolness between the Queen and her brother. The Emperor's opinions on the French Court: Louis XVI, the Comte d'Artois, the Comte de Provence. He severely criticizes the Queen's intimates. Portrait of Joseph II by the Comte de Provence. Discontent of the Choiseul party. Madame du Barry. Portrait of the Queen by Joseph II. Instructions left for Marie-Antoinette.

NECKER was the real successor of Turgot. He came from Geneva, from a school of skilful and honest bankers. He commenced his career in Paris in the house of a compatriot, bringing with him the solemn, formal **Necker and** spirit which flourishes on the banks of Lake **his Wife.** Leman, though it was modified and softened by his desire to attain a high position. He was greatly assisted by his wife, Suzanne Curchod, a Protestant minister's daughter, whom Gibbon had wanted to marry. Since 1765, Madame Necker had had a *salon* at which men of letters, aspiring to the Academy, appeared side by side with great nobles and most of the foreign diplomats. She shone more by her intelligence than by her grace. The Baronne d'Oberkich said of her that, " God when creating her dipped her in a bucket of starch." She remained a Vaudoise in the heart of Paris, and always had a trace of the provincial. Madame de Staël, to whom she bequeathed her wit though not her beauty, similarly failed to become absolutely French. But Madame Necker at least commanded respect by her virtue. One might say of her what Madame du Deffand said of the Duchesse de Choiseul, another virtuous woman : " She wished to be perfect ; it was her only fault and the only one she could have." If Madame Necker was not the woman she hoped to be, she at least set a fine example of philanthropy by the foundation of her hospital, with which she occupied ten years of her life. One of the innovations introduced in this hospital was that they nursed " the sick *in single beds* with every attention of tenderness and humanity, and without exceeding a fixed fee." The foregoing extract from a contemporary report testifies to the greatness of the service rendered by this worthy deaconess.

Necker at first mixed unobtrusively with the society with which his wife liked to surround herself ; he adopted the attitude of a spectator. On occasions, however, he **Necker's social aloofness.** jested, and called attention to some eccentricity or humorous incident. He lacked an essentially French characteristic, as Madame du Deffand observed to Walpole, which consists in " a certain ability to bring out the intelligence of those with whom one speaks. He gives no assistance to the development of one's thoughts, and one is consequently more stupid with him than when by oneself or with others." According to Marmontel, except for a few subtle phrases dropped here and there, he left his wife to maintain and enliven the conversation. When Necker married Mlle. Curchod the following remark was made : " They will be so bored with one another that it will give them an occupation." However, they did not bore one another, rather did they bore others by their adoration, and the incense they burnt to one another. Although Necker was not anxious to speak, he could write. As soon as his fortune was made he left the bank, and in 1773 published an *Éloge de Colbert,* which was crowned by the French Academy. He then got himself appointed representative of the Genevan Republic at the Court of Versailles, and thus received congratulations for two honours at once.

In his *Éloge* he made use of Colbert to paint a portrait of an ideal Finance Minister, "such as Colbert perhaps was, and **His Writings.** such especially as Monsieur Necker aspired to become," as Sainte-Beuve maliciously observes. Two years later appeared his work *Sur la Législation et le Commerce des Blés* (on Legislation and the Corn Trade), an attack on the theories and even the character of Turgot. In Necker's opinion, an administrator ought to have " a suave and pliant mind, an ardent soul, and a calm judgment." He was obviously thinking of himself. Necker delighted in compliments, " he used to fish for compliments," to use the picturesque English expression. He was vain-glorious, and in his effort to excite flattering comparisons his public acts were tainted with charlatanism. Thus at the time of his first loan, as it was fully subscribed in advance, he need not have made the public come to the Royal Treasury only to see an imposing guard. But it is only fair to say, with Droz, that his pride made him glory above all in services rendered to the State. If Turgot thought too much of theory, Necker was purely practical, and had no abstract ideas. His work on the Corn Trade proves this. The future minister did not pronounce for or against freedom in this trade, but he said enough to injure his predecessor's reputation. He came to no conclusions, and his policy was rather destructive than constructive. His style was pompous, verbose, and not easy to understand. Society called his work a " break-neck " (*casse-cou*) treatise, and Voltaire with some malice said " great application " was necessary to understand Necker " and deep knowledge to answer him." Turgot might have taken the able financier's advice with advantage, but a great gulf separated the two men, in spite of their ardent desire for the public welfare. The quarrels of their friends never ceased to embitter them and make them antagonistic to one another. At Clugny's death in October 1776, the King applied to Necker, believing that he had found a saviour.

There was a difficulty to overcome in the fact that Necker was a Protestant. Louis—to his honour be it said—was inspired by that spirit of toleration which his father **Necker in** the Dauphin and Turgot had shown ; he made **Power.** Taboureau des Réaux Controller of Finance, and gave the direction of this department to the " Genevan Banker," though without a voice in the Council of Ministers. A bishop called attention to the fact that the laws of the kingdom excluded Protestants from all official positions.

" We will give him up for your sake," said Maurepas, " if the clergy will pay the national debts."

246

THE EMPEROR'S VISIT

When Necker demanded the suppression of six Intendants of Finance, Taboureau sent in his resignation, his objection being that he did not wish to injure men whom he esteemed. Necker became Director-General on June 29, 1777, and remained in power for five years, until May 19, 1781. As he was rich he refused the salary attached to his office, a self-denial which made him very popular. But the flattery which was lavished upon him turned his head, and prevented him from seeing how serious were the times ; he was no statesman. One of his colleagues, the Comte de Vergennes, a man of considerable ability, showed he had more grasp of the situation than Necker when he said in a confidential communication to Louis : "There is no longer Clergy, Nobility, or Third Estate in France. The distinction is fictitious, purely representative, and without any real significance. The monarch speaks, all the rest are the people, and all obey."

One of the Director's first actions was to have recourse to a loan, which was justified by rumours of an approaching war with England, then at war with her American Colonies. This financial coup was a triumph for Necker. Nevertheless, he was criticized for not having given any guarantee to the lenders, nor introduced taxes to consolidate the loans. He answered that he was procuring the money at a lower rate of interest than ever before, and that this economic difference allowed him to ensure the satisfaction of all the liabilities he had contracted. Such a guarantee from an embarrassed treasury was somewhat illusory. In 1777 the successive loans amounted to 148,000,000 *livres*, and in the same year Necker resolved to reduce the number of posts in the Department of Finance, in spite of the opposition of the holders of those offices, who defended themselves "like devils." He established a commission with the object of reforming the hospitals, created Government pawn-shops (*monts-de-piété*) to compete with the moneylenders and pawnbrokers, who were very numerous among the office-holders. An opposition was formed against him. "It is because he interferes with the interests of the rich and powerful that he meets with continual obstacles," it was said ; "if he had attacked the poor only, all would go as he wishes." None the less he had more supporters than adversaries.

When the Emperor Joseph II came to France at this period, he had an interview with the celebrated Director and formed "the most favourable idea of his intellect" and "of his character, about which there is only one opinion."

This visit of the Queen's brother takes an important place in the history of 1777. Joseph II travelled incognito under the name of the Count of Falkenstein. He took care to keep strictly to his rôle, and whether he was in Paris or Versailles would only stay at an hotel. He endeavoured to escape the ovations inevitably showered on a prince whose liberal ideas and horror of prejudice were well known.

Visit of Joseph II.

Another brother of Marie-Antoinette, the Archduke Maximilian, had visited Versailles in 1775, but had not been a success. When Buffon offered him his works he said :

" Sir, I should be very sorry to deprive you of them." He was very young.

This foolish speech was duly retailed by the Queen's enemies. There were other grounds of complaint against Maximilian because, under the assumed name of the Count of Burgau, he had insisted that the Ducs d'Orléans and de Chartres and the Princes de Condé and de Conti should visit him first. The princes of the blood refused, and retired to their estates during the Archduke's visit.

But the visit of Joseph II, who was very popular, caused these unfortunate impressions to be forgotten. He saw Buffon and asked him for the books which his young brother had "forgotten," thus redeeming his brother's folly by his wit.

The Emperor was a grandson by marriage of Louis XV ; he had lost his wife, the Infanta Isabella, daughter of Don Philip, Duke of Parma, and of Louise-Elisabeth of France. It was thought that he had come to marry his wife's first cousin, Madame Elisabeth, sister of Louis XVI, but he did not succumb to the charms of the Princess, who later paid so dearly for her devotion to the King, Marie-Antoinette, and their children. For some time Joseph had renounced marriage, as much from an affected austerity as from natural coldness. In 1772 he wrote to his brother Leopold : " As for me, I am becoming rapidly less gallant and once more I am moping like an owl. The company of women becomes

Matrimonial Plans.

insupportable to a reasonable man after a time, and I may say that often the smartest and wittiest remarks turn my stomach." We have already seen something of this contempt for women in the famous intercepted letter, and we shall find it again in his conversations with the Queen.

Marie-Antoinette had reason to be disturbed by the Imperial visit. It was said that Joseph had a political object, that he had come to ask Vergennes to abandon Turkey and to consent to divide that kingdom between France, Russia, and Austria; but the Emperor's real object was to introduce harmony in the Royal Household. The choice of the Mentor was not a happy one.

The Queen refused to be governed, and showed herself stubborn when anyone tried to treat her with severity. Maria Theresa, as Marie-Antoinette herself once owned to Mercy, might say anything to her : "From my mother," she said, "I will take everything with respect, but as for my brother, I shall know how to answer him." The Queen's intimates had much to do with these declarations of revolt. The Austrian ambassador told Maria Theresa that Marie-Antoinette had been prejudiced against her brother ; "people had contrived," he said, "to fill her mind with fears and suspicions, and to prevent her from having any confidence in His Majesty the Emperor." Joseph caused some offence by his rather caustic remarks. He thought it extraordinary that the King and Queen did not know Paris better. The following conversation took place between Louis and his guest :

Friction between the Queen and her Brother.

"You possess the most beautiful building in Europe."

"What is that ? "

"Les Invalides."

"So they say."

"What ! have you never visited the building ? "

"*Ma foi*, no."

"Nor have I," said the Queen.

"Ah ! " said Joseph smiling, "I am not surprised in your case, sister ; you are so busy."

Another time Marie-Antoinette asked her brother to admire one of the enormous structures of hair, feathers, ribbons, and flowers which were then in fashion and were called *poufs au sentiment.*

" Is not my hair charmingly arranged ? " she asked.

" Yes."

" But that *yes* is very curt. Does not the style suit me ? "

" *Ma foi,* if you wish me to speak frankly, Madame, I think it is very light to bear a crown."

Thus far his criticisms were just and had been made with some wit.

But he exceeded all bounds when he advised the King to make a visit to some part of his kingdom, and told the Queen not to accompany her husband, because she would be useless. This insult was followed by others even more violent. Joseph objected to " the Queen's free and easy manner with her husband," to " her disrespectful language " and her " want of submission." * There were continual misunderstandings and serious quarrels between brother and sister. Marie-Antoinette displeased Joseph by defending Choiseul ; for she remained constant to the ex-minister, readily listening to her friends, the Duc de Coigny and the Comte Esterhazy, both devoted to the exile of Chanteloup.

Mercy records another scene between the Queen and the Emperor : " They went together to the Theatre of Versailles. When they were returning the Queen spoke of going to the Italian Theatre in Paris the next day. The Emperor observed that it was a fast-day, that the King did not dine, and that it would be wrong to make him wait too long for his supper. The Emperor also added other reasons which displeased the Queen, because they were given in the presence of two of the ladies of the Palace. On their return to the Château, the Queen quarrelled with the Emperor in the presence of the Comtesse de Polignac. . . ." Mercy took it upon himself to ask Joseph to be less harsh, and after that the quarrels came to an end.

But the impression remained. Neither the King nor the Queen was pleased. Louis was jealous of the popularity of Joseph, his affability, education, and his desire to see and understand new things. Marie-Antoinette retained some ill-

* Mercy to Maria Theresa.

feeling against her harsh Mentor. The Empress had foreseen the result of this visit, and before it took place she said to Mercy, " I am hardly counting upon the good effect of this journey. If I am not mistaken, one of two things will result from it : either my daughter will win the Emperor by her affection and charm, or he will irritate her by trying continually to teach her. . . . In either case we cannot hope for a happy result from the presence of the Emperor." Maria Theresa had expressed strong hopes that her son would not go to France.

Joseph's criticisms of the Court are interesting. According to the Chancelleries he declared : " I have three miserable The Emperor's brothers-in-law. The one at Versailles is an Criticisms. imbecile, the one at Naples a madman, and the one at Parma an idiot." All the same the Emperor wrote on July 9, 1777, to his brother Leopold : " This man (Louis XVI) is a little weak, but not an imbecile. He has ideas and a sound judgment, but his body and mind are apathetic. He converses reasonably, but he has no wish to learn and no curiosity ; in fact the *fiat lux* has not yet come ; the matter is still without form."

The Emperor liked gaiety and animation in others, and had a favourable opinion of the Comte d'Artois. Mercy was afraid that this might encourage the Queen to submit to the influence of her young brother-in-law. Joseph was well aware that Monsieur d'Artois was " a coxcomb in every sense of the word," but he was amused by him. He could not, on the other hand, get used to the extreme coldness of the Comte de Provence, and spoke of the two Piedmontese princesses in brief but unflattering terms.

He was also very harsh in his criticisms when he went to a party given by the Princesse de Guéménée, and was shocked " at the ill-breeding " of the guests and " the air of licence in this lady's house." He said plainly to the Queen, " that it was like a house of ill-fame." As for the Comtesse de Polignac, Joseph considered her too young and not sufficiently intelligent to be a useful adviser to the Queen, but he treated her indulgently, realizing that it would be inadvisable to cross his sister on this point.

The Emperor, in his turn, found a not too gentle critic in Monsieur, who wrote to Gustavus III : "He is very insidious

Monsieur criticizes the Emperor. and makes many protestations and vows of friendship ; his mind is adorned by the knowledge of many useful subjects. . . . That is what one sees at the first glance. On closer examination, his protestations and his open appearance hide his intent to do what is called *tirer les vers du nez* (extract information) and to conceal his own sentiments. But he is maladroit, for by means of a little flattery, to which he is very susceptible, far from his being able to see through anyone, it is very easy to see through him, and he then throws all caution to the winds. . . . He talks a great deal, and not in an attractive manner, but it amuses him and he repeats his stories mercilessly." This description receives some confirmation from Maria Theresa's criticism of her son : "He likes to please and to shine," and from the judgment pronounced by Frederick II : "The Emperor, though anxious for knowledge, had not the patience to learn. His importance made him superficial."

Joseph made enemies ; particularly the Choiseuls and their faction. The Duke still had some hope of returning to office,

Joseph II offends the Choiseuls. and he thought that there could be no better occasion to make an attempt than the visit of Maria Theresa's son, whom he had known at Vienna. Choiseul counted on the services he had formerly rendered to the Imperial Court. Everything was prepared magnificently at Chanteloup to receive the Emperor, who was to cross Touraine on his way to visit the ports on the west of France. From the first days after his arrival Joseph was expected there. He met the Duchesse de Gramont, Choiseul's sister, at Madame de Brionne's, and asked her which was the most fertile province of France.

" It is Touraine," she said, " my brother has a cottage there, he would be the happiest of men if he might receive Your Majesty."

The Emperor did not answer and changed the conversation. Maria Theresa was mortified at her son's attitude ; she regretted that he had disdained Choiseul, who was not the " man to provoke beyond endurance," as it was uncertain " whether

252

sooner or later he would not return to power." The Empress was no better pleased with her son's want of tact on another occasion : he went to Luciennes and asked to see Madame du Barry ; he was charmed with her. He met her in the garden, offered her his arm, and chatted with her very agreeably for a quarter of an hour. Maria Theresa found consolation in the fact that on his return the Emperor had passed without stopping at Ferney, where, as may be imagined, he was awaited with much impatience.

Such are some of the incidents of Joseph's visit, but it would not be fair to omit his final expression of opinion on the subject **Joseph II's** of his sister, which to some extent atones for the **Portrait of the** severity of the criticisms mentioned above. He **Queen.** wrote to his brother Leopold from Brest on June 9 : " She is a good and lovable woman, a little young and thoughtless, but she has a depth of goodness and virtue which, considering her position, is worthy of the utmost respect. With it all she unites an intelligence and a soundness of perception which have often surprised me. Her first impulse is always correct. If she would follow it up, think a little more, and listen a little less to the hosts of people of all sorts who advise her, she would be perfect. Her desire for pleasure is very strong, and as her taste is known, people take advantage of this weakness, and those who provide her with the most amusement find both hearing and favour." His French style is very Germanic, but it was a true portrait, and we recognize in all respects Marie-Antoinette as she is described by the most trustworthy accounts and as, it may be hoped, she has appeared in the preceding pages.

Joseph left very minute written instructions to his sister. One passage from them will show the Emperor's foresight : **His Advice to** " You are made to be happy, virtuous, and perfect. **his Sister.** But it is time, and more than time to reflect, to set up a rule of life and to act upon it. You are getting older and have no longer the excuse of extreme youth. What will you become if you wait longer ? An unhappy woman and a still more unhappy princess. . . . Acquire a reputation worthy of your virtues, your charms, and your character, but be true and firm ! Yes ! it is necessary to be inflexibly stubborn in the cause of right, and to oppose all seducers with courage and strength."

This was excellent and wise advice, but it was difficult to follow, like all advice, and as usual, was given too late; it dealt with evils that were ineradicable and a character already formed and no longer susceptible of modification from without. But a change was about to occur in the Queen's life, which for the time being was to have more influence than all the moral lectures in the world.

[PRINCIPAL SOURCES. Same as for preceding chapter.]

CHAPTER XIX

BIRTH OF MADAME ROYALE

Independence of the United States. Franklin in Paris. His presentation to Louis. War with England. The battle of Ouessant. The Bavarian succession. The policy of Louis and Vergennes. Birth of Marie-Thérèse-Charlotte. The crowd invade the Queen's chamber. Public disappointment. The education of the Princess. Marie-Antoinette's confessions to her mother. Family life. Marie-Antoinette and her children.

ON July 4, 1776, the English flag floating in the ocean breezes of America was replaced by the flag with the thirteen stars and thirteen stripes, which symbolized the independence of the thirteen United States. The " insurgents,"
American as they were called, found in Jefferson an able
Independence. orator, in Franklin a wise counsellor, and in Washington an incomparable administrator and general. They won France to their cause, for the latter had the courage to ally herself to them in the hope of avenging the disasters of the Seven Years War. The resulting operations were one of the brighter pages in the reign of Louis XVI. The King was ably assisted by Vergennes, who took charge of the more important diplomatic negotiations, among others, those with Charles III of Spain, who interfered by right of the Family Compact, and by the Marquis de La Fayette and a large staff of French officers, who crossed over to the New World and fought bravely side by side with the American colonists.

The Congress of Philadelphia sent ambassadors over to Europe to plead the American cause, and to bring about a
Franklin in reaction against England, who refused to allow
Paris. herself to be beaten. Franklin was sent to France. His pleasant manners and dignity helped to conciliate the scientists, the men of letters, the philosophers, the great nobles the Court, and the King. In February 1778, he secured the

signature of a treaty with the United States, a treaty which was to become an alliance in case England should declare war on France. Each party pledged itself to conclude neither peace nor truce without the consent of the other. The Independence was thus officially recognized, though even before, help had been secretly dispatched by Louis' order, under the auspices of Beaumarchais, a clever man of business as well as a brilliant author.

Franklin was presented at Versailles on March 20. The handsome old man made a picturesque figure, with his spectacles, his bald head, and his patriarchal appearance. People pressed about his path as though he were some strange novelty. It was not usual at the courtly ceremonies to see the homely honesty, the simple dress, and the absence of luxury characteristic of Franklin. The worthy American wore a brown coat and carried a stick in place of a sword. He was accompanied by two deputies, Silas Deane and Arthur Lee. The King was the first to speak, and he spoke with " more graciousness " than usual.

" Assure the Congress of my friendship," he said. " I hope that this will benefit both nations."

" Your Majesty," replied Franklin, " may count on the gratitude of the Congress, and on its fidelity to its engagements."

" It is certain," added Vergennes, " that nothing could be wiser or more circumspect than the conduct of these gentlemen when they were here."

The Duc de Croÿ, who records these remarks, makes the following commentary : " It was a treaty between nation and **War with** nation, the Congress was formally recognized, and **England.** with it the Independence by France before all others. To what thoughts does this great event give rise ! First, if successful, it was a cruel blow struck at England, and highly advantageous to French commerce. Secondly, it meant an implacable war, and perhaps the creation of a country vaster than France, which might one day subdue Europe."

It was, in fact, a declaration of war. Lord Stormont, His Britannic Majesty's ambassador, was recalled. The year 1778 was marked by French successes on the sea, such as the exploits of the *Belle-Poule* against the English frigate *Arethusa* off Brest, and the engagement of Ouessant on July 27, where the Comte d'Orvilliers, and with him Du Chaffault, Guichen, and La Motte-Piquet, distinguished themselves by their victory over Admiral Keppel. D'Estaing, however, was beaten on the sea off Rhode Island and off St. Lucia in August, and the English took Pondicherry in October.

At the same time another war seemed imminent in Germany over the succession to Maximilian Joseph of Bavaria, who had **The Bavarian** died on December 30, 1777. Joseph II, in his **Succession.** anxiety to establish ancient though shadowy claims and to increase his territories, aroused the susceptibilities of Frederick by occupying all Lower Bavaria and treating it as a fief of the Empire. The King of Prussia replied by putting two armies into the field and threatening to enter Bohemia. Maria Theresa, who did not approve of her son's warlike humour, believed the unhappy days of 1741 were about to recur, and that she would lose Bohemia as she had lost her dear Silesia. But all that happened was a few skirmishes; there were no sieges or pitched battles. However, Austria demanded of France the 24,000 troops stipulated by the treaty of 1756, or in default, 15,000,000 *livres*. The French ministers were fully occupied with the events in America and turned a deaf ear to this appeal. Marie-Antoinette received message after message from Vienna; at first she resisted, fearing that her brother might be playing his own game. But the Empress declared that the rupture of the Franco-Austrian alliance would " be her death." The Queen, in great distress, took the interests of her family in hand, saying that she was serving both her countries, but she did not understand the exigencies of the new French policy. She failed in her efforts.

The policy of Louis and Vergennes remained constant and wise, and was extremely creditable to them. " The ambition **Policy of** of your relations," said the King to Marie-**Louis XVI and** Antoinette, " will ruin all. They have begun **Vergennes.** with Poland; and now Bavaria is to be the second chapter. I am sorry for your sake. We are going to order the French ministers to inform all the Courts that this dismemberment of Bavaria is being done against our wishes, and that we disapprove of it." Neither the King nor his

Minister wavered from this line of conduct, and the Queen's tears had no effect on their resolution. Both did the right thing when at the time of the Peace of Teschen, May 13, 1779, which put an end to the Emperor's ambitions they acted as mediators between Prussia and Austria. The latter only secured some insignificant portions of Bavarian territory.

Thus a continental war was avoided. Vergennes honourably refused the advantageous offers of Joseph, who suggested that France should provoke Prussia and Holland by occupying the Netherlands. He thus guaranteed peace on land and was able to concentrate his attention on national and profitable schemes which he conceived and carried out in a statesmanlike manner.

At this crisis—on December 20, 1778—the Queen gave birth to a daughter, Maria-Thérèse-Charlotte, Madame Royale, **Birth of** afterwards Duchesse d'Angoulême, and the only **Madame** one of Louis XVI's family who survived the **Royale.** Revolution.* The crowd which invaded the young mother's chamber on the announcement of the event was so great that Marie-Antoinette was almost suffocated by the human flood. The Queen suddenly grew pale, her mouth was convulsed, and they thought her dead. The King himself opened the windows and ordered warm water for the bleeding, but in the press and confusion he could not get it. The surgeon lanced her foot " dry " ; the blood spurted out and the Queen opened her eyes. Fresh disturbance was caused when they sent the people out ; the Princesse de Lamballe was carried away fainting. The men-servants and the ushers took the indiscreet sightseers by the collars and pushed them out ; in the future this cruel etiquette was abolished and only the Princes, the Chancellor, and the Ministers were admitted in like circumstances.

When the young Princess was presented to the Queen she pressed her to her heart and said to her : " Poor little one, you were not wanted, but you will be none the less dear to me. A son would have belonged to the State. You will be mine ; you will be all my own, you will share my happiness, and soften my sorrows."

The Court and the town were in fact extremely disappointed.

* She lived until 1851.

They had hoped for a Dauphin. The projected fêtes did not take place; the King placed at the Queen's disposal 100,000 **Disappointment** *livres*, which she used to provide dowries for poor **of the Nation.** girls, to free some that were in prison for debt, and to distribute alms to the hospitals. The Town Council ordered the customary popular rejoicings : illuminations, fireworks, fountains of wine, distributions of bread and saveloys, and free spectacles at the theatres, but the joy was only half-hearted. When the King and Queen went to Paris on February 8, 1779, there were few cheers, and it was remarked that the main instinct of the populace was one of curiosity.

An innovation was made at the birth of Madame Royale due to the fact that the " return to nature " and " simplicity **The Education** of manners," as preached by Rousseau, were the **of the** fashion. All signs of pomp were kept from the **Princess.** Princess' sight at the request of Marie-Antoinette herself. Maria Theresa when she heard of this " reform " condemned it. She already saw her granddaughter transformed into a peasant girl, and she clung to the claims of rank even in the cradle. " It is an essential point," she wrote to Mercy, " especially with the French nation, as ardent as it is fickle." The Empress thought that the Sovereign and his family should differentiate themselves " from private persons by means of ceremony." However, the infant's household, though reduced, still numbered eighty persons entirely devoted to her service.

The Queen occupied herself with her daughter, her life became more serious and a new era commenced. The truth of this was shown by a confession she made to Maria Theresa, six months after the birth : " If I have done wrong, it was through childishness and lightness, but now my head is more steady, and she [the Empress] may rest assured that I fully realize my duties on this point. Besides, I owe it to the King for his tenderness, and, I may be permitted to say, his trust in me, on which I can only congratulate myself more and more." She spoke much of the little Princess ; to quote one charming instance, she wrote in March 1780 : " They are soon going to take her out of bed ; she is big and strong ; one would think her a child of two years old. She walks alone, stoops and straightens herself again without being held, but she hardly speaks at all. I am going to confide to my dear mother's tender heart a happiness that I had four days ago. I was with several other people in my daughter's room, so I told some one to ask her where her mother was. The little one, without anyone saying a word to her, smiled at me and came and held out her arms to me. It is the first time that she has deigned to recognize me. I confess that it gave me great pleasure, and I think I have loved her much more ever since."

If Marie-Antoinette had known earlier the happiness of being a mother, she would not have sought distraction from her want of occupation and ennui in futile amusements. She would not have had time to listen to flatterers and selfish advisers, nor to take part in intrigues and cabals. Calumny would have been disarmed, rendered powerless over an existence in which the smiles and the tears of her children are the mother's only joys and sorrows.

Marie-Antoinette loved her daughter and her sons tenderly, one might almost say intelligently, as is shown in her letters **The Queen's** to Madame de Tourzel, General Jarjayes, and **Love for her** especially in her beautiful letter to Madame **Children.** Elisabeth, which one cannot read but through a mist of tears. It is dated October 16, 1793, at half-past four in the morning : " I am writing to you, my sister, for the last time. I have just been condemned, not to a shameful death, for it is only shameful for criminals, but to rejoin your brother. . . . I am deeply grieved at having to leave my poor children.* You know that I exist for them and you alone, my kind and loving sister, . . . may my daughter realize that at her age she should always help her brother with the advice with which her wider experience and her love may inspire her ! May my son never forget his father's last words, which I repeat to this end : Let him never seek to avenge our death. Adieu, my kind and loving sister ! I hope this letter will reach you ! Think of me always ! I embrace you with all my heart, you and my poor dear children. Ah, God ! how heartrending it is to leave them for ever. . . ."

* Madame Royale and the Duc de Normandie, who was born in 1785 and became Dauphin at the death of his elder brother in 1789 ; he was the *Child of the Temple.*

CHAPTER XX

END OF THE AMERICAN WAR
1779–1783

Necker's economies. Abolition of rights of serfdom. Royal concessions. Projected invasion of England. Ségur and Castries. Maria Theresa's pupil. Capitulation of Yorktown. Fall of Necker. Joly de Fleury. Birth of the Dauphin. Festivities in Paris and Versailles. Death of Maurepas. Bankruptcy of the Prince de Guémenée. Overtures for peace. Siege of Gibraltar. Suffren in India. Treaties of Paris and Versailles.

WHILE the war lasted there was a complete renewal of confidence in the French armies and the policy of Louis and Vergennes. Economy was strictly imposed. The journeys of the Court were abandoned to purchase **Necker's** ships. Private individuals made public subscrip-**Economies.** tions to assist the Treasury to defray the enormous expenses which burdened the State. Necker taxed his ingenuity and effected numerous retrenchments in the budget; he abolished 406 posts in the King's Household, and reduced the number of Farmers of Taxes and Receivers-General. His economies extended over the royal candle-sellers and in allusion to this the Minister was accused of wishing " to burn the short ends " ; he was overwhelmed with pamphlets.

The financial relief caused by these reforms enabled the King to forgo the rights of serfdom and mainmorte.* Louis **Royal** had desired to go still further and abolish these **Concessions.** harsh relics of feudalism altogether, but the resources of the State were not yet sufficient to enable him to buy the rights of the nobles. He at least hoped to see his example followed and be in time " a witness of the complete enfranchisement of his subjects," who, as he asserted in his

* Mainmorte : a feudal custom by which serfs were not allowed to make a will, and if they died without heirs the lord succeeded.

edict of August 1779, *whatever the state in which Providence has ordained their birth, have equal rights to his protection and favour.* Necker in dictating these words to the King, remembered Turgot, and Louis in signing them won the just admiration of all the friends of philosophy. But these measures, though they gave an example to certain of the nobility, were not approved by either the higher Clergy or the Parliament.

Private interests superseded everything in this assembly composed of the owners of estates. In consequence the edict was only registered with the addition of express restrictions. The King's brothers, the Duc d'Orléans and the Prince de Condé were among the malcontents; they asserted that the innovations " injured their privileges," and that they " debased the Crown by depriving it of its prestige."

The liberal movement had commenced. Necker, profiting by this favourable tendency, prepared the way for other reforms which affected him more nearly. He demanded that Protestants should be allowed a civil status, and later that they should be eligible for public offices. However, this reform was not realized until 1788. But the new ideas took definite shape in acts of a humanitarian nature. The preliminary torture (*question preparatoire*) which was applied to the accused person to extort a confession of the crime imputed to him, was suppressed at this time, though judicial torture was not altogether abolished until 1788.

Thus royalty foreshadowed the reforms of the Revolution. The patriotic fervour of the nation was upheld by the conduct
La Fayette in of La Fayette, who returned from the New World
America. in February 1779, to urge the dispatch of troops to help the insurgents. He secured 4000 soldiers under the command of Rochambeau, and personally formed the project of an invasion of England. This expedition was to be supported by Spain. The preparations were extremely slow; France's allies made her wait for them at the rendezvous and so the project failed. The Comte d'Orvilliers, who had greatly distinguished himself in the engagement at Ouessant, returned to Brest in October 1779, having lost 50,000 men by disease. He was forced to send in his resignation. It was reported that d'Estaing had captured Grenada in the Antilles on July 16 and

that Saint Louis in Senegal, Gorea, and Saint-Vincent, had been taken, a small consolation, for d'Estaing himself was defeated at Savannah in Georgia and returned like d'Orvilliers, the object of general condemnation.

Hostilities were continued outside France by Spain on her own account. The sailors of Charles III thought only of them-
Siege of selves. Spain had not been mistress of Gibraltar
Gibraltar. since 1704, and she believed the moment had arrived to retake the fortress from the English. Vergennes promised the Spanish not to sign a peace until the desired capture had been effected ; but the enterprise could not contend against the hardihood of Rodney. In spite of the valour of Don Juan de Langara, it failed in January, 1780.

The Spaniards and French found themselves confronted by the same Rodney off the Antilles in June, but the engagements were negative, and there was no revenge as yet.

At the time of these events Necker was occupied with the delicate task of appointing two new Ministers—for the Navy
De Castries. and War. Sartine had occupied the former post since 1776 ; on his accession to power he had said " that he knew nothing of a ship " and that he had " very vague notions as to the four quarters of the world." But practice makes perfect, and it was recognized that " never had Minister built so many vessels or supplied the ports better." Necker, however, had to complain of the finances of his department, and secured Sartine's disgrace. He was succeeded by the Marquis de Castries, father-in-law of the Comte (now Duc) de Guines. The appointment was made by favour, but was justified by the services rendered by this able officer, the victor of Klosterkampen. He was devoted to his new task. His intervention in the Anglo-American conflict was successful, and he published certain salutary ordinances. In 1787 he gave up his place with honour to Montmorin.

Montbarrey, Sartine's colleague at the War Department, was notoriously incapable. The Marquis de Ségur took the office in
De Ségur. hand and he also distinguished himself by excellent reforms. Owing to him the monarchy bequeathed an army to the Revolution, an army which, by its discipline and devotion to duty, was to serve the Republican cause. In

justice it must be remembered that it is to him that the soldiers of Valmy and Jemmapes owed their prowess. It is true that Ségur has been reproached for his support of caste and his uncompromising decision of May 22, 1781, to exclude the *bourgeoisie* and many of the lesser nobility from military command. Thenceforward no one was eligible for the rank of officer unless he could prove his nobility for four generations. Nevertheless, with the assistance of Montalembert, who introduced a new system of fortification, and Gribeauval, who improved the efficiency of the artillery, Ségur organized great technical improvements. His successor, the Comte de Brienne, the Cardinal's brother, continued his work, and provided for the mobilization of the army in 1788 by dividing all the forces into twenty-one divisions and the divisions into brigades.

The Queen, still under the influence of the Polignacs, had a direct share in the appointments of Castries and Ségur, with which no fault could be found. Marie-Antoinette began to interest herself in affairs of State, but it was her intimates who reaped the advantage. There is little doubt that Mercy was right when he wrote to Kaunitz in June 1783 : " the Queen's influence, so widespread and beneficent in all other matters, is much less so in those which touch on politics, for the Queen has given her august husband only too much reason to presume that she knows little of affairs of State, and is unable to estimate their importance."

Mercy was now free, and dared to say here what he would not have said while Maria Theresa was living. The Empress **Death of** had died on November 29, 1780. Since 1774, she **Maria Theresa.** had urged her daughter to take part in the government, though on the whole her pupil responded badly to her lessons. Marie-Antoinette acted only by caprice and without reflection. She remained too much of a woman for it to be safe to entrust her with any serious undertaking. She had heart and feeling, but in politics these are not enough. The Queen's ascendency had always to be reckoned with after 1780, and everything tended to increase it. Louis' affection could refuse nothing to Marie-Antoinette, and his hopes of the birth of a Dauphin increased his tenderness for her.

There seemed to be the happiest auspices for this event.

France was cheered by the news of brilliant victories in America. La Fayette, Rochambeau, Guichen, and the Marquis de **Successes in** Saint-Simon served with success in Washington's **America.** cause during the year 1780, which culminated in the defence of Chesapeake Bay and the capitulation of York-town on October 19. Here 7000 men, forming the flower of the English troops in America, surrendered. The independence of the United States was assured, but to save her pride England would not own herself defeated. French arms and diplomacy triumphed.

In face of these great events the cabals which overthrew Necker seem paltry. It was commonly said that a battle lost would have been better for France than the Minister's resigna-tion, but it was not seriously meant. However, his fall was a disaster.

In January 1781, Necker made a great innovation which was his ruin. He issued his famous *Compte rendu* which for **Necker's** the first time enabled the public to read in black **Compte rendu.** and white the situation of the finances. Copies of it were greedily devoured and it was said that this " admirable " document " would mark an ever glorious epoch in the annals of the monarchy." But there were no lack of detractors ; some declared that the *Compte rendu* was the work of a con-ceited Minister infatuated with his own importance, others that it was the work of " a charlatan." The sudden light thrown on abuses alarmed the numerous and avaricious birds of prey who existed to the detriment of the Treasury, and Necker had to be sacrificed. In 1778 he had presented to the King, and to the King alone, a memorandum on provincial administra-tion. Relying on strict secrecy he allowed himself to use strong expressions against the Intendants, and still more against the Parliaments, with the object of awakening Louis from his apathy. But the document was divulged and copies came before the notice of those concerned. A violent criticism ap-peared, entitled *Lettre d'un bon Français.* Maurepas should **Fall of Necker.** have saved Necker, but he in fact helped to injure him with the King ; as usual, while outwardly approving the Director's system, he was chiefly instrumental in preventing its success. On May 20, Necker's resignation was

265

accepted, in spite of the Queen, who supported him to the end as " a man who had become so useful to France."

Louis declared, however, that " though he had changed his Minister he had not changed his principles." Joly de Fleury, Necker's successor, reversed his reforms and brought about a complete reaction. He re-established the Receivers-general, Treasurers, Farmers of taxes, and Officers of the King's household. This retrograde step advertised the uncertainty and contradictions of the Government.

But at this time the much-desired Dauphin was born, on October 22, 1781. Ephemeral heir to a tottering throne, he **Birth of the** only lived until 1789. The infant was greeted by **Dauphin.** magnificent and costly festivities, in which the people joined with sincere rejoicings, yet there were murmurings of hostility in Paris, and the police were vigilant and took extraordinary precautions for fear of trouble. Threatening placards appeared on the walls of the capital, in one of which it was said that the King and Queen " should be conducted to the Place de Grève under a strong escort, that they should go to the Hôtel-de-Ville and confess their crimes, and that then they should ascend a scaffold and be burnt alive." These grim words were posted on January 21, 1782, the day fixed for the festivities, and exactly eleven years before Louis' death.

At Versailles the Arts and Crafts of Paris came in a body to defile in picturesque procession before the Château with bands at their head. The sweeps, bedecked like players, had a chimney at the top of which was perched one of the smallest of their companions. The chairmen brought a nurse and a dolphin (dauphin), and the butchers a fat ox. The locksmiths beat an anvil. The shoemakers were making a pair of boots for the royal child and the tailors the uniform of his regiment. Finally came the gravediggers with the implements of their craft—a pleasantry which might almost have been inspired by the authors of the threatening placards. This element was quickly suppressed.

The Queen's influence increased, as has been already noted, but on occasion this influence was controlled. Thus when **Death of** Maurepas, old and broken in health, though **Maurepas.** witty still, died on November 21, 1781, Marie-Antoinette's circle in vain made an assault on the vacant

266

ministry. Louis XVI, as the Duc de Croÿ informs us, remained impenetrable, and would not allow any notion to get about as to the probable successor to this important post. "It was," he says, "one of the great crises of the reign and every one waited for him. Since there was not, on his part, the slightest suggestion or sign which could show what he intended to do, it was amusing for a philosophical spectator to see the astonishment of the intriguers, and their stupefaction." The Court was transformed. Vergennes, as became a skilled diplomat, gave evasive answers to the importunate place-hunters, who, not knowing to whom they should apply, found the door shut in their faces; their overtures, smiles, and bows were wasted on air. "To understand the general paralysis at Versailles," says de Croÿ with some subtlety, "it must be remembered that courtiers seem to find it absolutely incumbent on them to know on whom they should fawn, whether it be the Chief Minister, his confessor, his body-servant, or his friends . . . it is essential to fawn on some one. Judge then of their astonishment; *they knew no longer whither to turn.*"

Maurepas was not replaced. Louis was stronger than people thought. He managed to be firm on this occasion and he had an argument in his favour—the war, and a perfect adviser, Vergennes. It must be mentioned that the Court had just received a severe and most disconcerting lesson; the Prince de Rohan Guéménée was declared bankrupt with liabilities of 33,000,000 *livres*. The extravagant living and undisciplined luxury of this family, whose head was the unfortunate Maréchal de Soubise of the Seven Years War, had excited too much envy for their failure to awaken much sympathy. The Prince de Guéménée's fall left open the reversions of the offices of Grand Chamberlain and Captain of the Gendarmes of the Guard. His wife, who was Governess to the Children of France, was obliged to resign her functions, which were then offered to the Duchesse de Polignac. The scandal was immense; there was a general outcry among the people. The men of the Revolution bore in mind this fall of one of the most important of the princely houses.

The De Guéménée's Bankruptcy.

In the meantime progress was being made towards peace. England had defeated the French and Spanish fleets off the

Leeward Isles in February 1782 ; and being thus able to treat with honour, the British Cabinet was ready to open **Blockade of** negotiations. But Charles III wished to have the **Gibraltar.** last word at Gibraltar, and tired of the siege, he tried to blockade the impregnable rock. The allied forces were unable to cut off the food-supply of the English, so the result of their action was negative. Colonel d'Arçon's *floating batteries* were used during this campaign, but without success. The Comte d'Artois went as a volunteer to the army encamped at San Roque. He made a triumphal progress from Paris to the court of the King of Spain at San Ildefonso ; then he joined in the military manœuvres, without undue haste. But he had the good taste to be modest on his return. A flatterer, says the Baronne d'Oberkich, spoke to him of the dangers he had incurred.

" There was no glory there," he answered, " and I hold it very cheap. Of all my batteries, the one that did most harm during the siege was my *batterie de cuisine.* For the Spaniards, who are used to living on raw onions, a crayfish jelly was deadly poison."

Happily, Suffren performed marvels in India. He won three splendid victories and assured some Asiatic possessions to **Peace with** France, thus putting her in a good position on **England.** the eve of the peace, which was signed on September 9, 1783. The treaties of Paris and Versailles were the first treaties which had been profitable to France since 1738. The Chancelleries, and particularly that of Vienna, praised Vergenne's wisdom in stopping in time and showing himself satisfied with modest advantages. Dunkirk was freed from the presence of the English commissioner who was there to inspect the French ships. France gained Senegal, St. Pierre and Miquelon, St. Lucia, Tobago and five factories in India. These possessions, limited as they were in 1783, none the less paved the way for fresh conquests, and later it was seen that they were valuable open doors to new enterprises.

PRINCIPAL SOURCES. *Correspondance secrète du Comte de Mercy-Argenteau avec l'empereur Joseph II et le prince de Kaunitz,* published by M. le Chevalier Alfred d'Arneth and M. Jules Flammermont, 2 vols., Paris, 1889 ; Emile Bourgeois, *Manuel Historique de politique etrangère,* 1 vol., Paris, 1897 ; François Rousseau, *Règne de Charles III d'Espagne,* 2 vols., Paris, 1907.

CHAPTER XXI

THE QUEEN'S FIRST CALVARY
1785

The *Mariage de Figaro*. Mirabeau's book. Remarkable inventions. The Controllers of Finance. Calonne. Coldness of the Parisians towards Marie-Antoinette. Cagliostro and the Cardinal de Rohan. Intervention of Jeanne de Valois, Comtesse de la Motte. Oliva. Boehmer. The incident in the grove. The necklace. Arrest of the Cardinal. Rohan acquitted. The opening of the Scheldt. Vergennes' victory.

A FTER the American war there was a short period of calm marked by numerous manifestations of social activity. The peace seemed to give a new life to France. It was at this time that Beaumarchais succeeded in "Mariage de getting his *Mariage de Figaro* produced. The Figaro." Court and the town were amused and attracted by his wit, without suspecting the profound lesson concealed in the history of the Comtesse Almaviva and the lively Suzanne. They did not realize that the boastful barber is the mouthpiece of the small and weak, and that his words are formulæ which a few years later were to become proverbial and serve the cause of the malcontents—those malcontents who were ready to rise from their place behind the scenes where they were fostering the revolt against the aristocracy of birth.

The success of the piece was extraordinary. Applause marked each hit and sally. Noblemen laughed at their own expense, and made others in the audience laugh with them. Beaumarchais showed the nobility a caricature of themselves and they replied : " Yes, indeed, it's very like us." Strange unconsciousness ! The significance of the work became evident as time went on, but it practically escaped its first audience. Beaumarchais had no idea of causing a revolution, he amused himself as much as his hearers. However, the King had fore-

269

seen the danger and said : "It is detestable, it must never be performed ; the Bastille will have to be destroyed if we are to save ourselves from inconsistency in allowing this play to be acted. . . . This man makes a jest of everything which should be respected in a government." But Louis had to yield to the Polignac group. To obtain their end, these latter had said with Figaro : "It is only little minds that fear little writings." After delay the piece was performed at the Comédie Française sixty-eight times in succession, a rare event in the eighteenth century.

Thus it became more and more general for people to say what they thought. President de Bachaumont's chroniclers record an interesting conversation between Louis and Richelieu. The Marshal had just been ill and the King congratulated him on regaining his health :

"For you are not young, you have seen three centuries."

"Not quite, Sire, but three reigns."

"Yes. And what do you think of it all ? "

"Sire, under Louis XIV no one dared to say anything ; under Louis XV they spoke in whispers ; under your Majesty they speak out loud."

His toleration was one of his good characteristics. It was not in vain that Mirabeau published his *Lettres de Cachet*, an **Mirabeau's** eloquent attack on the system of arbitrary im- **"Lettres de** prisonment without trial. The prison of Vin- **Cachet."** cennes was evacuated, and all Paris went to see in this fortress the relics " of ancient barbarism." A few years before the executioner would have publicly burned a book in which the author dared to show that despotism in a State does not depend on the individual character of the sovereign, but on the insufficiency of the laws, " that there is no mean between the absolute reign of despotism and the absolute reign of law."

Minds, said Ségur, are, as it were, " drunk with philanthropy." The institutions of the Abbé de l'Epée and Valentine Haüy were patronized ; the severe winter of 1784 aroused charitable feelings in every one ; the King gave 3,000,000 *livres* for the relief of the distressed ; the Queen caused 200,000 *livres* to be distributed. Their example was generally followed. Public rewards, gold medals, and sums of money were instituted to encourage work. " Prizes are given for all virtues," we read in the records of Bachaumont.

Remarkable inventions were recorded. Did not they think in 1784 that they had conquered the air by means of balloons ? **Remarkable** Blanchard crossed the Channel in a balloon and **Inventions.** enabled the French flag to wave over England. This was enough to make people talk of flying to America. Attempts were also made to walk on the water ; the word " impossible " was not allowed. *Speaking animals, flying birds,* and *feeding ducks* were constructed. Finally, Mesmer bewildered every one with his marvellous tubs, and it was generally believed that the times of Pâris, the deacon, were come again, and that magnetism was a miracle which would cure all ills. " Truly," writes Ségur, " when I think of that period of illusive visions and learned madness, I compare the state we were in to a person on the top of a tower who is made giddy by the sight of an immense horizon and in a few minutes will have a terrible fall."

In the meantime daring increased with freedom ; if those in power made a mistake, they were recalled to their senses by **Controllers of** unusually forcible reminders. This time the blow **Finance.** fell on Calonne, the most baneful Minister of the reign, and through him on the Queen. After the conclusion of Peace the office of Controller of Finance had become of the first importance. Joly de Fleury failed to retain the post ; Ormesson, who succeeded him, was a young Counsellor of State without any great ability. He only remained in office for seven months, from April 1 to November 2, 1783. He was the seventh financial administrator since 1774. The Minister on whom at that moment the stability of the Government depended should have been chosen with the greatest care, but the King allowed himself to be seduced by the intrigues of Madame de Polignac. The Queen who, according to Augeard, was "*very recalcitrant,*" was won over first. Marie-Antoinette since the fall of Joly de Fleury had desired the recall of Necker, but she allowed herself to be persuaded by Madame de Polignac and Baron de Breteuil, Minister of the King's Household, who " after much argument, persuaded their Majesties to make an appointment which was one day to result in the total destruction of their kingdom, and their own end on the scaffold." These are the exact words of Augeard, one of the Queen's two private secretaries, spoken in all sincerity; he gave his sovereigns many proofs of devotion at the beginning of the Revolution. The history of Calonne's ministry shows how right this faithful servant was, although his expression was perhaps exaggerated.

Calonne was as unscrupulous as he was attractive. In his first interview with Louis, he played the saint; he confessed that his debts amounted to 220,000 *livres*, that a Controller-General could always find means of paying them off, but that he preferred to owe everything to the King's kindness. Louis took out the sum from a desk and gave it to Calonne. The new Minister had been Intendant of Flanders and Artois, and had distinguished himself there by his love of display. " No one," writes the Duc de Lévis, " understood better than he how a room should be decorated, or how a fête should be organized." He was very skilful in deceiving the public; his speech to the magistrates of the Chamber of Accounts before whom custom obliged him to take his oath, was considered " a model of well-chosen and manly eloquence," breathing " patriotism " and revealing " the statesman." Like Necker, he had recourse to loans in the form of lotteries; he borrowed 100,000,000 *livres* to begin and he could have obtained a still larger sum, since every one was ready to subscribe. He used part of this money to begin some important constructive works in Paris and the large towns. He established a sinking-fund, by means of which, in twenty-five years, the debt was to be paid off. This last was only a snare, for the scheme was never put into operation. But boundless confidence was felt in a man who developed his plans with such conviction and who seemed to have reorganized the whole financial system. Louis called his minister " his dear Controller-General," and when it was known what use Calonne made of the State's money, people were not wanting who said that the Controller-General was indeed *dear* to France. For three years he cleverly concealed his methods, and his credit seemed inexhaustible; he gave and gave unceasingly, and assumed the rôle of public benefactor without any scruple. Maurepas had once said of Calonne, who had long coveted the post of Controller: " Why! he is a fool, a spendthrift. If you put the finances into his hands

the Royal Treasury would soon be as empty as his purse."
This prophecy was fulfilled. In 1785 the loans amounted
to 487,000,000 *livres*, the debt was 101,000,000, and the deficit
100,000,000 *livres*, but the secret had been well kept. Every one
took advantage of this mad prodigality; no Minister had ever
so completely satisfied the increasing rapacity of the "privileged." One noble said: "When I saw every one holding out
their hands, I held out my hat." At this time Rambouillet was
bought for the King and Saint-Cloud for the Queen. The Prince
de Guéménée sold Lorient to the Crown for 11,000,000 *livres*.
The debts of Monsieur and the Comte d'Artois were paid, but
Calonne's personal expenses surpassed all. The public funds
were squandered in the most extravagant fashion. The Controller's answer to a request for money was: "If it is possible
it is done. It if is not possible it will be done." The Pactolus
flowed on and no one enquired how. Calonne's principles were:
"A man who wants to borrow must appear to be rich; but to
appear rich, he must dazzle people with his expenditure." This
sophism had succeeded in his private life and now the new Controller applied it to his public career.

Pamphlets fell thick upon Calonne, but nothing was more
influential than Necker's book on the *Administration des
Finances*. It was a new *Compte rendu*, in which definite figures
proved the existing financial disorders. Twelve thousand copies
of this book were sold in one month. Calonne defended himself
and showed a bold front; it took more to shake his courage.

He appealed to the clergy, who made him a "freewill
offering" of 18,000,000 *livres* in return for the suppression of the
Calonne's   edition of Voltaire's *Works* published under the
dubious   auspices of Beaumarchais. The repeated loans
Devices.   tired the speculators; Calonne resorted to the expedient of reminting the gold coins, a disguised fraud which brought
in more than 50,000,000 *livres*. Murmurs grew louder and were
addressed particularly to the Queen, who was held responsible
for the Controller's prodigality. Marie-Antoinette realized this
to the full in May 1785, when she went in great pomp to Notre
Dame de Paris to thank God for the birth of the Duc de
Normandie,* which took place on March 27, 1785. She was

* The future martyr of the Temple, the so-called Louis XVII.

S

received in icy silence and said tearfully : " What have I done to them ? " Times had changed and the minds of men seemed in revolt. Owing to skilful calumnies and odious insinuations the **Unpopularity** popular hatred had been turned against a woman **of the Queen.** full of youth and innocence, whose fault had been to inspire those around her, her brothers-in-law and aunts, with a fierce jealousy, which found expression in libels not only in Versailles, but among the people. Gradually the pin-prick became a bludgeon-blow, destined to culminate in the knife of the guillotine.

Marie-Antoinette was to undergo her first Calvary this year.

For some time past the occult sciences had attracted great attention. Both Mesmer and Cagliostro found eager dupes ; the latter pretended to cure all maladies. " As he did not take money," said the Baronne d'Oberkich, " and on the contrary, gave much away to the poor, he always attracted a large crowd, notwithstanding the failure of his panacea. He only cured those who were well, or at least those whose imagination was strong enough to assist the remedy." Cagliostro unveiled the past and revealed the future. Among his celebrated clients was the Cardinal de Rohan, who was entirely captivated and proclaimed everywhere the " miracles " of the magician. Showing a great solitaire on which were engraved the arms of the House of Rohan, he said : " He (Cagliostro) did it, do you understand ? He made it out of nothing. I saw it ; I was there with my eyes fixed on the crucible ; I watched the whole operation. . . . That was not all; he made gold. There in the roof of the palace he made about 5000 or 6000 *livres'* worth before me. He will make me the richest prince in Europe. **Cagliostro and** These are not dreams, Madame : they are proofs. **De Rohan.** His prophecies are realized, and the cures he has effected are wonderful ! I tell you he is the most extraordinary and the most sublime man, and his wisdom is only equalled by his goodness. What alms he gives ! What good he does ! It passes all imagination."

His clever interlocutrix, the Baronne d'Oberkich, answered : " Ah ! Monseigneur, this man must expect to secure some very dangerous sacrifices from you if he has bought such boundless confidence. In your place, I should take care : he will lead you far. . . ."

But Cagliostro alone could not have played enough upon de Rohan's credulity, or led his Eminence sufficiently far. The magician was introduced by his admirer to Jeanne de Valois, Comtesse de la Motte, a clever adventuress, well able to turn the situation to account. She made use of Cagliostro's ascendency over the Cardinal and saw where to strike.

The Cardinal de Rohan, before becoming Grand Almoner of France, had been ambassador at Vienna when Marie-Antoinette was the Dauphine. His mad expenditure, his inexperience, his tactlessness, his foolishness, and even his conduct, which scarcely conformed to his ecclesiastical status, had greatly displeased Maria Theresa, who with some difficulty managed to get rid of this strange representative of the Court of Versailles. Marie-Antoinette shared her mother's antipathy, and in spite of numerous attempts, the Cardinal never gained access to her. Rohan was chagrined at this and his friends knew how ardently he desired to regain her favour. The Comtesse de la Motte knew this better than anyone, and saying that she was an intimate friend of Marie-Antoinette, she offered to obtain an interview for him which should bring about a reconciliation. The adventuress had infinite resources, she took in hand the threads of the intrigue and surrounded herself with the necessary confederates ; she was a wonderful stage manager.

She wanted some one who resembled Marie-Antoinette and she found her. This was Marie-Nicole Leguay, the so-called Baronne d'Oliva. The Comtesse was aware that Boehmer, the jeweller, had put all his capital into a single piece of jewellery worth 1,600,000 *livres ;* it was a necklace of incomparable diamonds which could only be bought by a princess. She knew also, like every one else, that Marie-Antoinette could not resist the attraction of jewellery, and that her jewel cases were never numerous enough for her.

Such were the seemingly incongruous elements with which Madame de la Motte, relying on the credulity of Rohan and the prestige of Cagliostro, formed the scaffolding of a romance never equalled by Anne Radcliffe, Walter Scott, or Alexandre Dumas.

She it was who conceived the scene in the grove. One evening the Cardinal was conducted to the Park of Versailles ; **The Affair of the Necklace.** suddenly in the twilight a woman appeared, who had the form and bearing of the Queen. It was d'Oliva, the " street-walker " whom the Comte de la Motte had met in the gardens of the Palais Royal. Oliva murmured some unintelligible words and let fall a rose as she passed. Rohan thought he heard : " *You may hope that the past will be forgotten !* " He was convinced that the Queen had pardoned him. Then Madame de la Motte told him that Marie-Antoinette wanted to buy Boehmer's necklace and that she had chosen him to nego-tiate the affair secretly. The Comtesse next forged instructions for the purchase, using the Queen's name. No one can think of everything, and she signed the orders " Marie-Antoinette *de France*," though the Queen never signed documents or letters in that way. A more intelligent man would have seen through the trick, but Rohan was an easy prey. Advised by Cagliostro, he bought the necklace on credit, and gave it to an accomplice, whom he thought to be a domestic of the Palace, on February 1, 1785. The Comtesse kept the necklace, sold the separate stones, and squandered the proceeds, amounting to hundreds of thousands of *livres*. The jeweller, who was paid nothing, sent in a claim to the Queen. Marie-Antoinette was convinced that Rohan had made use of her name to obtain the necklace by fraud, and induced the King to order the Cardinal's arrest on August 15, 1785.

The Queen was naturally annoyed, and in her desire for revenge she did not stop to reason. She thought the Cardinal **Arrest of Cardinal de Rohan.** was to blame and must be punished. Her letters to her brother Joseph show how unguarded was her anger : " All had been agreed to between the King and myself. The Ministers knew nothing, the King had the Cardinal summoned and questioned him in the presence of the Keeper of the Seals (Miromesnil) and the Baron de Breteuil. I hope that this affair will soon be ended. But I do not know if it will be sent to the Parliament, or if the culprit and his family will trust themselves to the King's clemency." This was written on August 22, 1785. Then on September 19, 1785, she wrote : " The Cardinal used my name like a vile and maladroit coiner. It is possible that pressed by want of money, he thought he could pay the jewellers by the date he had agreed on, without anything being discovered." And on December 27, 1785 : " The charlatan Cagliostro, La Motte, his wife, and a certain Oliva, a street-walker, are accused with him (Rohan). He must be confronted by them and answer their reproaches. What associates for a Grand-Almoner and a Rohan Cardinal ! "

There was a solemn festival at Versailles on August 15, the day of the Assumption, when France commemorated the vow of Louis XIII and the Queen's fête. The Cardinal de Rohan was there, ready to say Mass, in a cassock of watered scarlet silk and a rochet of English point lace, when he was brought before the King.

" Cousin," said Louis, " what about this purchase of a diamond necklace that you are said to have made for the Queen ? "

" Sire, I see I have been deceived, but I have not deceived."

The prelate was given time to write his defence, but it was impossible to unwind the tangled skein of this intrigue in a few lines. Rohan's statement satisfied no one, and the proud and angry Queen least of all.

There was a crowd in the apartments from the Œil-de-bœuf to the Cabinet of the Clock—an anxious crowd which did not understand why Mass was not being said. The door of the inner room where this tragic scene was being enacted then opened ; Rohan, very pale, advanced, followed by Breteuil, who cried to the Duc de Villeroi, Captain of the bodyguard : " Arrest Monsieur le Cardinal."

The next day the Grand-Almoner was in the Bastille. This hasty decision was an irreparable mistake, but it was impossible Acquittal of to check the nervous tenacity of the Queen, en-
De Rohan. couraged by the hatred that Breteuil bore towards Rohan. One man, Vergennes, might have saved the situation, but he was not at the Council when the question was decided. The Queen was the first victim of this impulsive action. The trial took place before the Parliament, the Cardinal was acquitted, and it was judged that he had been the dupe of the

Comtesse de la Motte, who alone was condemned on May 31, 1786. The Rohans triumphed and declared themselves avenged for the failure of the Prince de Guéménée, but they complained loudly when they heard that the Cardinal was exiled to his Abbey at La Chaise-Dieu, and that he had been forced to resign the office of Grand Almoner. The public joined them in their indignation at this treatment of a man whom justice had acquitted. The Rohans, to whom were allied the Soubises, Marsans, Brionnes, and the Prince de Condé, who had married a Rohan, in their turn put Marie-Antoinette on trial. The poor Queen, who was already unpopular, heard all round her murmurs of blind hatred. The mass of the people thought her guilty, seeing that the Cardinal was innocent, and thus the reprisals of '93 began. When Madame de la Motte underwent the degrading punishment of being branded in the Cour du Mai before the Palais de Justice, public sympathy was on her side and against the Queen. The Crown of France had already begun to roll in the revolutionary gutter. As Goethe says, Marie-Antoinette then lost in the minds of the people that moral support which made her person inviolable.

In 1777 Maria Theresa wrote to Mercy : " I confess that my fears are redoubled at the thought of how much harm **The Queen** a man of this kind (Rohan) would be capable **discredited.** of doing if ever he secured an established position at Court." And the Empress had said to Marie-Antoinette : " The post that Rohan is to occupy alarms me. He is a bad man to have as an enemy, both on your account and on account of his principles, which are quite perverted. Under an affable, easy, and prepossessing exterior, he has done much harm here. Yet I am to see him at the King's side and at yours ! He will scarcely do honour to his office as Bishop." We are forcibly reminded of these predictions by the story of the necklace. Maria Theresa was clear-sighted, but she could hardly have imagined all the harm to be wrought by Rohan's stupid credulity and her daughter's regrettable blindness. The Queen wept and watched the approach of dark days ; joy and repose for her were things of the past. Meanwhile complications started by her brother, the Emperor, nearly provoked another Continental war. Urged by Joseph and his

278

Minister, Chancellor von Kaunitz, Marie-Antoinette championed
the Austrian cause, personally conducted her case with the
King and his Ministers, dictated dispatches, kept back couriers,
informed her brother of all resolutions and thus allowed him to
act with a strong hand.   Too faithful to her mother's principles,
she forgot, or rather did not understand, that the alliance of the
Bourbons with her family was not the beginning and end of
French policy.

In 1784 Joseph, in spite of his treaties with Holland, demanded the opening of the Scheldt and the possession of
The Opening of Maestricht.   The Emperor was rather energetic
the Scheldt.   than clever, and he had a mania for territorial
aggrandizement.   Poland had so easily become part of the
Hapsburg patrimony that everything seemed permissible, and
now Flemish succeeded to Bavarian dreams.   To the first overtures of her brother Marie-Antoinette replied by a " confession "
which she said was " not very flattering to her self-esteem."
" I do not deceive myself," wrote Marie-Antoinette on September 22, 1784, " as to my power, especially in politics.   I
have not a great ascendency over the King's mind.   Would it
be prudent for me to have quarrels with his Ministers on subjects
on which I am nearly certain the King would not support me ?
Without ostentation or falsehood, I allow the public to believe
that I have more influence than I really have, because if I were
not believed to have some, I should have less still."   This essentially feminine way of thinking shows considerable insight.
Joseph in his reply thought it useless to lecture one who showed
such candour and dexterity.   " You should avoid scenes with
any of the King's Ministers," was all he said.   " To tell a pretty
woman who combines tact with wit and ability as you do, how
she ought to act when she knows all the people concerned and
is anxious to succeed in her purpose, would be waste of time,
and might make you laugh. Consistency, perseverance, grasp of
detail, patience, complaisance, and a little constraint are the
sex's true weapons and its most powerful and infallible method
of influencing our wills.   But these means must be prepared
beforehand, for one does not always win the game just at one's
own time."   This is a great change from the Joseph who reprimanded his sister so brutally that Maria Theresa intercepted

his letter, but when the Emperor had need of the Queen of France he knew how to flatter her successfully. In his heart he did not believe that Marie-Antoinette was capable of helping him, as his correspondence with Mercy proves. His judgment of her in his confidential letters to the ambassador is always severe.

Joseph wished to secure the King's support. The opening of the Scheldt was only to be the prelude to the cession of Dutch Flanders to Austria in exchange for a " rectification of frontiers advantageous to the Republic." It was also possibly a step towards the annexation of Bavaria, if Holland would agree to this. It was all to the interest of France to favour these negotiations, since they would give her two safe ports, instead of one, in the Austrian Netherlands. She was reminded of the considerable services which the port of Ostend had rendered her commerce in the last war. This was the theme of Mercy's **Successful Diplomacy of Vergennes.** propositions to Vergennes. The French minister replied that he would refer the question to the Dutch ambassadors, that he desired to be on good terms with the Republic, and it was not his business to dictate laws to them. The negotiations were interminable. Vergennes was firm ; he kept the King equally so, and pursued the wise policy which had enabled him to re-establish France, at least in her external relations. Marie-Antoinette's influence remained negative, in spite of her unceasing efforts to pilot her brother's ship as she wished, and to secure the dismissal of Vergennes. The King would not sacrifice him to his conjugal affection. Victory remained with the minister ; he again calmed the Emperor's exuberance, and on November 8, 1785, he prepared the Treaty of Fontainebleau between Joseph and the Batavian Republic, thus enabling France to intervene in the honourable rôle of mediator. The Emperor demanded payment of 10,000,000 *livres* from the States-General of Holland, because his standard had been insulted, but the Dutch obstinately refused to give more than half. Vergennes agreed to 5,000,000 *livres*, and signed a private treaty with the United Provinces, which were thus relieved of the English influence and gave France great advantages in return. It was a small price to pay for the peace of Europe, for these few millions saved the expenses of a war. But the public did not understand Vergennes' political skill. It was everywhere proclaimed that French money was being expended for the benefit of the Queen's brother ! The idea still haunted the Republicans, who, on the audit of the accounts by the Constituent Assembly, were astonished to find no trace of the fabulous sums believed to have been squandered for the Austrian cause. These same men when they entered the Trianon, expected to find there the room studded with diamonds and the twisted columns ornamented with sapphires and rubies, invented by malignant imagination.

Vergennes made one mistake in allowing himself to be deceived by Calonne and in believing with Louis XVI that the Controller-General would find a solution for the financial difficulties. Their blindness had lasted too long, but the veil was at length to be torn aside.

PRINCIPAL SOURCES. Grimm's *Correspondance* ; *Mémoires* of Bachaumont, Ségur, Augéard, La Fayette, Bailly and Governeur Morris ; *Correspondance secrète du Comte de Mercy-Argenteau avec l'Empéreur Joseph II et le Prince de Kaunitz*, 2 vols., Paris, 1899 ; Funck Brentano, *L'Affaire du Collier*, Paris, 1901 ; Lacour-Gayet, *Voyage de Louis XVI à Cherbourg*, Paris, 1906.

CHAPTER XXII

THE DAWN OF THE REVOLUTION
1786–1789

The King's journey to Cherbourg. Convocation of the Assembly
of Notables. Public sarcasms. Calonne's speech. He creates
an opposition in the Assembly. Loménie de Brienne in power.
His portrait. The new Minister's concessions. Dismissal of the
Notables. Attitude of the Parliament. The Queen's conversation
with Besenval. Exile of the Parlementaires. Joseph's letter to
his sister. The Duc d'Orléans in opposition to the Court.
Brienne's rapacity. The decree of May 3. Espréménil. Agitation in Paris. The King decides to convene the States-General.
Fall of Brienne. Return of Necker.

A FEW days after the termination of the necklace incident,
Louis, perhaps calling to mind the advice of Joseph II,
undertook a journey. He went to Cherbourg from
June 20 to 29, 1786, his object being to view the works then
The King's   carried on in the harbour and the roadstead,
Visit to   which had been commenced after the signing of
Cherbourg. the peace in 1783. Royal journeys, beyond the
annual visits to Compiègne and Fontainebleau, were rare. It
was remembered that Louis XIV had only spent one day at
Dunkirk, and Louis XV only three at Havre. The navy had
been one of Louis XVI's chief concerns, and people were pleased
to see the monarch interested in so glorious a work. " Two
things were particularly noticeable," we read in Bachaumont,
" one, that the King is perfectly well informed in all which
concerns the navy, and shows himself ignorant neither of the
construction, the equipment, nor the handling of ships . . . the
other, that the King questioned each officer who was presented
to him, mentioning to him the actions in which he had been
engaged during the war, and singularly flattered these gentlemen
by the excellence of his memory. . . ."

To repeat Louis' own words, the day of his coronation and that of his arrival at Cherbourg were " the two happiest days of his life." His reception was enthusiastic. To the cries of " Long live the King ! " Louis replied with " Long live my people ! " At Caen he ordered his carriage to proceed at a walking pace, and allowed every one to approach him. He delighted in saying repeatedly : " They are my children." The rejoicings were sincere on both sides.

On his return to Versailles a second daughter was born to Louis—on July 9, but this princess lived scarcely a year. Then **Birth of a** he was swept away into the whirlpool of State **Princess.** affairs; again he had to bear the burden of government, which seemed so heavy to him. His people, whom he loved and whom he wished to see happy, fell a prey to ministerial intrigues ; and Louis had not sufficient penetration to reject the bad counsels that were to ruin him. Following Vergennes' advice he signed a commercial treaty with England on September 26, 1786, which was advantageous from an economic point of view, but he fell once more under the influence of Calonne's artifices, subterfuges, and lies.

At the end of his resources and at enmity with the Parliament, Calonne was obliged to reveal the situation ; in spite of **The Notables** loans to the extent of 487,000,000 *livres*, the debt **convoked.** was 101,000,000, and the deficit 100,000,000 *livres*, but he threw the blame on his predecessors, and as he feared to alarm Louis, once more deceived him. He showed him a plan, as a last resource, which, he asserted, would ensure unlimited prosperity. He asked and received a promise of secrecy from the King. An Assembly of Notables was to be summoned, and proposals for the reform of abuses were to be placed before it. This idea, reminiscent of Henri IV, caught Louis' fancy. There were a hundred and forty-four Notables, among them princes of the blood royal, archbishops, bishops, dukes and peers, councillors of State, deputies from the provinces (four from the clergy, six from the nobility, and only two from the Third Estate), and municipal officials. The majority were natually upholders of the abuses which were to be remedied. Calonne, from motives of vanity, affected to choose among these Notables some of the most prominent of his enemies, such as the Archbishop of Toulouse, Loménie de Brienne, a candidate for the ministry, who was said to be an able administrator. Calonne did not wish his victory to be unattended by risk. Brienne duly took care to discover difficulties and to create opposition.

On December 29, 1786, the King announced to the Conseil des Dépêches * that on the 29th of the following month he was summoning an assembly composed of persons " *of various classes who were the best qualified in his kingdom, and that he would communicate to them his plans for the relief of his people, the restoration of order in finance, and the reformation of many abuses.*" Louis was still under his Controller's influence and he wrote to him the next day : " I did not sleep all night, but it was from pleasure."

The public was much excited. At Court fears were expressed as to the result of this new authority ; a young noble, the **Popular** Vicomte de Ségur, cried : " The King is resign-
Sarcasms. ing." In the town there was little confidence in a minister like Calonne, and a section of the population rejoiced in the certainty that the Assembly would fail. Nothing was known as to the subjects which were to be discussed in the Assembly, but satirists were not far wrong when they distributed pamphlets announcing the spectacle in these terms : " You are informed that Monsieur le Controleur-Général has formed a new company of actors, who will begin to play before the Court on Monday, the 29th of this month. Their principal production will be *False Confidence*, and their second one *Forced Consent*. These will be followed by an allegorical ballet-pantomime composed by Monsieur de Calonne, entitled *The Cask of the Danäids*."

At this time *Théodore* was played in the presence of the Queen at Versailles. The principal character in the piece is a King, who goes on a journey. At a certain place the King's equerry says to his master that there is no more money ; they are both troubled and ask each other what is to be done ? At this moment a voice cried from the pit : " *Assemble the Notables*."

The first sitting, which had been fixed for January 29, was postponed owing to the illness of Calonne and the death of

* The Council for Internal Affairs.

Vergennes on February 13, 1787. The latter's influence over the King would have been very valuable at this time. At length, however, the Assembly opened on February 22 at the Hôtel des Menus. On his way there the monarch received neither cheers nor applause.

But the Controller was full of hope ; he had divided the Assembly into seven boards, with the princes as presidents and the Councillors of State as reporters. There was not one of these princes that Calonne " had not obliged with several millions."

The reforms proposed by the Controller were inspired by those of Turgot and Necker. They were drawn up in vague **Calonne's** terms and in a pompous style which made the worst **Speech.** impression on the Notables and on the public, among whom his speech at the opening was widely distributed.

Calonne had said that his plans, which were known and approved by the King, had become his Majesty's own plans. An altercation followed this, and Dillon, Archbishop of Narbonne, said in angry tones : " Do you take us for sheep and imbeciles that you call us together simply to obtain our sanction to plans which are already settled ? "

The members of the Assembly all demanded to know the exact amount of the deficit before voting the land taxation, which was disapproved by the privileged classes. They insisted on knowing the state of the finances. Calonne refused, saying that it was their duty to decide on the form of the tax and not on its basis. The Notables held firm, and some even spoke of a Convocation of the States-General. The Controller thought that audacity would once more save him, and he distributed in Paris and instructed all the *curés* to read as a sermon an appeal to the people, representing the Notables as upholding opinions which were opposed to the monarch's purpose and to the happiness of his subjects. In the Assembly this caused a tempest of accusations and complaints against this shameless minister. He was confronted with his embezzlements and thefts. La Fayette, the hero of America, demanded a " rigorous " examination of the minister's expenses, saying that " the fruit of the sweat, tears and, perhaps, blood of the people " should not be abandoned to cupidity. Calonne was lost. He had prepared thirty-three *lettres de cachet* with which to strike his adversaries ; he secured the dismissal of Hue de Miromesnil, Keeper of the Seals, and replaced him by Lamoig-

Exile of Calonne. non, President of the Parliament ; he tried to over- throw Breteuil, the Queen's *protégé*, but it was himself that was doomed. He was exiled to Lorraine, but he did not feel safe there, as the people of Metz had hanged his effigy, so he was allowed to retire to Flanders, and thence to England in April 1787. There was some talk of reinstating Necker, but Louis refused to listen to the supporters of the Genevan banker, and a Court intrigue brought a prelate into power. This was Loménie de Brienne, Archbishop of Toulouse,

Loménie de Brienne. who had been since youth a great friend of the Queen's reader, the Abbé de Vermond. He had given proofs of ability ; the construction of the *Brienne Canal* was due to him, and he had won the approval of Turgot and Malesherbes. Joseph II had met him during his visit in 1777, and since then had not ceased to praise him. It seemed a propitious moment to have recourse to the intelligence of a man who was so highly esteemed. He had secured public opinion in his favour as a victorious adversary of Calonne, whose fall he had helped to encompass by his brilliancy in the Assembly of Notables. Marie-Antoinette was, like many others, dazzled by this so-called saviour, and secured his appointment as head of the Financial Council, with a young Master of Requests, Laurent de Villedeuil, Intendant of Rouen, as Controller-General in subordination to him. The Queen was supported by the Keeper of the Seals, Lamoignon, Vergennes' successor, the Comte de Montmorin, and the Baron de Breteuil. Brienne had tried to satisfy his ambition on various occasions. It was common knowledge that he had solicited the succession to Christophe de Beaumont in 1781, when Louis XVI had said : " We must at least have an Archbishop of Paris who believes in God." He was known to be unscrupulous in the means he used to attain his ends ; he had secretly favoured the philosophers, but had never compromised himself. He laughed at miracles and relics even though he sent an elbow-bone of Saint Thomas Aquinas, to the Duke of Parma, first cousin to Louis and brother-in-law of Marie-Antoinette. He was adroit, clever, competent to play a part, and could easily assume the absorbed appearance of a man who is busy with great affairs. He offended no one and flattered every one's particular vanity, and this was all that was necessary to secure him a place beyond his deserts in the public estimation. Louis XVI had been deluded by Calonne's **His Con-** brilliant ease ; Marie-Antoinette in her turn was **cessions.** deceived by Brienne's simulated intelligence. The Archbishop-Minister consented to disclose the state of finances to the Notables, thus with some skill granting what Calonne had refused, and thereby gaining the favour of the Assembly. It was discovered that the deficit had reached 140,000,000 *livres !* Brienne proposed to the Parliament a loan of 60,000,000 *livres,* promising to economize in the King's Household to the extent of 40,000,000 *livres,* instead of the 20,000,000 *livres* promised by his predecessor. The edict was registered on May 10, 1787. The Notables, however, did not wish to vote the necessary taxation (a tax to be levied on all lands and a stamp tax) ; on this point they trusted to the " wisdom of His Majesty." They formulated their wishes, which were that preventive measures should be devised to meet the financial disorders, that a report should be published annually, which should be audited by capable men *who did not form part of the Government,* and that the civil and criminal laws should be revised. This programme seemed to be a preface to the demands which were said to be imminent. La Fayette suggested that a National Assembly should be convened for 1792.

" What ! Monsieur," cried the Comte d'Artois, " you desire the convocation of the States-General ? "

" Yes, Monseigneur, and *even more than that."*

The Notables were dissolved on May 25. " As might have been expected," said Bailly, " in the case of men who had only **Dismissal of** the right to advise and no authority," they left **the Notables.** things almost exactly as they found them. But the popular excitement was increasing. Every one had been interested in the discussions of the delegates. La Fayette told Jay, an American friend of his : " The French have acquired the habit of thinking about public affairs."

The struggle had begun, and at this juncture the Parliament entered the lists to strike a fresh blow against the royal Acropolis, already trembling from the first shock.

Some administrative edicts, which were proposed by Brienne, were passed without opposition. The provincial Assemblies, which had been founded during Necker's term of office in Berry and Haute-Guyenne, were definitely established. These Assemblies were a successful and liberal step towards decentralization. They were composed of forty-eight members, twelve from the clergy, twelve from the nobility, and twenty-four from the Third Estate, of whom twelve were deputies from the towns and twelve from the country proprietors. Their duties were to assess and collect the taxes and to supervise public works. Next the *corvée* was suppressed. But when the stamp tax **Attitude of** was proposed, the Parlementaires were unusually **the Parliament.** violent in their opposition and attacked the extravagance of Calonne and the Court. They demanded statements of receipts and expenditure to assist them in their decision. Brienne refused, since he had shown them to the Notables. The King supported his Minister. The only reply of the Parliament was to draw up a remonstrance, in which it petitioned the King to withdraw the stamp edict and expressed the desire " to see the nation assembled before there was any fresh taxation." The remonstrance was at once printed. The public saw in it the trial of the Government, and realized that all confidence had been lost. The Parliament was considered justified and recovered its former popularity. The agitation spread to the provinces, and all the provincial Parliaments rallied round that of Paris. Brienne had resort to a *lit de justice,* but this " instrument of despotism " was ridiculed, and victory still lay with the magistrates. On August 14, 1787, Mercy gave a graphic description of the situation in a dispatch to Joseph II. The turn which internal affairs are taking, he said, places the King, Queen, and Ministers in the most embarrassing position. The obstinate resistance of the Parliament to the designs of the Court has influenced men's minds. By degrees all classes of society are joining in the struggle.

It is difficult to imagine the audacity with which people even in public places spoke of the royal family, and especially the Queen, against whom violent insults were directed. Marie-Antoinette became *Madame Deficit,* and the Lieutenant-General warned her not to let herself be seen in Paris. The idea of summoning the States-General found universal support, for it was said the country no longer had a guide. The police were powerless to repress the movement ; even if they had put the people in prison by thousands it would have had no effect ; insurrection would have broken out. The King's prestige was deeply shaken. If the Court of Versailles at this time had had the misfortune to be dragged into a war—and the negotiations between Holland, Prussia, and Great Britain were full of menace to France—any measures which might have been taken for safety would have been useless, and a general bankruptcy would have been unavoidable.

The country henceforward took the place of the Parliament and itself made war on Royalty.

Meanwhile the Queen went to Trianon to seek a short rest In the shade of the park, Besenval, one of her confidants, gave **Besenval warns** her advice, and in his own way revealed the **the Queen.** dangers of this critical time. He advocated boldness and wanted the King to show himself master and not to fear to use his authority ; " *otherwise*," he said, " *his Majesty will have to put down his crown, never again, perhaps, to replace it on his head.*"

" Ah ! " cried the Queen, " what harm Monsieur de Calonne has done the country with his Notables ! " This was the cry of the ardent Royalists, but were there many of them left ?

During the night between August 14 and 15 the Ministers decided to banish the Parliament to Troyes, an antiquated **The Parliament** stratagem of another age, and now only a display **banished.** of impotence which increased the popularity of the magistrates. In exile they received the support and encouragement of the various Courts of Paris and even of the University. Reprimands, which almost amounted to orders, were sent from the provinces to Versailles. The King was irresolute, and Brienne profited thereby to get himself appointed Prime Minister. His excuse was that he wished to concentrate the executive power, and his vanity made him think he could pacify the disorders. Lamoignon wished to imitate Maupeou and dreamed of suppressing all the refractory Parliaments, which were fixed in their desire for the *Convocation of the States-General ;* such was the expression which was echoed from one end of France to the other. It was heard at Rennes, Rouen, Bordeaux,

Dijon, Besançon, Grenoble, Toulouse, and Pau. The Convocation was indeed to be, but the Parliament had no suspicion that when it came it would mean the extinction of itself as well as of the monarchy.

Brienne yielded and pardoned the Parliament, and by a declaration dated September 20 brought the exiles back to Paris. Four days later another declaration was published, revoking the stamp duties and the territorial subvention. It was a complete retraction. But the return of the Parliament and these concessions had no calming effect. As before, insulting notices disgraced the walls of Paris. Calonne was burnt in effigy in the Place Dauphine ; an effigy of " the Polignac " was burnt also, and the Queen came near to suffering the same indignity, according to Bachaumont and Hardy. But the unhappy Marie-Antoinette found her severest critics in her own family. On October 6, 1787, Joseph had no compunction in writing to Mercy : " I am *extremely curious* to learn how the disorder which reigns in France will end. I am sorry for the *vexation which it causes the Queen.* . . . I speak of it in the accompanying letter to her, and I touch in passing on the subject of her intimates, whose cupidity brings *all this unpleasantness* upon her. But I am aware that it will have no effect, *for when one has no resources in oneself, the fear of ennui prevails over every other consideration.*" What a tone at such a moment ! He was utterly heartless, and it was only to further his own and the Austrian interest that he recommended the Archbishop of Toulouse to the unfortunate Queen.

The financial measures had so far been illusory. So Brienne formed the plan of issuing a loan of 420,000,000 *livres*, redeemable in five years, and of promising the States-General for 1792. On November 19 the edict was read to the Parliament in the King's presence. **Promise to convoke the States-General.** After a sitting of nine hours, Louis failed to obtain the support he needed, but he none the less caused the registration of the edict to be pronounced, following the formula used at the *lits de justice*. This decision was received with many murmurs. The Duc d'Orléans declared that this form of registration was illegal, that the Assembly was not a *lit de justice*, but an ordinary royal session with right of free discussion. Two councillors, Fretcau

290

and the Abbé Sabattier, uttered words which were " indecent." They were taken to prison, while the Duc d'Orléans was exiled to his Château of Villers-Cotterets. This Prince had at one time been popular at the Court, but he became one of the bitterest enemies of the King and Queen. He even voted for Louis' death ; he himself was to perish on the scaffold.

Fretcau, Sabattier, and Orléans were championed by the Parliament, which demanded their liberation. A quarrel ensued and Louis persisted in his refusal. The loan failed, the taxes were not voted, and the situation became more and more complicated. Brienne had no governing idea, no initiative, and none of the talents with which he had been credited ; his attitude displayed nothing but feebleness and uncertainty. He conceived the idea of summoning the Queen to the Committees and of giving her a preponderating voice in their decisions. Neither by her education nor by her tastes was Marie-Antoinette fitted to give useful counsel. The Archbishop admonished her ; though he may have thus increased his prestige, observes Besenval, " such conduct could only have the effect of compromising the Princess and of making her the object of ridicule."

Brienne did not neglect his own interests. On one occasion he thought he would be obliged to resign his ministry, owing Rapacity of to a severe illness ; even while in bed he coveted Brienne. the Archbishopric of Sens, rendered vacant by the death of Cardinal de Luynes, and the Abbey of Corbie, and he secured both. " Added to this," said Besenval, was " a right to cut down trees to the value of 900,000 francs," which was sufficient to pay his debts. " It was forgotten," said the same writer, " that they were adding fuel to the popular hatred by thus showering money on one who extracted it from everybody and enriched himself whilst he preached economy." Brienne already possessed an income of 700,000 *livres* from his ecclesiastical benefices alone, but he was insatiable and wished in addition to his wealth to have the honour of the Cardinal's purple.

The Archbishop's youngest brother, the Comte de Brienne, replaced De Ségur as Minister for War. He was said to be honest, but he was shallow and very ignorant He had the best intentions, but his efforts ended in his allowing himself to be led without having any clear idea where he was going. He attempted some reforms, wishing to make a complete reconstruction of the army and its discipline, but his attempts soon degenerated into mere personal questions and came to nothing.

In April 1788 the fever spread over the whole country. Governors of provinces were directed to return to their posts, **The Protest of** and the army was ordered to support them. The **May 3, 1788.** King said aloud that he was tired of being under the " tutelage of citizens," and that he wished to " free himself from them." A *coup d'état*, in the shape of a dissolution of the Parliament, was suggested. On May 3 the Parliament made a violent protest against the proposed measure, and declared that " if force reduced it to powerlessness," it would maintain the constitutional principles of the monarchy and would resign " the sacred trust to the King, the States-General, and to each of the united or separate orders which formed the nation." A comedy had been witnessed when the Notables were assembled, but people began now to fear that it had been " the first act of a tragedy." The promoters of this protest of May 3 were Espréménil and Goislard de Montsabert ; on the following night an attempt was made to arrest them, but they took refuge at the Palais. They were followed there by the Swiss and French Guard. The captain of the latter did not know the two councillors and asked where they were : " We are all d'Espréménils and Goislards," was the answer of the entire assembly. The captain retired and returned with a fresh order ; the two offenders gave themselves up and followed the officer. The meeting had lasted thirty hours, and the magistrates separated with violent protests against the arrest of two of their members, who had been " violently torn from the sanctuary of law."

Louis continued his policy, and by the six edicts of May 8 reduced the Parliament to nullity, instituted new Courts of Justice under the name of *Grands Bailliages*, created the Plenary Court, which alone was authorized to verify and register laws, and reserved for himself the power of raising loans at will. The Chief President bitterly opposed this " despotic authority," which royalty claimed, but which *the French nation would never adopt.*

In the provinces there were the same protests and a like refusal to submit to the new edicts. Everywhere agitation was at its height. "A palace for sale, ministers to be hanged, and a crown to be given away," was to be read on the walls of the Parliament which had been turned into barracks. Pamphlets were dedicated "to the sovereigns who are so pleased to see their kingdom become a republic." In the theatre allusions of all sorts were made. The Court used the same weapons and published libels and pamphlets against its adversaries. The promoters of sedition were arrested, and the police were active everywhere. An explosion was expected. Brienne then said these celebrated words : " I foresaw everything, even civil war ! " He tried to struggle against the clergy who deserted him and only granted 180,000 *livres* out of the 8,000,000 he had expected, against the army who disobeyed him, and against the Parliaments and all the supreme courts. On August 8 the King convened the States-General for May 1, 1789, thus condemning the Archbishop's policy. The Prelate declared the nation bankrupt. He hoped to secure Necker as his saviour and colleague ; but the honest Genevan did not wish to work with an unscrupulous minister who had even had recourse to charity and hospital funds, and who with his colleague Lamoignon, was now about to overdraw on the Treasury * as a final impropriety, leaving there only 200,000 francs. At last, on August 25, Brienne sent in his resignation, or rather he was forced to resign : " I think that this was necessary," said Marie-Antoinette to Mercy on the same day ; " I have just written three lines to Monsieur Necker to ask him to come here to me at ten o'clock to-morrow. There is no time for hesitation. If he can begin work to-morrow so much the better. . . . *I tremble—excuse my weakness—that it is I who am recalling him. I am fated to bring misfortune ; and if infernal machinations make him fail again, or if he lessens the King's authority, I shall be still more detested. . . .*" For the future the Queen never ceased to tremble.

The news of Brienne's departure, quickly followed by that

Fall of Brienne.

* By means of Treasury Bills.

of Lamoignon, caused immense joy to the Parisians and all France, and the crowd wished to set fire to the houses of the two ministers. Besenval says that the Place Dauphine was like a field of battle, petards were thrown about, carriages were stopped on the Pont Neuf, and men were obliged to kneel down in front of the statue of Henri IV and cry, " Vive Henri IV ; to the devil with Brienne and Lamoignon ! "

Necker returned to power and immediately restored confidence. He undid all that Brienne had done, repealed the **Return of** edicts, liberated the exiles, reconstituted the **Necker.** Parliament and revoked the edict of bankruptcy, promising his own fortune as a pledge for loans made to the State. In a declaration on September 23 the King fixed the meeting of the States-General for an earlier date, January 1, 1789. But Necker thought it would be wise to call the Notables together again to decide questions relative to the three Orders, and thus months passed away.

The new era began on May 5, 1789, with the assembly of the representatives of the country. The Revolution was born and was already lusty when the procession of deputies, the funeral procession of the monarchy, passed through the streets of Versailles.

" It is with the person of kings," said Rivarol, " as with the statues of gods : the first blows strike the god himself, the last fall only on the disfigured marble."

PRINCIPAL SOURCES. Same as for the preceding chapter.

FIFTH PART

THE ARTISTIC AND LITERARY MOVEMENT

CHAPTER XXIII

I

THE ARTS

Watteau, Quentin de La Tour, Chardin, Greuze, Coysevox, Bouchardon, Pigalle, Caffieri, Falconnet, Lemoyne, Houdon, Clodion, Gabriel, Rameau.

TWO great painters dominate the eighteenth century—Watteau and La Tour. Watteau was a true creative genius and owed everything to his own talent. Where among those who went before him can we find his easy grace, his delicate charm, or his delicious tones and **Watteau.** design? He had no doubt studied Rubens and admired the Venetians in the Crozat Gallery, and perhaps he owed to them something of his life, but not his colour, for a sense of colour is innate. He had seen Terburgs, Teniers and Van Ostades, and from them he may have borrowed the smallness of his canvases. But he owed nothing else to anyone. The poetry which flutters through his *scènes galantes*, the essentially French air which appears in the expressions on his faces, the landscapes which harmonize so well with the character of the actors—all these reveal an exquisite imagination and a finished art ; all these are unique.

His influence, on the contrary, was great. All through the century we see painter after painter more or less directly inspired by Watteau's work : Lancret, his friend, who was more sober, more deliberate, and who lacked his light fancy and picturesque feeling ; Pater, who came from Valenciennes as did the poet of the *Embarkation* and was for a time his pupil ; Van Loo, whose *Halt of Sportsmen* is in the Louvre, and Jean-François de Troy, whose *Oyster Feast* is at Chantilly ; Natoire, who painted the decorations in the Hôtel de Soubise (Archives

Nationales) which are still so fresh, and a whole series of panels now in the Museum of Troyes, but originally executed for the castle of Prince Xavier of Saxony ; * Boucher, who had time in his long life sometimes to be a true artist, as for instance in the ceiling of the Council Chamber at Fontainebleau, but has left behind him too many insipid canvases without any real beauty ; Lagrenée and Le Prince, who were only second-rate painters ; and above all, Fragonard, the last to come, who was borne at Grasse beneath the sun of Provence, and brought to life again the brilliance, the warmth of colour and the consummate art of the poet of the Regency. From one end of the century to the other Watteau and Fragonard join hands, and enclose the host of imitators who serve to emphasize their consummate mastery. Both celebrated and transmitted the *fêtes galantes* of the eighteenth century ; they revive that time of splendid carelessness, whose children smiled and frolicked, and inhaled the perfume of roses without thinking of the catastrophes which were to dispel their charming dreams, fugitive and illusory, like all things human. . . .

Others also followed this school : Ollivier, for instance, the Prince de Conti's painter in ordinary—his pictures are rare, but his *Thé à l'anglaise* in the Louvre is sufficient to show the delicacy of his brush. Eisen, Portail, Cochin, Gravelot, Baudoin, Saint-Aubin and Moreau have shown in engravings, sketches, and vignettes their persistent anxiety to imitate Watteau.

In the eighteenth century before La Tour there were portrait-painters who are not to be disregarded : Tournières, an excellent **Quentin de** physiognomist ; Belle, to whom we owe the charm-**La Tour.** ing portrait at Versailles of the Infanta betrothed to Louis XV ; Rigaud and Largillière, and an artist inferior to them, Vivien ; Nattier, who was popular with ladies ; the beautiful as well as the ugly flocked to him knowing that they would be well treated ; Tocqué, who painted the delicate portrait of Marie, wife of Louis XV, in the Louvre. But the

---

* Natoire said to Vien : " What is the good of painting from Nature ? What difficulty is there in taking a model and copying it ? " This negligence is perceptible in Natoire's work, although their decorative effect is so charming.

pastellist of Saint-Quentin is incontestably the most marvellous representative of the art of portrait-painting in France. Not that he knew how to compose, but he had a better gift, for he could give to a face something intangible, expressive life, brilliance and truth. We must go to his native town and study his sketches—simple heads drawn from models—to see how beautifully a face may be reproduced, not only in its physical but in its moral aspects.

La Tour said himself : " My models think that I catch only the features of their faces, but I search into the depths of their hearts without their knowing it, and I take the whole of them away with me." These sketches, most of them anonymous, which are kept in the silent provincial sanctuary, were used by the artist to enable him to repaint at leisure an elaborate portrait, which was not always equal to the first eager record, set down in an hour or two. At Dijon there is to be seen a head of the artist painted by himself, in which perhaps all the qualities of his talent are displayed, and a very beautiful sketch of Joseph Vernet. To obtain an insight into the art of the pastellist these sketches should first be studied. It is then easier to appreciate the finished works which are to be seen in the Louvre and some of the museums of the large towns of France. Although the portrait of Madame de Pompadour is not worthy of all the praise that has been bestowed on it, the same cannot be said of the portraits of Marie Lesczynska and Marie-Josèphe of Saxony, the Dauphiness, in the same room at the Louvre, which so admirably suggest the resignation of the former and the goodness of the latter, and give us at the same time a complete idea of La Tour's versatility and the perfection of his art. The means by which the painter achieved his results are forgotten in the impression of life that they produce ; the princesses seem to smile at us as though they were about to entrust us with a secret !

La Tour's character was as individual as his art. He was frank like his pastels. He sent a message to the Marquise de **His original** Pompadour when she asked him to come to Ver- **Character.** sailles, saying, " Tell Madame that I do not paint in a town." However, he consented to go to her on condition that no one should interrupt him. This he was promised. When he arrived he unfastened his shoes, his garters and his collar, took off his wig and hung it on a girandole, put a silk skull-cap on his head, and in this picturesque *déshabillé* began the portrait. At the end of a quarter of an hour Louis XV came in.

" You promised, Madame," said the painter, " that your door should be closed."

The King laughed heartily and told the artist to continue.

" It is impossible for me to obey Your Majesty," answered this original, " I will return when Madame is alone."

He got up, took his wig and garters, and went grumbling into another room. He was heard to say several times :

" I don't like to be interrupted."

Louis took a very witty revenge. La Tour, who was a politician and a philosopher at times, took the liberty of saying to the King : " Sire, we have no ships."

" You forget those of Vernet," replied the monarch.

There is no worse trial for a painter than to be discontented with the model he is forced to paint. This was the case when La Tour undertook the portrait of the celebrated financier, De La Reynière, who missed his appointment one day and sent his servant to tell La Tour that he had not time to come.

" My friend," said the painter to the domestic, " your master is an imbecile whom I ought never to have painted. . . . Your face pleases me, sit down, your features are intelligent, I am going to paint your portrait. I tell you again, your master is an idiot."

" But, sir, bethink you ! If I don't go back to the house I shall lose my place."

" Never mind ! I will find a place for you . . . let us begin."

La Tour sat down to his easel. Monsieur de La Reynière dismissed his valet the same evening. The servant's portrait was exhibited in the Salon and the anecdote was told everywhere ; every one wished to know the hero of the affair, and soon there was rivalry as to who should obtain him for a servant.

Amongst the portrait-painters contemporary with La Tour was his friend Perronneau, whose colour is conventional but whose drawing is attractive. He is cold, and his coldness gives him a style and dignity which are respectable. There were also Aved and Duplessis, the latter of whom is brilliantly represented in the Museum at Avignon and the Museum at Carpentras, his native town. There are portraits of Louis XVI and his brothers by him at Versailles, but they give less pleasure than his portrait of his compatriot, the sculptor Péru, in the Calvet Museum. Here Duplessis surpasses himself and is the **Madame Vigée-** precursor of the romantic painters. Madame **Lebrun.** Vigée-Lebrun, who has left several portraits of Marie-Antoinette and the charming picture in the Louvre in which she represents herself holding her daughter in her arms, must not be forgotten, though her art is not perhaps very original. She possesses charm but not sufficient fidelity, for her portraits are not very like their originals, and this fault is not redeemed by her method, which is uninteresting, nor by her colouring, which is more a process than a reproduction of nature.

Another woman, Madame Guiard, had a virile and realistic talent, and many of the qualities which Madame Vigée-Lebrun lacked, but her chief excellence was a robust technique.

Side by side with the genre painters, the creators of a land of poetry, and the protrait-painters, we find historical painters, the successors of Le Brun and Le Sueur. The King encouraged them from habit and a sense of veneration. State commissions still went to such painters as Jouvenet, Coypel, Subleyras, **Historical** Pierre, Doyen and Vien. How futile were **Painters.** the efforts made under the vigilant eyes of an official Mæcenas, the Duc d'Antin, Tournehem, Marigny, or the Comte d'Angivilliers ! Louis XIV or Louis XV could not have dispensed with an official painter. Mariette, in his *Abecedario*, records a significant remark of Gersaint, Watteau's master, who said : " It is to be regretted that Watteau's first studies were not historical paintings. It is to be presumed that he would have become one of the greatest painters of France." To think that Watteau might not have been Watteau is to imagine that a rose-bud might develop into a thistle. People were blinded by the prestige gained by the daubers of enormous canvases ; they did not think that one day Gersaint's regrets would contribute to his pupil's apotheosis.

In this century of frills and furbelows, of the Pompadour, of laughter and grace, of the return to nature, historical pictures were an anachronism. The heroes of Athens and Rome were

301

too remote ; their cold appearance in the seventeenth century had created nothing ; the arid soil could produce no more ; it needed a redeemer ; David came in the epic time at the end of the century and in the midst of the triumphs of Napoleon, threw off the leading strings of his classical education and constituted himself a bold and victorious innovator. But it is not within the scope of the present work to recount that period of France's glory ; we must be content to record the birth of a new genre, cleverly grafted on traditional convention.

We must further note particularly the fathers of modern landscape painting, and after them the painters of popular **Beginnings of Landscape Painting.** scenes, before completing this brief study of our debt to the eighteenth century. A tendency to show the time of day in the open air, in a park, or at the outskirts of a forest is already to be seen in the hunting-scenes of Desportes and Oudry, though they are timid attempts in which people and animals are still the most important points. Joseph Vernet was the first to strike the right note ; he seemed to prepare the way for Corot with his little views of Rome, the *Ponte Rotto* enveloped in the morning mist, and the *Castle of Saint Angelo* with its delicate greys and its golden tints, the treasures of one of the rooms of the French School at the Louvre. When looking at these pictures we recall the naïve criticism of Mariette : " *It is by studying from nature* and by working with the greatest application, that he (Vernet) has acquired so beautiful a touch, and has learned to render so truthfully the light and shade and the effects produced on the air by the vapours which rise from the earth or the water, drawn upwards by the sun." It is in studying from nature ! This was the great innovation of this period, in some ways so artificial. The series of the *Ports de France*, which Vernet painted by command of Louis XV, are still in the Louvre. In detail they are very delicate, but as a whole they have an air of official monotony.

Italy brought luck to Vernet, and it was there, also, in the shade of the Coliseum, that Hubert Robert found his vocation. He brought back from Rome, from the studio of Panini, a taste for ruins and a talent for painting them. Robert knew how to compose with intelligence and art, he put sun, a real sun, on his ancient stones, he lightened his palette, gave depth to the sky, and poetry to the silence of ruined temples.

France has her Canaletto in Pierre Antoine de Machy. He was less brilliant and spontaneous than the Venetian master, but his views of Paris, of which there are a great number in the Carnavalet Museum, have a certain interest, although they are perhaps cold. Comparing Hubert Robert and Machy, Diderot in his Salon of 1761 made this very just remark : " I watch Machy, ruler in hand, drawing the grooves of his columns. Robert has thrown all such instruments out of the window and has only kept his brushes." This was a good exposition of the verve and warmth of the true painter, and the dry precision of the architect.

The cottage also had its exponents. A shepherd, Simon Mathurin Lantara, displayed his powers in some very interesting works, landscapes of the neighbourhood of Béziers, Blois, and even Trieste, which, save that they lack the perspective of fine palaces and the outlines of large ships, might compete with those of Claude Lorrain. With these happy creations, moonlight, setting sun, and mist effects, may be classed the pictures of Lazare Bruandet, Louis Gabriel Moreau's fresh landscapes round Paris, and Jean Louis de Marne's beautiful perspectives ; they have a historical significance. The origin of the French School of 1830, the School of Rousseau, Troyon and Jules Dupré, must be sought among these early landscape painters, as well as in the famous Constable in the Louvre.

Two artists remain to be mentioned, not equally appreciated, but both very popular, one beloved of connoisseurs, and the other the favourite of the Sunday public at the Louvre. Chardin and Greuze have still their ardent admirers. Chardin has brought before us with splendid power the poorer classes, their surroundings and atmosphere. Without him we should know but little of the modest existences he has so lovingly reproduced in pictures now hanging in places of honour in the various museums. If we were to judge the eighteenth century solely from the point of view of its painters, we should get a very incomplete idea of it without Chardin. It is a pleasure to see his picture of the good mother setting her children down to table and asking a blessing

Chardin.

on the food. Her clothing is graceful, but displays nothing fanciful, no false elegance ; she is a true *bourgeoise*. This composition is exquisitely simple ; it is drawn with a broad and able brush, without any harsh notes ; its sober harmony is perfect. How much is due to Chardin for having painted with such feeling and delicacy what he saw every day, instead of wandering in some operatic Olympus, some dream country, instead of bedizening his figures in the finery of past generations ! He was a true child of his century ; he gives us a clear impression of the familiar people who lived around him ; and as he had no imagination, he had sufficient wit not to force his talent. It was incontestably wise of Chardin, who was naturally an unpoetical painter, to be content with prose. Besides his interiors he has left pictures of still-life which are a feast for the eyes. In them the light caresses the objects and puts them into high relief; beautifully shaped fragile porcelain, flowers, fruit, and articles of food, form so many pretexts for giving us a lesson on art, for showing us that the most commonplace object is capable of expressing correctness of drawing and the magic of colour. When Chardin had grown old and rich in experience, he began to paint pastel portraits, amongst others his own and that of his second wife, Marguerite Pouget, now in the Louvre. They hang near the collection of LaTours, and bear this proximity bravely. It must be admitted when looking at the works of this faithful master that the eighteenth century was not entirely the beribboned reign of affected *pompadoureries*. Diderot has given an excellent definition of his art. " One stops before a Chardin," he says, " almost instinctively, as a traveller who is tired with a long journey sits down, practically without realizing it, in a spot where there is a green bank, silence, water, shade and freshness."

Chardin was content with scanty remuneration ; he was accustomed to live on very little. One day he was painting a hare when his friend, Le Bas the engraver, came in upon him. Le Bas admired the hare and wanted to buy it.

" It can be arranged," said the painter ; " you have a jacket which pleases me very much."

Le Bas took off his coat and carried away the picture.

Diderot tells of a conversation of Chardin's in which he

Thus Lalande and the Abbé Lacaille determined the distance between our planet and the moon, and the result of their calculations was definitively accepted. Lacaille spent four years, from 1751 to 1755, at the Cape of Good Hope at the expense of the State. His whole mission, including the cost of his instruments, cost 9144 livres 5 sous. When he went for payment to the Treasury agents, these functionaries were greatly surprised, not being accustomed to deal with accounts which revealed such honesty. Money mattered nothing to the savant, who thought himself sufficiently rewarded by the success of his lofty researches.

The study of astronomy advanced in England more especially. Bradley and Herschel made important discoveries for the general benefit, such as the circular movement of the earth and the insertion of Uranus and the satellites of Saturn in the chart of the heavens.

Again, it was foreigners who established the great physical laws. But Réaumur in 1730 applied them to the thermometer, Réaumur. and the brothers Montgolfier to aerostatics in 1783. Modern chemistry is indebted to Lavoisier, who was born in 1743 and died on the scaffold in 1794, and to Berthollet. The former discovered oxygen, and the latter expounded the laws of chemical affinities. Their progress necessitated a methodical nomenclature, which was proposed by Guyton de Morveau in 1782, and adopted by Lavoisier, Berthollet, and Fourcroy in 1786. This introduced light into chaos and caused a rapid advancement in practical utility and numerous industrial applications.

The best known among the men of science was Buffon. In his masterly *Histoire naturelle* he founded Anthropology and Buffon. Ethnography, and in his *Époques de la nature* he anticipated Cuvier's system in many respects. The Jussieus, Lacépède and Daubenton were his collaborators. Buffon is an admirable writer and he even had time to give the secret of his talent. His *Discours sur le style* is a classic and a literary achievement of the highest merit. Before him Fontenelle had already expounded science to the ignorant, but not quite so ably.

Medicine was still backward and decidedly empirical with

its eternal bleedings, ridiculed by Beaumarchais no less sharply than by Molière. An Englishman, Jenner, introduced vaccination, and a Genevan, Tronchin, decided to become a hygienist rather than a dispenser of remedies. Once when summoned to the Dauphiness, Marie-Josèphe of Saxony, he had breakfast with the princess and found that she ate too fast. La Breuille, her physician-in-ordinary, intervened, and said that the meal usually took seven minutes.

" It must be fifteen," replied Tronchin.

The Dauphine declared that she was accustomed to eat fast and could not do otherwise.

" You must learn, Madame, for good digestion depends on it."

Society was not accustomed to such authoritative statements, or to such simple precepts, which seemed to show so little learning. Consequently Tronchin had to defend **Tronchin.** himself against his *confrères* in Paris. He caused a revolution and excited much jealousy. The apothecaries were forced to lay down their arms. The Genevan met with great success, and every one wanted to consult him. The Æsculaps of the period laughed when Tronchin placed the Duc de Gramont on a diet of cold meat, and ordered Monsieur de Puysieulx to rub himself with pomade, explaining that his internal condition was sound, but that his skin, which he termed the " pie-crust," was too dry, and that this dryness prevented perspiration. They laughed again when the foreign doctor recommended exercise for women, were it only to sweep out their own rooms. But the sick were all the better for following his wise prescriptions, and the mockers were made to look foolish.

A new science—Political Economy—was created in the eighteenth century ; it was based on material phenomena and the social interests dependent on them ; it studied **Quesnay.** the productive forces of nature and reckoned with the needs and aspirations of man. Madame de Pompadour's doctor, Quesnay, was the real pioneer of Political Economy, and his aims are summed up in Turgot's motto : " Freedom of labour and barter."

D'Alembert and Diderot conceived the idea of combining scientific ideas and all that was known of the various branches of knowledge in an historical work. Such was the origin of the *Encyclopédie* or *Dictionnaire raisonné des sciences, des arts et des* métiers, the great Palladium of the century. The first volume appeared in 1751, and the seventeenth in 1765. Those who are wrongly termed philosophers and should be called the secret enemies of metaphysics, made use of this vast store of knowledge to deny everything that was not founded on reason alone, forgetting that though certain facts may be inexplicable, they are none the less worthy to be considered and discussed. A leader of modern thought has made the excellent criticism that " the Encyclopædists knew everything except the *indescribable something*. . . . Their science distinguishes things as snow distinguishes objects ; it isolates and freezes them. . . ."

The Encyclopædia.

Supernatural belief, and at the same time traditions, were overthrown, and scepticism became the fashion. The light which these new men diffused for the future enlightened a merely rationalistic world ; the benefits of their physical discoveries compensated humanity to a certain extent, but they forgot that the soul as well as the mind needs comfort and support. Their work was not completely successful ; it was lacking in the immortal flame of aspiration towards a future life. To deny a thing does not destroy it. Neither a nation nor a morality can be killed, in spite of the faults and errors of their representatives.

D'Alembert and Diderot attracted a Pleiad of famous collaborators : Montesquieu, Rousseau, Buffon, Turgot, and Condillac, each in his own department dealt with purely scientific questions from an uncontroversial standpoint. We may cite Montesquieu's article on *taste*, Rosseau's dissertation on music, or Turgot's essays on social and administrative economy. After them Voltaire and Holbach were more aggressive, for they took the bull by the horns without always raising their masks ; here the *Encyclopédie* becomes an arena wherein the champions, apparently ashamed of the blows they struck, used the weapon of anonymity. In this they were only half French, for they had no courage.

Voltaire was the cleverest advertiser of his times ; no one knew better than he did how to secure the success of a work,

especially if it were his own. There is a very witty passage
of his in which he praises the usefulness of the *Encyclopédie*,
pointing out carefully all the good points and cleverly glossing
over the bad ones. Under Louis XV at a little supper a
discussion arose on ignorance.

" It is funny," said the Duc de Nivernais, " that we amuse
ourselves daily killing partridges in the Park of Versailles and
sometimes killing men or being killed on the frontier, without
knowing exactly what it is that kills."

" Alas ! it is the same with everything in the world,"
answered Madame de Pompadour. " I do not know what the
rouge which I put on my cheeks is composed of, and I should be
much embarrassed if some one asked me how the silk stockings
which I am wearing are made."

" It is a pity," said the Duc de la Vallière, " that his Majesty
has confiscated our *Dictionnaire Encyclopédique*, which cost us
each a hundred pistoles. We should soon have found in it
the key to everything."

The King sent for the seventeen volumes and they learnt
from them all they had wished to know.

" Ah ! what a splendid book ! " cried the Marquise, " Sire,
did you confiscate this *depository of all useful things* so as to be
its sole possessor and the only savant in your kingdom ? "

" Really," answered Louis XV, " I do not know why I was
told so much against this book."

" Well ! Do not you see, Sire," answered the Duc de
Nivernais, " it is because it is excellent ? People never object
to the mediocre and dull in anything. If women try to make
a newcomer look ridiculous, it is because she is prettier than
they."

" Sire," went on the Comte de Coigny, " you are very happy
that men have been found in your reign who know all the arts
and can transmit them to posterity. Everything is here ; from
the way a pin is made to how to cast and point a cannon, from
the smallest to the greatest things. Thank God that your
kingdom is the birthplace of those who have served the entire
universe. The other nations must buy the *Encyclopédie* or
imitate it. Take everything I have, but give me back my
Encyclopédie."

" All the same," said the King, " they say that there are
many faults in this necessary and admirable work."

" Sire," said the Comte de Coigny, " there were two badly
made ragoûts at your supper. We did not eat them, and yet
we have had plenty. Would you have liked the whole supper
to have been thrown out of the window because of those two
ragoûts ? "

This scene gives a sparkling summary of a royal conversation.
As for the comparison at the end, it was too generous. Except
for about fifty articles the famous *Dictionnaire raisonné* is of
very little interest. Besides the articles which are out of date,
there are many more than two " badly made " articles in the
seventeen volumes. For the rest, Voltaire was quite correct
when he said that the *Encyclopédie* was a harlequin's coat, with
a great many pieces of good material, but also a great quantity
of rags.

III

LITERATURE

Voltaire, André Chénier, Destouches, Piron, Gresset, Marivaux,
Beaumarchais, Montesquieu, Jean Jacques Rousseau.

THE literature of the eighteenth century is the mirror of
this positive, seditious period, in which ideas were everything
and their expression very little. The traditions of beautiful
style remained, but the heritage was not always respected.

Such philosophical times do not breed poets, and the
springs of Hippocrene were dry. The age had the poets that it
deserved. Voltaire, whose name immediately

Voltaire.
suggests itself when any manifestation of brilliance
is under discussion, has left epistles, stanzas, and short poems,
and even an epic poem and a shameful burlesque ; but practically his one poetic talent lay in correct rhyming and scansion.
His malice and ingenuity appear in some of his verses and give
them a certain attraction ; he knew how to write a madrigal,
but he flattered every one and knocked at all doors at the same
time, with the result that his able rhetoric is quite lacking in
sincerity. He flattered in turn the Regent, the young King,

Frederick II, the Queen, the Dauphines, the favourites, from Madame de Prie to Madame du Barry, a strange medley of contradictory eulogies—and of substantial benefits.

Voltaire wrote to the King of Prussia :

> O philosophe roi, que ma carrière est belle !
> J'irai de Sans-Souci, par des chemins de fleurs,
> Aux champs élysiens parler à Marc-Aurèle
> Du plus grand de ses successeurs.
> A Salluste jaloux je lirai votre histoire.
> A Lycurgue vos lois, à Virgile vos vers :
> Je surprendrai les morts ; ils ne pourront me croire ;
> Nul d'eux n'a rassemblé tant de talents divers.*

He sent the same exaggerated compliments to Louis XV, George I, Maria Theresa, Catherine II, and Gustavus III.

But poetry was not Voltaire's forte ; prose was necessary to his lucid mind.

The other poets of the period are forgotten. No one reads La Motte-Houdard, Thomas, Bernis, Saint-Lambert, Roucher, Lebrun, Malfilâtre, or Lefranc de Pompignan now. Some, like Jean Baptiste Rousseau, Gilbert, Gresset, and Delille, still have a place in anthologies, but their verses are like dried flowers in a collection. Others, such as Parny, Gentil-Bernard, Dorat, and Piron, are excluded altogether ; their licentious verses have been relegated to the back of the bookshelf, safe from youthful **André Chénier.** curiosity. One true poet only, André Chénier, was living at the end of the century. He was born at Constantinople. His mother was Greek and his father French, and he seemed predestined to say :

> Sur des pensers nouveaux faites des vers antiques.†

He defended the French language, which had been stigmatized by versifiers who thought to excuse themselves by complaining of the instrument they did not know how to use :

* O philosopher King, how fair is my prospect ! I shall go from Sans Souci by a flowery path to the Elysian fields to speak to Marcus Aurelius of the greatest of his successors. To jealous Sallust I shall read your history, to Lycurgus your laws, and to Virgil your verses. I shall surprise the dead ; they will not be able to believe me ; none of them have combined so many different talents.

† Antique verses on new thoughts.

LITERATURE

Il n'est sot traducteur, de sa richesse enflé,
Sot auteur d'un poème ou d'un discours sifflé . . .
Qui ne vous avertisse, en sa fière préface,
Que si son style épais vous fatigue d'abord . . .
Si son vers est gêné, sans feu, sans harmonie,
Il n'en est point coupable : il n'est pas sans génie ;
Il a tous les talents qui font les grands succès ;
Mais enfin, malgré lui, ce langage français,
Si faible en ses couleurs, si froid et si timide,
L'a contraint d'être lourd, gauche, plat, insipide.*

Chénier had that " unpremeditated expression " which " has its birth with the inspiration," and is inseparable from it. He could always find the rhythm, the imagery, and the form which suited his ideas ; all these came to him at once and thus he was a true poet. The secret had been lost for a hundred years and Chénier rediscovered it. He makes the gentle kingfishers weep over Myrto, the young Tarentine, and over the young captive whom he endows with an emotion long unknown. Harmony had been forgotten, when all at once sounds like these were heard :

Je ne suis qu'au printemps, je veux voir la moisson ;
Et comme le soleil, de saison en saison
    Je veux achever mon année.
Brillante sur ma tige et l'honneur du jardin,
Je n'ai vu luire encor que les feux du matin,
    Je veux achever ma journée.†

He made the blind poet, the divine Homer, live again in an atmosphere of beauty ; he repeopled the poetic desert with his visions of Greece and his noble enthusiasm ; he reawakened the soul of France with the magic of his melodious words. He had

* Every foolish translator puffed up with his wealth, every author of a poem or of a discourse which has been hissed . . . tells you, in his pompous preface that if his heavy style tires you at first, . . . if his verses are awkward, without fire and without harmony, he is not to blame : he is not without genius ; he has all the talents necessary for a great success. But in spite of himself, this French language, so weak in colour, so cold and so timid, has forced him to be ponderous, clumsy, dull, and insipid.

† I have only seen the spring, and I wish to behold the harvest : like the sun from season to season I wish to finish my year. Shining on my stalk, the honour of the garden, I have seen as yet only the morning fires ; I wish to finish my day.

faults, it is true, his verses are sometimes violent and rhetorical, and he perhaps relied too much on myths. But, though he sometimes indulged too freely in periphrase, he made prosody more flexible and freed it from restraint.

André Chénier died on the scaffold on the 7th Thermidor, at thirty years of age, when Fouquier-Tinville had ceased to keep count of his innocent victims. The poet Roucher was on the same cart with him, and the two friends exchanged this conversation :

" You," said Chénier, " the most irreproachable of our citizens ! A father ! an adored husband ! They are sacrificing you ! "

" You," answered Roucher, " you, virtuous young man ! They are leading you to death glowing with genius and hope ! "

" I have done nothing for posterity," answered Chénier, and then he struck his forehead and was heard to add : " *All the same, I had something there.*" They both talked of poetry until the last moment, and recited a scene of *Andromaque*, borrowing the words of Orestes and Pylades as if to take courage under the protection of Racine :

Oui, puisque je retrouve un ami si fidele . . .*

The dramatists endeavoured to maintain the prestige of tragedy, and poured forth their alexandrines. But their dramas,

Tragedy. though often well designed, had more regard for the tastes of the public, for whom they had been composed, than for art ; however, they enriched their authors and the booksellers, and gave excellent opportunities to excellent actors. With the exception of Voltaire's *Zaïre*, an imitation of Shakespeare, which was the masterpiece of the Louis XV style, and his *Mérope*, nothing of this vast repertory has survived. Who would think of reviving Crébillon's tragedies with their improbable scenes founded on incognitos, or those of Lemierre, La Harpe, Belloy, who wrote *Le Siège de Calais*, or Saurin ? Ducis with his feeble adaptations of Shakespeare was well intentioned, but artless and ridiculous.

Comedy in verse was more honourably upheld ; not that any

* Yes, as I find again so faithful a friend . . .

pleasure can be derived from glancing at the works of Destouches. It is better to go back to the source from which he draws his material, La Bruyère. Having borrowed his character, such as the Ungrateful, the Irresolute, the Calumniator, or the Boaster from the latter, he dramatized it as well as he could with a setting of supernumaries and puppets. Let us give Destouches the credit due to him for the following line, which is so often attributed to Boileau :

> La critique est aisée, et l'art est difficile.*

Destouches had the further distinction of being preferred to Molière by Lessing in his *Hamburgische Dramaturgie*.

Satirical comedies, such as Piron's *Métromanie* and Gresset's *Méchant*, raised the standard of the theatre. Piron drew the character of a poet who could see nothing but **Comedy.** poetry in everything, very wittily. His metromaniac pursued the passers-by with his verses, and was always dreaming abstractedly ; he did not live in the same planet as mankind. The plot of this comedy is very complex, but it shows its superiority in its natural and expressive style. The famous quotation " J'ai ri, et me voilà désarmé " † is from *Métromanie*. Gresset, the author of *Vert-Vert*, tried his hand at comedy and had some success. His *Méchant* says :

> Les sots sont ici-bas pour nos menus plaisirs, ‡

and the whole play is merely a development of this clever line. Cléon takes a malicious pleasure not only in laughing at exhibitions of foolishness, but in provoking them. A young coxcomb thinks it fine to follow his example and there is an extremely funny dialogue between the *Méchant* and his pupil. The five acts are filled with familiar and much-quoted verses :

> L'esprit qu'on veut avoir gâte celui qu'on a . . .§
> L'aigle d'une maison n'est qu'un sot dans une autre. . . .‖
> Elle a d'assez beaux yeux pour des yeux de province.¶

---

* Criticism is easy and art is difficult.
† I laughed and so I was disarmed.
‡ Fools are here below for our distraction.
§ The wit one wishes to have spoils that which one has.
‖ The eagle of one house is but a fool in another.
¶ Her eyes are fairly beautiful for provincial eyes.

There were no real successors to Molière and Regnard.
Piron and Gresset, however, were able to amuse their contemporaries, and they created some types which amuse us also.

But two dramatists, Marivaux and Beaumarchais, struck
an entirely new note and seem to sum up all the wit of the
eighteenth century as perfectly as Watteau and La Tour.

There were some attempts at sentimental comedies and
popular dramas. La Chaussée and Diderot were in this respect
the somewhat tedious and solemn ancestors of melodrama. They
outlined a genre which was to develop later with a liberal admixture of laughter and tears. But Marivaux and Beaumarchais
left a definitive work with strongly marked individuality ; they
seem to have had no masters and to have formed no pupils. It
is difficult to imitate the charming subtlety of the former and
the audacious impertinence of the latter. The mark of the
creative writer is that he cannot be imitated.

The author of *Fausses Confidences* was so original that a
word had to be coined to describe his talent and wit. This
Marivaux. word is *marivaudage*, and by it his comedies may
be recognized, as all his actors *marivaudent*, that
is to say, speak with an ease, grace, and irony that can scarcely
be met with elsewhere. They are all akin, the Luciles and
Dorantes, as well as the Lisette and Lubins, the countesses and
coxcombs, as well as the maids and valets. This may be a fault
from the standpoint of dramatic truth, but he takes his reader
into a romantic dream, into a rose and blue world, and we must
become familiar with the exceptional beings who people this
realm of poetry. A great critic, Paul de Saint-Victor, has so
well expressed the enchantment produced by Marivaux's plays,
that we cannot refrain from quoting him. He tells a pretty
story about them : " A fairy entered, at midnight, the great
hall of an old castle hung with high warp tapestries. The shepherds of the *Astrée* and the nymphs of the *Aminte* were playing
their flutes or drawing their bows, enthroned on clouds or conversing in green arbours all along walls transformed into idyllic
gardens. But the autumn of centuries had passed over this
spring of colour, the sky was getting yellow, and the figures
themselves had begun to fade. . . . All these frail people were
falling away, stitch by stitch, showing the inner void. A few

days more and their fictitious existence would be over. The fairy touched this fading phantasmagoria with her wand and suddenly a magic life animated it. . . . That is the miracle which occurs at each revival of Marivaux comedies, which are now as faded as ancient tapestry. This society of which he has recorded the fleeting brilliance in a silver and silken style is a thing of the past. The characters are as strange to us as the inhabitants of the planet Venus. . . . Yet whenever this Eldorado is staged the charm works and the enchantment is complete. . . . We once more fall in love with this exquisite world, these delicate metaphysics, and the gentle maids whose subtle loves make one think of the marriage of flowers and the interchange of their perfumes." '

One of the dialogues will give a better idea of *marivaudage* than any commentary. The following takes place between Lépine, the Marquis' valet, and Lisette, the Comtesse's maid, who exchange gallant remarks :

LISETTE. I am busy, and I shall leave you.

LÉPINE. Gently, Mademoiselle, wait a minute. I think it time to tell you of a little accident that is happening to me.

LISETTE. Well ?

LÉPINE. As a man of honour, I had not realized your charms. I was not acquainted with your appearance.

LISETTE. What does that matter ? I can say the same about you : I have only just got to know yours.

LÉPINE. The lady thought that we loved each other.

LISETTE. Well, she thought wrong.

LÉPINE. Wait : this is the accident. Her words made my eyes rest on you more attentively than usual. . . . It is certain that my master has very tender feelings for your mistress. This very day he told me that he contemplated telling you of his sentiments.

LISETTE. Just as he likes. The answer that I shall have the honour of communicating to him will be short.

LÉPINE. Let us note, by the way, that the Comtesse likes the society of my master and that it delights her to see him. You will say that our people are strange creatures and I agree with you. The Marquis, who is a simple man and not at all daring in his speech, will never venture to make a declaration, and the Comtesse is terrified of declarations. In this conjuncture I consider we had better encourage these two. What will happen ? They will love each other honestly and simply, and they will marry in the same way. What will follow ? That when you see me your comrade you will make me your husband, from the sweet habit of seeing me. Well then ! speak ! are you willing ?

If the Comtesse and Lisette had said " Yes " immediately, the comedy would have been finished too soon, and there would have been no *marivaudage.* But our author has to follow a labyrinth before arriving at a foregone conclusion, and that is the secret of his subtle art and his sentimentality. His conversations, in which there is never a raising of voices, never anything dull, are a pleasure to readers even more perhaps than to spectators—a pleasure similar to that which we feel when looking at a scene by Watteau. He revives the age of elegance and refinement.

Beaumarchais' comedies are so intimately connected with the social movement of the century that it has already been necessary to refer to them in connection with the *Mariage de Figaro,* which created such a sensation in 1784. It announced the new era in clarion notes.

Beaumarchais had given evidence of his talent before this brilliant satire. On February 23, 1775, the *Barbier de Séville* **Beaumarchais.** was produced, in which Figaro, created to utter caustic aphorisms, prepared the public for the audacities to come. He begins with such dicta as : " The great do us sufficient good when they do us no harm," and " Considering the virtues required of a domestic, does your Excellency know many masters who are fit to be servants ? " As he began, so he continued. In the *Mariage* he put away all restraint and openly pleaded the cause of the oppressed. " Because you are a great noble you believe yourself to be a great genius ! Nobility, fortune, rank, place, all these make men proud ! What have you done for all these fine things ? You have done nothing but give yourself the trouble of being born : in other respects you are quite an ordinary individual ! While I, who am lost in the crowd of the obscure, have had to display more science and more calculation merely to exist than have been expended

LITERATURE

for the last hundred years in the government of all the Spains ! "
Figaro's description of his existence in the famous monologue
in the fifth act ends with an extremely pessimistic confession :
" Now master, now servant, as it pleases fortune, made ambitious
by vanity and laborious by necessity, but delighting in idleness !
I have seen everything, done everything, worn out everything.
Then my illusions were shattered and I am disabused . . .
Disabused ! " We can see what this *Folle journée* means, how
its comic humour and reckless wit will speedily lead to the
abandonment of principles. These two comedies, though one is
scarcely more than a timid preface to the other, are the whole
of Beaumarchais. The rest of his plays are unimportant ;
neither his first two productions, *Eugénie* published in 1767 and
Les Deux Amis published in 1770, nor his last comedy, *La Mère
Coupable,* a sequel to the *Mariage de Figaro,* can be compared
with the masterpieces which still charm us, though we have
forgotten the moment at which they were written, and the
influence they had on the already doomed reign of the unhappy
Louis XVI.

Beaumarchais broadened the theatrical horizon. He made a
rostrum of the stage. The prose-writers, moralists, philosophers
Montesquieu. or historians who are next to be dealt with show
where the dramatist found his inspiration ; he
was the brilliant mouthpiece of the ideas of Montesquieu,
Voltaire, and Jean Jacques Rousseau, to quote only the great
leaders. Charles le Secondat, Baron de la Brède et de Montesquieu
published his *Lettres Persanes* in 1721 in the middle of the
Regency. This nobleman, who was President of the Bordeaux
Parliament, made his first appearance with a book which was
apparently light, but which, nevertheless, foreshadowed the
author of the *Esprit des Lois*. His Persian who was so anxious
to know Paris was a shrewd observer, a witty satirist, and had
read La Bruyère. He made jokes, but he touched on grave
social, political, and religious questions. In his *Considérations
sur la grandeur et la décadence des Romains* and the *Esprit des
Lois* which followed it, serious though these works are, we are
sometimes astonished to find reminiscences of Usbeck's vein of
humour. Madame du Deffand called the *Esprit des Lois*
" witticisms on the laws " (*de l'esprit sur les lois*) and Voltaire

asked if it were seemly " to make jokes in a work on jurisprudence."

But these echoes of the style of the *Lettres Persanes* in no
way detract from the value of these books, and Montesquieu's
exposition of the philosophy of modern history. " It is not
Fortune which governs the world," he says. " There are general
causes either moral or physical which raise, maintain, or overthrow each monarchy. All the incidents are in subjection
to these causes. If the loss of a battle, that is to say, a particular
cause, has destroyed a State, there must have been a general
cause which made it possible for this State to perish as the
result of a single battle. In short the general tendencies
bring about all the particular incidents." Montesquieu upset
Bossuet's " divine " theory and explained how laws are formed
under the influence of government, climate, religion, and
custom. His style gave jurisprudence a place in literature,
just as the brilliant writer Buffon gave Natural History a claim
to rank as such.

Voltaire, at the age of twenty-five, in 1719 had his *Œdipe*
produced, and until his death in 1778 he wrote indefatigably
Voltaire's for the public and his friends. His letters in
Prose. many volumes form nearly a third of his works,
and are attractive reading. In these he faithfully portrays
himself with this enthusiasms, weaknesses, love of his neighbour
and himself, his temperament, and his infirmities. They all
have intense vitality ; the language is marvellous, limpid, and
clear ; the tone by turns tender, violent, or witty. They are
the psychological index of the most active existence the world
has ever seen. Voltaire the man did not sufficiently resemble
Voltaire the writer ; his character was mediocre. Under the
cloak of an apostle of noble and generous ideas, the dress of the
courtier is always to be seen. Across that face of a superb
classic ugliness immortalized by Houdon, flits a disconcerting
ironical smile. It is indeed the face of a man who has scoffed
at holy things. And yet Voltaire was a king. At the end of
his life he reigned supreme over men's minds, and all the in-
tellectuals felt this influence which was prolonged through so
many generations.

A quarrel may be said to have decided Voltaire's vocation.

LITERATURE

He was beaten by the Chevalier de Rohan's servants, put in the Bastille, and only released after a fortnight on condition that Voltaire in   he would go to England (May 2, 1726), whence England.   he brought back his *Lettres Philosophiques*, which were published in 1734. These letters created a great stir ; they popularized English ideas and caused more to be known about Bacon, Locke, and Newton, the religious sects, and the English Constitution. They also revealed Shakespeare to the French. Voltaire's sarcastic temperament could not resist comparisons between the liberties of one country and the privileges of the other. He said : " A man because he is noble or a priest is not exempt here from paying certain taxes. Every one pays. Every one gives, not according to his rank (which is absurd) but according to his income."

" The English nation is the only one in the world which has succeeded in regulating the power of kings by resisting them."

" If there were only one religion in England, its despotism would be a menace ; if there were two they would cut each other's throats ; but there are thirty, and they live happily and in peace."

Men denounced the " horrible consequences " of maxims predestined to " arm subjects and foment revolts." The Abbé Molinier thus defines his adversaries', the *philosophers'*, profession of faith : " It is a new sort of monster in society, which acknowledges none of the claims of custom, propriety, politics or religion. Anything may be expected from these gentlemen." Voltaire began the campaign which was to last through the whole century.

By a decree of June 10, 1734, the Parliament ordered his *Lettres* to be publicly burned. This made him nervous and he Voltaire at   took refuge at Cirey-sur-Blaise with the Marquise Berlin.   du Châtelet, the celebrated mathematician ; once there, as it was near the frontier, he could cross into Lorraine at the first sign of danger. At Cirey the young philosopher began his *Siècle de Louis XIV*, thus continuing his historical work, which had had so successful a beginning in his *Charles XII*. He regained favour at Court, was made Gentleman in Ordinary and Royal Historian, and finally was elected to the Académie

Française in 1746. When Madame du Châtelet died, he decided to accept the King of Prussia's repeated offers, and went to Potsdam to him whom he had called the " Solomon of the North." He was delighted with his host and his Court. " A hundred and fifty thousand victorious soldiers," he wrote, " no Public Prosecutor, opera, comedy, philosophy, poetry, a philosophical and poetic hero, grandeur and grace, grenadiers and Muses, trumpets and violins, Platonic repose, society and liberty. Who would believe it ? All this is true." This dream was to last three years. At first Voltaire said : " I give an hour each day to the King of Prussia to polish up his prose and poetical works ; I am his grammarian, not his chamberlain." Then when a quarrel arose about Maupertuis, the geometrician, President of the Berlin Academy, he remarked that his duty was " to wash the King's dirty linen," whilst Frederick declared cynically : " one squeezes the orange and throws away the skin."

Voltaire went in search of liberty to the territory of the Genevan Republic, and took an estate at Saint-Jean which he called Les Délices. It still exists near the gates of the town. But here he came into collision with the narrowness of certain Calvinistic ideas. Lekain came to Les Délices and gave some performances which aroused the susceptibilities of the Consistory, the enemy of " innovations so contrary to religion and morals." Then began, in 1755, Voltaire's quarrel with Rousseau about the *Poème sur le désastre de Lisbonne.* Jean-Jacques wrote a defence of Providence which Voltaire answered with his *Candide.* This finished the discussion. But Les Délices had lost its charm, **Voltaire at** and Voltaire went to live at Ferney in the district **Ferney.** of Gex, and there for twenty years he combined the rôles of nobleman, somewhat unscrupulous speculator, and literary man. He still held the Tourney estate which had been presented to him by the President de Brosses, and he used to say : " I am of every nation." He certainly possessed a large tract of land stretching into Switzerland, Geneva, France, and the Duchy of Savoy. He wrote to his friend Thiérot : " It brings in altogether about 10,000 livres of annual income, and it saves me more than 20,000, for these three estates practically pay all the expenses of a household, in which I have more than thirty people and more than twelve horses to feed."

LITERATURE

Ferney is now a pilgrimage for all travellers who stop at Geneva. There is the château in the " Doric style " of architecture, on the frieze of which *Voltaire fecit* was inscribed. The rooms are spacious and filled with souvenirs, and the park is especially stately. Voltaire could say with justice : " Ferney has become one of the pleasantest spots on earth. I have made gardens which are like the tragedy which is forming in my head. They are like nothing else. Vines in festoons stretch away into the distance ; four rustic gardens at the four cardinal points, the house in the middle, practically no regularity." To-day the trees have grown, the hedges are thick and well kept, the walks are shady, and the great green arbours have all the poetry of beautiful old things. In such a spot it is easy to conjure up visions of the life of a man supremely happy in that he was conscious of his good fortune. From Ferney Voltaire sent forth many works : *Le Dictionnaire Philosophique* in 1764, *Histoire de la Russie sous Pierre le Grand*, and philanthropic pamphlets such as the *Commentaire des délits et des peines*, *Le Cri du sang innocent* and others connected with his celebrated vindications of Calas, Sirven, and Lally-Tollendal. In February 1788 the " patriarch " went to Paris where an enthusiastic reception awaited him. The people crowded into the streets to see him pass, the horses were taken out of his carriage, which was then drawn by his admirers. Visitors flocked to him, among them deputations from the Comédie Française and the Académie, Glück, Madame Necker, Madame de Polignac, representing the Queen, Madame du Barry, and ambassadors, such as Franklin, whose grandson he blessed saying : " God and Liberty." On March 30, after the sixth performance of *Irène*, the actors crowned the bust of the dramatist before a crowd of enthusiastic spectators.

" You wish then to kill me with glory," said the poet. He did not know how truly he was speaking. He died on May 30, **Death of** at the house of his friend the Marquis de Villette, **Voltaire.** at the corner of the Rue de Beaune and the Quai Voltaire, formerly the Quai des Théatins. He passed away terrified at the thought of the great mystery. He received priests, but only made a lay confession : " I die adoring God, loving my friends, not hating my enemies, and loathing persecution."

327

His name has been a political watchword under different *régimes*, but in this respect times have changed, and it has now lost its prestige. A master of modern criticism, Monsieur G. Lanson, has said with justice : " It seems to me incontestable that if Voltaire continues to exercise any influence on our France it must be a purely literary and intellectual influence. . . . Since the downfall of naturalism and the symbolistic crisis, the evolution of prose must be towards brilliant light, that is to say, the eighteenth century and Voltaire."

If the patriarch of Ferney was happy, Jean Jacques Rousseau was the most unhappy man of his times. He was sickly from **J. J. Rousseau.** a child ; all through his life he suffered both in body and mind ; he was strange, brusque, surly, and full of pride, and yet he was timid, sympathetic, and kind, and he inspires a profound pity, and the consideration which one feels for the irresponsible and the unbalanced. Rousseau, in spite of everything, forces us to admire his literary powers. It is impossible to deny his genius as a writer, the novelty of his harmonious diction, and the emotions—slightly morbid —which he felt in contemplating nature. He rendered prose poetical, and putting green on his palette, unfolded the beauties of the country ; he was the forerunner of a generation of stylists numbering among them Bernardin de Saint-Pierre and Chateaubriand. Madame de Sévigné had introduced " la feuille qui chante " ; * but that was a mere solo ; Jean Jacques gave the whole symphony.

He was born at Geneva in 1712 ; his education was neglected ; he had no fortune and had consequently to think of making his own livelihood. He tried everything ; he was scribe, engraver, teacher, practically a domestic servant, secretary, and copyist of music. His existence was a paradox, like his thoughts and his work. He began to write when he was nearly thirty, and his first success was the *Discours sur les Sciences et les Arts,* which was crowned by the Dijon Académie in 1750. In this he set himself against society and civilization. Next he wrote the *Nouvelle Héloïse* and *Émile,* that strange contradictory treatise written for other people's children by a man who repudiated his own. *Émile* was rewarded by a decree of arrest.

* The singing leaf.

He left Paris by favour of the Maréchal de Luxembourg, and took refuge first in Switzerland and then in England. Afterwards he returned to France and accepted the hospitality of the Marquis de Girardin, as he accepted the hospitality of so many nobles whose kindness he abused. He died at Ermenonville in 1778, some weeks after his cruel enemy Voltaire.

Rousseau was the most personal of the philosophers. The general idea of all his books is that man was good and that society made him wicked, that he was free and that society made him a slave, that he was happy and that society made him miserable. He preached for the good of all, but in reality he was defending his own cause. His defence was all the more sincere. He sought remedies for the existing state of things, and set them forth in the *Nouvelle Héloïse*, but unfortunately he did not find them for himself. From the point of view of politics, he explained in the *Contrat Social* what society should be, and his book formed the gospel of the Constituent Assembly ; in it they found the principles of equality, liberty, and fraternity and adopting the *Profession de foi du Vicaire Savoyard* they maintained the omnipotence of God, the source of moral energy. Thus an entire creed was evolved by this troubled life and excited brain. Its details are sometimes contradictory, but as a whole it shows complete unity. To Rousseau's credit it must be said that he never disowned his books, and never, like Voltaire, wrote anonymously.

From a social point of view some people hold the eighteenth century to be the great century. This sketch of the writers of the period shows the new elements they introduced into literature and the conceptions they gave to the world. In this respect they are great. Voltaire, Montesquieu, Rousseau, and Beaumarchais spoke with infinite brilliance and eloquence ; each in his own way upheld the complaints of the people against the privileged classes. But they saw their work accomplished, and their works are retrospective witnesses thereto. Under Louis XIV the masterpieces of Bossuet, Racine, Molière, Corneille, Pascal, and La Bruyère soar above their times and will be always a source of pure artistic delight. The beauty and eternal interest of the *Oraisons funèbres, Andromaque, Le*

Misanthrope, le Cid, Les Pensées, and *Les Caractères* have no true parallels in the eighteenth century.

IV

THE SALONS

The Duchesse du Maine, the Prince de Conti, the Marquise de Lambert, Madame de Tencin, Madame Geoffrin.

THE society which devoured the works of the philosophers and rushed in crowds to the theatre when Beaumarchais was played, claims a place in this last chapter. The salons, where authors expounded their ideas before having them printed, give an insight into literary manners and complete the picture. These gatherings date really from the death of Louis XIV. Until then courtiers were contented with one The Duchesse circle, and the homage went to one person alone. du Maine. Madame du Maine marks the transition from the seventeenth to the eighteenth century. Sceaux was still a court. It was there that the *Grandes Nuits* were instituted, meetings devoted to gaming, and literary diversions whose subject was always praise of the mistress of this semi-royal household. One evening a deputation from Greenland made a surprise visit : " Renown," said the chief, " has told us of the virtues, charms, and inclinations of Your Most Serene Highness. We have seen that she abhors the sun . . ." and they offered the crown of Greenland to the princess. Another time the diversion was astronomic ; savants had discovered a new star and that star was Madame du Maine.

Her intimates, who were responsible for these flatteries, were numerous. First of all Malezieu, ex-tutor to the Duc du Maine, who combined the rôles of secretary and savant. " His decisions," said the brilliant Madame de Staal-Delaunay, attendant on Madame du Maine, " were as infallible as were those of Pythagoras amongst his disciples. The hottest disputes ended the moment that anyone asserted : *he said so !* " Then there was the Cardinal de Polignac, titular professor of philosophy to the little court. He was the author of the *Anti-Lucrèce,* a Latin poem written in defence of morals and theology. Another was the President de Mesmes, who unbent so far as to perform comedies for the Duchess' diversion. There were others among them who were genuine men of letters, such as the Abbé de Chaulieu the poet, Fontenelle, and Voltaire.

On one occasion some one asked Fontenelle in the Duchess's presence :

" What is the difference between a clock and Madame du Maine ? "

" One tells the hours, the other makes one forget them," replied Fontenelle.

Voltaire, to redeem a forfeit, made the following well-known enigma :

> Cinq voyelles, une consonne
> En français composent mon nom,
> Et je porte sur ma personne
> De quoi l'écrire sans crayon.*

Everyone was in ectasies when the Duchesse guessed *oiseau* (a bird).

It is strange that the Cellamare conspiracy should have originated in this atmosphere. But this opera-goddess naturally aspired to play a part in a tragi-comedy.†

We may pass over the Regent's Court at the Palais Royal, celebrated for its suppers and orgies ; the next salon of importance was that of the Prince de Conti, who received a select society at the Temple. In Ollivier's little picture in the Louvre we are shown the Princesse de Beauvau, the Comtesse de Boufflers, the Comtesse d'Egmont, the Maréchale de Luxembourg, the Maréchale de Mirepoix, the Président Hénault, the Baillé de Chabrillant, Pont-de-Veyle, Trudaine, and others. The child Mozart is at the harpsichord, and beside him is Jélyotte singing and accompanying himself on the guitar. This picture is a most precious document ; it shows the atmosphere of sober elegance which reigned at the meetings of all these great ladies, clever men, and artists.

The Prince de Conti was that Louis-François de Bourbon

---

* Five vowels and one consonant compose my name in French, and I carry on my person that with which to write it without a pencil.

† See chap. iv, pp. 46, 47.

who was for a long time candidate for the throne of Poland, and was concerned in the secret diplomacy of Louis XV. His Versailles was the Château de l'Ile-Adam. According to a contemporary he was very well made, and in that respect he was unlike the rest of the Contis, who had an hereditary hump. His bearing was noble and majestic, his features handsome and regular, his face agreeable and intellectual, and his looks proud or gentle as occasion demanded He expressed himself on every subject with considerable warmth and power.

He had conducted many brilliant campaigns, particularly in Italy in 1744 ; he was even compared to his ancestor, the hero of Lens and Rocroi. He was one of the protectors of Rousseau, Beaumarchais, and the Chevalier de Florian. The Prince de Conti will always be the type of a witty and intelligent patrician.

But it was private individuals, and even ladies of the middle classes who gave the tone to society. With them there was more conscious freedom and less feeling of restraint. In their houses there was a sort of republic on Athenian lines, composed of men of the world and men of letters. We will enter some of their doors, and the Marquise de Lambert, Madame de Tencin, and Madame de Geoffrin shall in turn disclose the histories of their little " kingdoms."

The Marquise de Lambert. The Marquise de Lambert was a woman of considerable attainments. This fact is proved by her *Avis à sa fille,* her *Avis à son fils,* and her *Traité de la Vieillesse.* Her ideas were shrewd and her style good, if a trifle laboured, and she was a judge of character. Some of her maxims, which date from the end of Louis XIV's reign, anticipate Vauvenargues and Rousseau. For instance : " Accustom yourselves to show kindness and consideration to your servants. An ancient writer once said that they should be regarded as unfortunate friends." " By the word conscience I mean that inward sense in an honourable man, which tells him whether he has anything with which to reproach himself." " I exhort you, my son, to improve your heart far more than to perfect your mind. Man's true greatness is in his heart."

She lived in a part of the old Palais Mazarin which she rented from the Duc de Nevers. There, on the Tuesday and

Wednesday in each week from 1710 to 1733, a chosen circle of aristocratic and literary guests met together. Members of the Academy were welcomed, and they readily listened to Madame de Lambert's suggestions. People were scarcely admitted under the " Cupola " " unless they had been presented at her house and by her." Thus said Argenson, and he knew better than anyone. He frequented her salon most assiduously and has left some lines on the death of the Marquise, giving his impressions in the form of a funeral oration : " I have just sustained a great loss in the death of Madame la Marquise de Lambert at the age of eighty-six. . . . It was an honour to be admitted to her house. I went there to dinner regularly on Wednesdays, which was one of her days. In the evening she held her reception, where the guests conversed and there was no more question of cards than at the famous Hôtel de Rambouillet, so much praised by Voiture and Balzac. She was rich and made good use of her wealth by generosity to her friends, and particularly to the unfortunate." This compensates for Marais' mockery and Lesage's banter of " the Marquise de Chaves " in a chapter of *Gil Blas*.

Under the Regency, Madame de Lambert maintained the traditions of politeness and good taste. These were not always **Madame de** predominant in Madame de Tencin's salon, for **Tencin.** there intrigue prevailed, and the hum of conversation became an uproar. " She was," said Marmontel, " a woman of profound sense, but her good-natured and simple exterior made her look more like the housekeeper than the mistress of the house." Marivaux owed much to this lady. In his *Vie de Marianne* he sketched some of the features of his benefactress' society. " Marivaux," said Marmontel, " often embarrassed his hearers by sophisms which were sufficiently subtle to appear simple, and Madame de Tencin was always embarrassing Marivaux by observations which hid wisdom under extreme simplicity."

One day some ludicrous verses by Collé were read in Fontenelle's presence. Fontenelle did not quite understand and asked that the couplet should be read again.

" Why you great imbecile ! " cried Madame de Tencin, " do you not see that it is only nonsense ? "

" It so resembles," replied Fontenelle, " all the verses I hear read and sung here, it is not astonishing that I made a mistake."

Madame de Tencin died in 1749. She knew Madame Geoffrin and left her this advice : " Do not discourage people ; even though nine people out of ten will not take an atom of trouble for you, the tenth may become a useful friend." Suard says that she knew how to use a fool as well as a wise man. She foresaw that Madame Geoffrin would one day take her place, and she said to her friends in her middle-class way :

" Do you know what the Geoffrin comes here for ? She comes to see what she can pick up out of my inventory."

Madame Geoffrin's salon was the most characteristic of the eighteenth century ; the mingling of the classes began there **Madame** more than anywhere else. " Her house," said **Geoffrin.** the *Mémoires secrets*, " is the rendezvous of savants, artists, and famous men of all sorts. Foreigners especially considered they had seen nothing in France if they had not been presented to this celebrity."

At Madame Geoffrin's everything was done with as much regularity as in a public office ; there were two dinners a week, the one on Monday for artists such as Van Loo, Vernet, Boucher, Vien, Soufflot, and Lemoine, and the other on Wednesday for men of letters like d'Alembert, Marivaux, Marmontel, Morellet, Saint-Lambert, and d'Holbach. Madame Geoffrin kept the conversation well under her control ; if it strayed on to vexed questions such as religious belief, although she approved of the Encyclopædists, Madame Geoffrin stopped the discussion with, *That is all right,* and it was useless to say more as this was known to be her last word, and they were obliged to go and *make their Sabbath* elsewhere. She herself talked little, though when she did she spoke sensibly, and either introduced a maxim or some well-told anecdote. She once said to the Chevalier de Coigny, who was telling an interminable story : " Would you be so good as to carve this capon ? " and as the young man took a very little knife out of his pocket, she added : " To succeed in this country, one must have large knives and little stories."

Her wit was particularly used against bores, whom she could not endure, and importunate visitors who stayed too long.

One day when she saw the good Abbé de Saint-Pierre settle himself down in her drawing-room for a long winter's evening, she was for the moment appalled, and then she rose to the occasion and drew him out to such an extent that she made him amusing. He was astonished, and when she complimented him on his conversation, he answered as he took leave :

"Madame, I am only an instrument on which you have played well."

Chatterers made her turn pale and "feel like death," and yet she managed to put up with them if, as she said, "they were simply chatterers, and only wished to speak without expecting any answer. My friend Fontenelle, who pardoned them as I did, said that they gave his lungs a rest. They confer another benefit on me : their insignificant buzzing is to me like the noise of bells, which does not prevent one from thinking and often stimulates thought." She was good and charitable, but a little crabbed ; there was a certain egotism about her generosity, as the following reflexion of hers shows : "Those who rarely do things for others have no need of maxims, but those who are continually doing things for others should do them in the way which is most agreeable to themselves, *because one must do comfortably anything that has to be done every day.*" Her motto should, however, be remembered ; it was *give and lose.*

There were other well-known hostesses, such as the Marquise du Deffant, Julie de Lespinasse, the Maréchale de Luxembourg, Madame d'Epinay, Madame Necker, Madame Helvétius, and many other celebrated women. But the most interesting galleries are those in which the pictures are not too crowded. Madame de Lambert and Madame Geoffrin, one about 1730 and the other about 1760, are the best representatives of the wit of their times, and with them we may fitly conclude a study of the Eighteenth Century.

INDEX

Y

INDEX

INDEX

341

INDEX

INDEX

343

INDEX

INDEX